Palgrave Advances in Regional and Urban Economics

Sock-Yong Phang

Policy Innovations for Affordable Housing In Singapore

From Colony to Global City

palgrave
macmillan

Sock-Yong Phang
School of Economics
Singapore Management University
Singapore, Singapore

Palgrave Advances in Regional and Urban Economics
ISBN 978-3-030-09208-5 ISBN 978-3-319-75349-2 (eBook)
https://doi.org/10.1007/978-3-319-75349-2

Cover illustration: Ivan Nesterov / Alamy Stock Photo

Printed on acid-free paper

This Palgrave Macmillan imprint is published by the registered company Springer International Publishing AG part of Springer Nature.
The registered company address is: Gewerbestrasse 11, 6330 Cham, Switzerland

For my husband Andrew and
our daughters Rachel and Christine

Foreword

An ancient Chinese proverb asserts that while a government has strategies, citizens have counterstrategies. Those words concisely frame the challenge society faces in choosing from among the range of possible government policy regimes. In a market economy, equilibrium prices and quantities as well as the distributions of wealth and income that they generate depend on a government's tax and regulatory policies. The challenge is to choose a policy regime that produces equilibrium prices and quantities that maximize an accepted measure of social welfare. Designing policy well requires a good understanding of how citizens' counterstrategies depend on government strategies: it requires an economic theory that works.

This book tells how public authorities in Singapore designed and adapted policies for allocating land, capital, and labor in order to create good places for Singapore citizens and residents to live and work, setting the infrastructure for people in Singapore to create a poster-child East Asian economic miracle of the late twentieth century. The book describes economic models underlying policy makers' strategies, their purposes, and their expectations. It sorts through intended and unintended consequences, and how policy makers adapted to unintended ones. The book is, among other things, a fascinating analytical economic history about how Singapore purposefully deployed a suite of interrelated public policies about land use, life-cycle savings, taxation, regulation, and ethnic toleration.

A personal note: because Harvard's late John R. Meyer advised both of our PhD theses, Professor Sock-Yong Phang is my (much younger) academic sister. John Meyer was a master at combining economic theory, data, and econometrics to discover how things worked. In Sock-Yong Phang's book, I think I see a part of John's legacy that he would like. John was very interested in US economic history and, with Alfred Conrad, wrote a founding paper about the economics of slavery in the United States. I think that the striking contrast between how the US federal government gave away vast holdings of lands or sold it at below market prices and Sock-Yong's detailed account of the very different way that Singapore has managed its land would fascinate John. I know that it fascinates me.

New York, NY, USA
February 19, 2018

Thomas J. Sargent

Preface

As a global multiracial city-state with a land area of 720 square km and a population of 5.6 million, Singapore has managed to develop a framework for affordable housing that has resulted in a high homeownership rate of 91%. How did Singapore manage to achieve this in a fiscally sustainable way? What were the roles of land acquisition and land use planning policies? How was homeownership subsidized and financed? How did market deregulation impact house prices? What policy instruments were used to contain housing price bubbles? How did policymakers deal with ethnic preferences for segregation? What has been the impact of housing policies on wealth distribution? How do elderly homeowners extract home equity for retirement financing? What can other countries learn from the experience of Singapore?

I have spent much time over the past three decades researching the above issues from the perspective of an urban economist. This book is the culmination of my previous publications and current research on Singapore's housing policies. In this book, I distil the key housing policy innovations, provide implementation details, analyse the impact of these polices, explain the local context as well as necessary conditions for these policies to work, and conclude with an assessment of their transferability. In the process, I provide the answers to the above questions by presenting the history and policy innovations introduced into Singapore's housing policy framework over five decades. The reader should note that part of

Singapore's housing history has already been covered in some of my earlier publications (as well as by other authors); however, repeating part of the history is necessary for this book as it would not tell the full story otherwise.

In sharp contrast to the situation in Singapore, the availability of affordable housing for low- and middle-income households is a challenging social problem that many countries and cities continue to grapple with. Recent rapid house price inflation has further deepened the divide in urban societies between those who own properties and those who do not. New housing sector regulations to curb housing demand by foreigners have been recently implemented in several hot-spot cities across the world.

Although it is a small city-state, Singapore's experience in transforming its housing sector since independence can be relevant to larger countries as the urban housing market is a highly localized market. Singapore's experience has also been of particular interest to Commonwealth countries, as it inherited a western institutional structure from the British colonial government when it gained independence. Developing as well as former socialist economies that are exploring alternative systems of affordable housing can also draw useful lessons from Singapore's experience. This book provides an in-depth economic analysis of Singapore's housing policies and it is my hope that it will be a useful reference for policymakers, city leaders, students and academic researchers in universities, think tanks, and international organizations who work on affordable housing policies.

Singapore, Singapore Sock-Yong Phang

Acknowledgements

In the process of researching and writing this book, I have accumulated many debts along the way. First, I would like to thank Mr Liu Thai Ker (Chairman of the Centre for Liveable Cities, CEO of the Housing and Development Board between 1979 and 1989, and CEO and Chief Planner of the Urban Redevelopment Authority between 1989 and 1992) who suggested that I write a book on the economics of Singapore's housing system in 2014. This prompted me to sketch the first outline for the book. However, numerous other commitments in the intervening years led me to put off embarking on a book-length project. In the interim, I accepted several invitations to write and speak on Singapore's housing policies from the Asian Development Bank Institute, China Executive Leadership Academy in Pudong, Fudan University, Hong Kong University, Korea Development Institute, Korea Research Institute for Human Settlements, the Lincoln Institute of Land Policy, the *Singapore Economic Review*, Southwestern University of Finance and Economics, Tsinghua University, and the World Bank Institute. I would like to thank these organizations for their interest in my research on Singapore's housing policies and my co-authors during this period, David K.C. Lee, Kyung-Hwan Kim, and Matthias Helble for helping to shape my views.

I am also grateful to Zhi Liu for the invitation to give a series of lectures on real estate policies at the Peking University-Lincoln Institute Center for Urban Development and Land Policy in the summer of 2017. Preparing the material for these lectures helped me conceptualize Chap. 5 on land use planning and regulations. My colleague, Wen-Tai Hsu, provided extensive comments on the chapter and I have benefited greatly from his valuable suggestions as well as our discussions on the regulatory tax.

I delivered the Celia Moh Chair Professor public lecture at the Singapore Management University (SMU) on March 23, 2015 on the topic of "Superstar Cities, Inequality and Housing Policies", upon which Chap. 8 is based. I would like to thank my colleagues at SMU, in particular, SMU President Arnoud De Meyer, then Provost Rajendra Srivastava, and Dean Bryce Hool, for conferring upon me the honour.

Chapter 9 is based on a talk, "Monetization of Housing: 3 puzzles", that I gave at the Housing Roundtable organized by SMU's Centre for Research on the Economics of Ageing (CREA) on August 16, 2017. I am grateful to Professor Bryce Hool, Director for CREA and Dean of the School of Economics at SMU, who has been the key person behind CREA and the Singapore Life Panel® survey from which the statistics used in Chap. 9 are drawn. The research for Chap. 9 (which draws on data from the Singapore Life Panel® survey) was supported by the Singapore Ministry of Education (MOE) Academic Research Fund Tier 3 grant MOE2013-T3-1-009.

The book only came together when Laura Pacey approached me in 2016 to consider publishing a second book with Palgrave Macmillan. She has been a very patient and supportive editor, and I am grateful to her for getting me to embark on the journey. I am grateful to Stephen Hoskins and Naqun Huang at SMU for excellent research assistance. I would like to thank Hites Ahir, senior research officer at the International Monetary Fund, for very kindly reading the manuscript in its entirety and providing helpful comments and edits.

I am deeply honoured that Professor Thomas J. Sargent very graciously agreed to write the Foreword for the book. I have learned a great deal more than economics from Professor Sargent who is not only a man of exceptional learning but also embodies the enormous generosity and kindness that are the hallmarks of a true scholar.

As always, my husband Andrew, my constant cheerleader, critic, and sounding board, read the entire manuscript. His advice, comments, and encouragement have been extremely helpful and his enthusiasm for the project helped to spur me on. This book is dedicated to him and to our daughters Rachel and Christine.

Contents

Abbreviations

ABDS	Additional buyer's stamp duty
AHG	Additional Housing Grant
BSD	Buyer's stamp duty
BTO	Build-To-Order
CBD	Central Business District
CC	Construction cost
CPF	Central Provident Fund
CPF LIFE	CPF Lifelong Income For The Elderly
DBSS	Design, Build and Sell Scheme
DC	Development Charge
DGP	Development Guide Plan
DTI	Debt service-to-income
EC	Executive Condominium
EIP	Ethnic Integration Policy
FHA	Federal Housing Administration
GDP	Gross Domestic Product
GLS	Government Land Sales
GST	Goods and Services Tax
HDB	Housing and Development Board
HECM	Home Equity Conversion Mortgage
HELOC	Home equity line of credit
HOS	Home Ownership Scheme
HPF	Housing Provident Fund

HUD	U.S. Department of Housing and Urban Development
HUDC	Housing and Urban Development Company
IUP	Interim Upgrading Programme
KHFC	Korea Housing Finance Corporation
LAA	Land Acquisition Act
LBS	Lease Buyback Scheme
LTV	Loan-to-value
LUP	Lift Upgrading Programme
MAS	Monetary Authority of Singapore
MC	Management Corporation
MIR	Monthly mortgage payment to gross monthly household income ratio
MRT	Mass Rapid Transit
MUP	Main Upgrading Programme
NIMBY	Not-in-my-backyard
NPV	Net present value
NTUC	National Trades Union Congress
OCBC Bank	Oversea-Chinese Banking Corporation Limited
PAP	People's Action Party
PCP	Project Completion Period
PHG	Proximity Housing Grant
PIR	Median house price to median annual household income ratio
PM	Prime Minister
PPP	Public Private Partnership
PR	Permanent resident
REIT	Real Estate Investment Trust
RM	Reverse mortgage
S&CC	Service and conservancy charges
SARS	Severe acute respiratory syndrome
SERS	Selective En bloc Redevelopment Scheme
SHB	Silver Housing Bonus
SHG	Special Housing Grant
SIT	Singapore Improvement Trust
SLP	Singapore Life Panel®
SOE	State-owned enterprise
SPR	Singapore Permanent Resident
SSD	Seller's stamp duty
TDSR	Total Debt Service Ratio
URA	Urban Redevelopment Authority

Unless otherwise stated, $ in this book refers to nominal Singapore Dollars. The reader may refer to the Appendix on page 201 for data on Singapore's Consumer Price Index, exchange rate vis-à-vis the US Dollar, and interest rate for housing loans for 1988 to 2017.

List of Figures

List of Tables

1

Introduction

The Affordable Housing Challenge

The issue of affordable housing cuts across geographical as well as economic lines. The problem has become particularly pronounced both for cities in developing countries facing rapid urbanization and in global cities that are magnets for immigration and global capital. A shortage of adequate and affordable housing for low- and middle-income households has risen to the top of the social and political agenda across cities in China and India, as well as in hot spot cities of London, Paris, New York, San Francisco, Vancouver, Toronto, Sydney, Melbourne, and Hong Kong.

This is not surprising for a number of reasons: economic and population growth is unevenly distributed across metropolitan areas, there has been increased global capital flows into real estate investments, and housing constitutes the largest expenditure item for the majority of households. Tenure choice—whether to rent or own—is a major financial and investment decision for most households. In many Asian countries, there is a societal premium placed on homeownership and it is homeownership affordability that is a major source of concern for young households.

S.-Y. Phang, *Policy Innovations for Affordable Housing In Singapore*,
Palgrave Advances in Regional and Urban Economics,
https://doi.org/10.1007/978-3-319-75349-2_1

Owning a property, however, often requires an overall outlay that involves multiples of the annual income for the average household. Given the high cost of a long-life asset, and the attendant long-term commitment of a mortgage as well as the substantial transaction costs involved, the decision to purchase a property is not to be taken lightly.

Government Interventions for Affordable Housing

To resolve the problem of housing affordability, government interventions are widely accepted as necessary in order to channel resources into housing and cope with the challenges of market failures, cross-border capital flows, misaligned incentives, and, paradoxically, regulatory distortions and failures. Governments intervene in housing finance, production, transaction, and service delivery processes in multifaceted ways that differ from country to country. Phang (2013) provides a review and discussion of the range of well-intended housing market interventions that have been utilized, with outcomes that have, on occasion, been unexpected. In some contexts, such as the US subprime mortgage crisis of 2007, the consequences have been devastating, requiring massive interventions by governments. This raises policy questions on the appropriate role of the government in the housing market, again with answers that vary greatly across the world.

The International Monetary Fund (IMF) (2011) estimated an index of government participation in housing finance markets for 33 advanced and emerging economies. The index is a measure of the breadth of government intervention and is based on the presence or absence of the following eight policies to facilitate homeownership: (i) subsidies to first-time or other buyers up front; (ii) subsidies to buyers through savings account contributions or through preferential fees; (iii) subsidies to selected groups, low income; (iv) provident funds early withdrawal for house purchase; (v) housing finance funds or government agency that provides guarantees/loans; (vi) tax deductibility of mortgage interest; (vii) capital gains tax deductibility; and (viii) state-owned institution majority market player greater than 50%. Amongst the 33 countries in the IMF study, Singapore topped the rankings for government participation in both housing finance as well as homeownership.

Another recent study by Renaud et al. (2016) compared government interventions in housing markets in six East Asian economies, namely, Japan, China, South Korea, Taiwan, Hong Kong, and Singapore, paying particular attention to housing supply interventions. The authors assessed Korea to have the most intense degree of government intervention into real estate, with Singapore second, and Hong Kong the least. Amongst the six economies however, Singapore was exceptional in relation to the share of housing built by the government agency, the Housing and Development Board (HDB), as a proportion of the total housing stock. While the 2016 figure is 73% for Singapore, the figures for the other economies are much lower: Hong Kong (29%), China (< 10%), Korea (5%), and Taiwan (1%). Singapore is thus unique in its housing supply regime in both the dominance of the HDB as a housing developer and the sale, rather than rental, of HDB-supplied housing on a 99-year leasehold basis. The dominance of the government has not precluded a vibrant resale market as owners of subsidized new HDB flats are able to sell their housing at market prices after a minimum period of 5 years of occupancy.

Housing Affordability in Singapore

Introduction

From the general backdrop outlined briefly above, I turn now to the thrust of the present book. Put simply, it focuses on the role of innovative policies adopted to solve the housing affordability problem in the Singaporean context. However, it is hoped that some of the policies that have been implemented in Singapore would not only be of general comparative interest to other jurisdictions but might also prompt possible practical reforms (by way of ideas, if not direct application) in some of these jurisdictions as well. In this last-mentioned regard, a caveat is of course necessary. In particular, it is acknowledged that each jurisdiction, however, is different and the policies implemented to deal with the problem of housing affordability must necessarily be relevant to the local circumstances of the jurisdictions concerned.

In the next section, I will briefly compare housing affordability in Singapore with other cities and over time using the housing price-to-income ratio. Following this backdrop, I will furnish the reader with an overview of the present book, which discusses and analyses the various policy innovations that have enabled Singapore to achieve housing affordability and a sizeable homeownership rate despite its severe physical constraints. In this regard, the section will summarize the thrust of each of the ensuing chapters of this book and how they relate to each other.

Housing Affordability Indicators for Singapore

As "ownership of housing built by HDB" is the dominant form of housing tenure arrangement in Singapore, this requires that housing affordability indicators that are reported by various sources for purposes of international comparison be interpreted with care. The most widely used indicator of homeownership affordability is the median house price to median income ratio (Median Multiple or Price-to-Income ratio (PIR)), due to its simplicity and consequent ease of understanding. The aggregative data website, Numbeo, compares PIR for 267 cities across the world, and estimates Singapore's price- to-income ratio for 2017 as amongst the highest in the world—at an astronomical 22.18 (Numbeo 2017). This figure is, however, based on the price of a 90 square metre apartment in the *private* housing sector and net average salary (multiplied by 1.5). *However, 80%* of resident households in Singapore do *not* reside in the *private* housing sector, but in the HDB sector instead.

A more reliable source for international housing affordability comparisons is the *Demographia International Housing Affordability Survey.*[1] The 2017 edition of the survey provides PIRs for 406 metropolitan markets in nine countries for 2016. The authors of the *Demographia Survey* consider a PIR of between 4.1 and 5.0 as "seriously unaffordable", and 5.0 and over as "severely unaffordable". The survey estimates the median multiple for

Singapore to be 4.8—in the "seriously unaffordable" category. In comparison, data from the survey show several "severely unaffordable" housing markets (PIR > 5.0) in the US, Australia, UK, Canada, New Zealand, with Hong Kong topping the list with a median multiple of 18.1.[2]

In 2016, the annual median income for resident Singapore households was S$93,000 and the median price of a 4-room HDB flat in the resale market was S$451,000 (giving a PIR of 4.8). Eligible first-time citizen homeowners in Singapore, however, enjoy subsidies in the form of housing grants when purchasing existing HDB flats in the secondary market. A housing grant of S$30,000 in 2016 was available to first-time homeowners purchasing a 4-room flat and this reduced the ratio to 4.5. Additional housing grants are given to lower-income households (see Chap. 8) as well as households that choose a resale flat with or close to their parents or married child.

Moreover, the majority of first-time citizen homeowners purchase new flats directly from the HDB at prices below market prices, together with additional housing grants that vary with household income. Table 1.1 shows the PIRs that are reflective of these non-market transactions for

Table 1.1 Price-to-income ratios (PIRs) for HDB flats at Sengkang Town, 2017

	New flat applicants'	(A) Resale flat		(B) New flat		(C) New flat		
HDB flat type (size in sq m)	median annual household income (S$)	Market price (S$)	PIR	List price (S$)	PIR	Price minus grants (S$)	PIR	MIR[a] (%)
2-room (45)	21,600	n.a.	n.a.	115,000	5.3	40,000	1.9	7
3-room (65)	30,000	342,000	11.4	180,000	6.0	110,000	3.7	17
4-room (90)	51,600	415,000	8.0	290,000	5.6	240,000	4.7	22
5-room (110)	72,000	438,000	6.1	360,000	5.0	360,000	5.0	25

Notes: Sengkang town is about 17 km travel distance by road from the CBD

Data sources: HDB website at http://esales.hdb.gov.sg/hdbvsf/eampu09p.nsf/0/17AUGBTOSK_page_8557/$file/pricing.html, http://www.hdb.gov.sg/cs/infoweb/residential/buying-a-flat/resale/resale-statistics. Accessed 1 Nov 2017

[a]MIR refers to monthly mortgage payment to monthly household income ratio

Sengkang town in Singapore. Column A shows PIRs using market resale prices, column B shows PIRs using listed prices of new HDB flats, while column C shows PIRs for households eligible for housing grants that vary with household income of applicants. The PIR for new HDB flats with grants is estimated at 1.9 for households purchasing 2-room flats and the PIR increases to 5.0 for higher-income households purchasing 5-room HDB flats. Housing affordability is thus much better for *new* flats purchased from the HDB and also better for lower-income households buying smaller new flat types.

Although the PIRs for new flats are substantially below those based on resale flats, an eligible household needs to be successful in balloting at a project launch and then wait for 3 to 4 years for the project to be completed. Similar to rent-regulated housing markets, housing *affordability* in price-regulated markets therefore do not necessarily imply housing *availability*. Singapore's housing affordability based on new flat prices masks market disequilibrium when demand exceeds available new supply. When the allocation method was on a first-come-first-served basis, the length of the waiting list and waiting period before flat allocation would indicate the extent of disequilibrium. When the allocation method was changed to a registration for ballot for individual projects (in order to determine if there is adequate demand), the ratio of those unsuccessful in the ballot to available units provided a measure of unmet demand.

Another indication of unmet demand in the new HDB flat sector would be HDB *resale* prices, as households that are repeatedly unsuccessful at ballots or do not wish to wait a few years for a new flat could purchase a resale flat. The median resale price of a 4-room HDB flat minus the housing grant available would thus be the appropriate market price by which to estimate PIRs. Figure 1.1 shows the trends in PIR between 2000 and 2016, estimated using the weighted average of median resale prices of a 4-room HDB flat net of family housing grant of $30,000. (The family housing grant was increased to $50,000 in 2017.) There are two reported median household income series that are available: one for all resident households and the other for employed resident households. The upper line shown in Fig. 1.1 indicates the PIRs calculated using median household income for all households. Lower PIR values are obtained

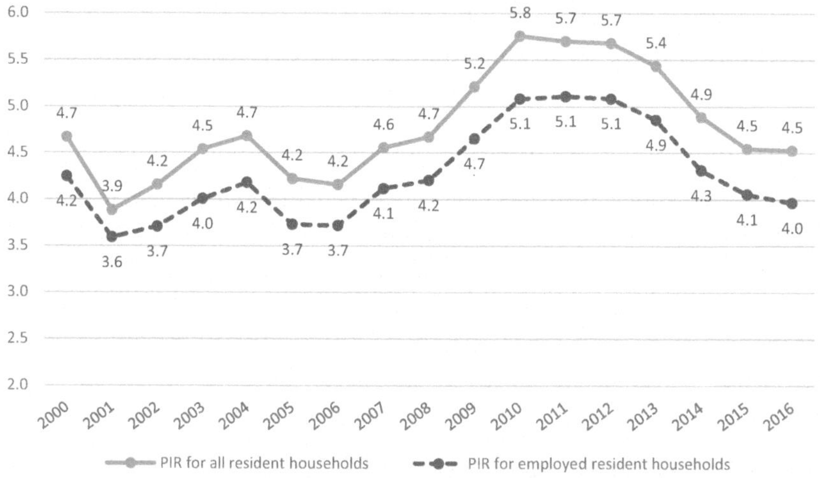

Fig. 1.1 Housing price-to-income ratios for Singapore, 2000–2016 (Notes: For estimation of PIRs, I used the weighted average of median resale price across HDB towns net of housing grant for a 4-room HDB flat in 2016. The prices in earlier years (2000–2015) are derived using the HDB resale price index. The income data is the median household income inclusive of employer's CPF contributions for (i) all resident households, and (ii) employed resident households; Data sources: HDB and Singapore Department of Statistics websites)

when employed household income data is used. For the series based on all households, the range for PIR varies from a low of 3.9 in 2001 (when there was an excess supply of new HDB flats) to a peak of 5.8 in 2010. It entered the "severely unaffordable" range of above 5.0 between 2009 and 2013, leading to a roll out of a basket of demand-side cooling measures and a ramping up of housing supply (see Chap. 6).

Given the multiples of home prices over income, homeownership affordability is also dependent on the availability of *housing loans* (Phang 2013) and the terms at which these loans are offered. Low-income households that are assessed to be at higher risk of default may find difficulties with obtaining a mortgage loan from financial institutions. Subprime mortgages in the US are offered at higher interest rates and are also insured by the federal government.

In contrast, the HDB provides mortgage loans to buyers of its flats, thus making it the largest mortgage lender in Singapore in terms of number of households served. HDB loans are offered based on loan-to-value ratio of up to 90%, a maximum tenure of 25 years, and at a standard interest rate of 2.6% that does not discriminate against the low-income borrower. The monthly mortgage payment to gross monthly household income ratio (MIR) is widely used as a measure of mortgage affordability and is also used by mortgage underwriters or lenders to determine how much a household will be allowed to borrow. MIRs of 25% to up to one-third are generally considered as the upper limits of mortgage affordability. The last column of Table 1.1 shows the MIRs for HDB new flats after grant subsidies. These vary from 7% to 25%, increasing with household income and size of housing purchased.

Policy Innovations for Affordable Housing

Bearing the above backdrop in mind, this book discusses and analyses the policy innovations that have enabled Singapore to achieve sustainable housing affordability and a homeownership rate of 91% for its resident households despite its severe geographical land constraint.

The foundations of Singapore's present housing policy framework were laid in the 1960s during a critical period of transition to postcolonial independence. Singapore shares with several Commonwealth countries historical roots, legal systems, and political institutions inherited from the British colonial period. However, unlike most former colonies, it is an island city-state with no rural hinterland, occupying only 720 square kilometres of land. With a population of 5.6 million, it is amongst the most densely populated countries in the world.

In the decades since the first elections were held in 1959 for self-government and since independence in 1965, Singapore has been governed by the People's Action Party (PAP). For a brief 2-year period between 1963 and its independence as a nation state in 1965, Singapore was part of the Federation of Malaysia. Political stability has been further enhanced by political leadership continuity with only three Prime Ministers (PM) having led the country since 1959: PM Lee Kuan Yew from 1959 to 1990; PM Goh Chok Tong from 1990 to 2004; and the present PM Lee Hsien Loong since 2004.

It is widely acknowledged that Singapore's economic performance since independence has been remarkable. With a 2016 nominal GDP per capita of US$53,000, it ranks amongst the top 10 high-income countries in the world. There is a large body of literature on Singapore's economic development history.[3] Similar to strategies for Singapore's economic development, its housing policies have not been founded on ideology, but, rather, upon a pragmatic assessment of constraints and strengths. The 1960s constituted the critical juncture when the newly elected government made amendments to legislation and institutions to address the problems of unemployment as well as housing crisis faced by a newly independent state.

The policy innovations for land, housing supply, housing finance, and land use planning are covered in Chaps. 2, 3, 4, and 5. Chapter 2 discusses the changes to land acquisition legislation that removed the constitutional right to private land ownership in Singapore and allowed the government to acquire land at below market values. Chapter 3 reviews the transformation of public housing from a social rental model under the British to a homeownership model under the HDB. The achievements of the HDB and its organizational structure and practices that have enabled it to avoid the inefficiencies common to state-owned enterprises will be analysed in this particular chapter. Chapter 4 discusses how the HDB homeownership programme was complemented by changes to the Central Provident Fund (CPF) in 1968. The fund was transformed into a housing finance institution for financing homeownership when legislation was enacted to permit withdrawals from CPF accounts to finance the purchase of housing sold by the HDB.

Land use and housing regulations have major implications for housing affordability and inclusiveness of urban neighbourhoods. High housing prices in several cities can be attributed to regulatory obstacles to new construction and higher density. In Chap. 5, we discuss how Singapore's land use planners did not follow the British land use planning model and, instead, adopted planning practices that facilitated economic growth and increases in housing supply. In the aftermath of the Global Financial Crisis in 2008, macro-prudential regulations became a new buzzword in

Central Banking circles. Chapter 6 reviews how the Singapore government has devised and experimented with a wide range of policy tools in order to mitigate housing speculation since the 1970s. Similar to other global cities, Singapore has relatively high-income inequality as well as residents from diverse racial and religious backgrounds. Chapter 7 describes how housing regulations have been carefully crafted in order to build mixed income and racially inclusive neighbourhoods.

Chapter 8 further describes how housing policies have been used to mitigate wealth inequality and to ensure homeownership is affordable to the lowest income group. The outcome is a housing wealth distribution that is close to the ideal wealth distribution described in Thomas Piketty's 2014 seminal book, *Capital in the Twenty-First Century*. Housing wealth, however, is relatively illiquid. With a rapidly ageing population, a significant portion of household wealth in housing and few affordable rental options, there is a need for instruments to help households monetize their housing wealth in the face of retirement and problems related to ageing. Chapter 9 discusses the options available to Singapore's ageing homeowners, amongst which is a 2009 policy innovation in the form of a Lease Buyback Scheme. While the scheme has not been particularly popular, it provides insights into the challenges of monetizing home equity in a leasehold context.

From its British colonial legacy, Singapore has evolved into an institutional structure that is quite different from most other western countries and that has contributed to its economic performance as well as housing outcomes. How the reforms were made and implemented would be of particular interest to other countries in the Commonwealth that share a common colonial legacy. Singapore's experience has also been of interest to socialist economies in transition to more market-oriented systems. These include economies in Asia such as China and Vietnam as well as countries in other parts of the world that are exploring alternative systems of affordable housing. It is in this context that Chap. 10 concludes the book with an assessment of the transferability of Singapore's housing policies.

Notes

1. *The 13th Annual Demographia International Housing Affordability Survey 2017* covers 406 metropolitan housing markets in nine countries for the third quarter of 2016. A total of 92 major metropolitan housing markets (with more than one million population) are included, including five megacities (Demographia and Performance Urban Planning 2017). The OECD (https://stats.oecd.org/Index.aspx?DataSetCode=HOUSE_PRICES) and the United Nations (https://unhabitat.org/national-sample-of-cities/) also produce PIRs. Accessed 28 Feb 2018.
2. *Ibid.* The PIRs for the most unaffordable major cities were: Sydney 12.2, Vancouver 11.8, Auckland 10.0, San Jose 9.6, Melbourne 9.5, Honolulu 9.4, Los Angeles 9.3, and San Francisco 9.2.
3. More recent publications on Singapore's economic development strategies include Peng and Phang (2018), Perry (2017), Koh and Mariano (eds. 2005), Wilson (ed. 2011), and Lim (ed. 2016).

References

Demographia and Performance Urban Planning. 2017. *The 13th Annual Demographia International Housing Affordability Survey 2017*. http://www.demographia.com/dhi.pdf. Accessed 1 Nov 2017.

International Monetary Fund. 2011. *Global Financial Stability Report*. Washington, DC: International Monetary Fund.

Koh, Winston T.H., and Roberto S. Mariano, eds. 2005. *The Economic Prospects of Singapore*. Singapore: Prentice Hall.

Lim, Linda Y.C., ed. 2016. *Singapore's Economic Development: Retrospection and Reflections*. Singapore: World Scientific.

Numbeo. 2017. *Property Investment Rankings*. http://www.numbeo.com/property-investment/rankings.jsp. Accessed 1 Nov 2017.

Peng, Nathan, and Sock-Yong Phang. 2018. Singapore's Economic Development: Pro- or Anti-Washington Consensus? *Economic and Political Studies* 6 (1): 30–52.

Perry, John Curtis. 2017. *Singapore: Unlikely Power*. New York: Oxford University Press.

Phang, Sock-Yong. 2013. *Housing Finance Systems: Market Failures and Government Failures*. Basingstoke: Palgrave Macmillan.

Piketty, Thomas. 2014. *Capital in the Twenty-First Century*. Cambridge: Harvard University Press.

Renaud, Bertrand, Kyung-Hwan Kim, and Man Cho. 2016. *Dynamics of Housing in East Asia*. Chichester: Wiley Blackwell.

Wilson, Peter, ed. 2011. *Challenges for the Singapore Economy After the Global Financial Crisis*. Singapore: World Scientific.

2

Land Acquisition for "Any Public Purpose"

An important policy innovation for Singapore was radical land reform through the enactment of the Land Acquisition Act of 1966 (LAA). The LAA and subsequent amendments conferred on the state enormous new powers to compulsorily acquire land for "any public purpose" from private landowners at below market prices (between 1973 and 2007). This constitutes the backbone of the large public housing programme. More than 90% of land in Singapore currently belongs to the state.[1] This chapter discusses the justification for such draconian action, and the process by which the government acquired land and implemented resettlement.[2] Government control over scarce land resource was, and remains, an important and under-appreciated part of Singapore's economic development in general and its housing programme in particular.

Historically, English land law was received in Singapore together with other English law and doctrines from 1826.[3] By the early twentieth century, large plots of land outside the city had been sold to some individuals and large private corporations mostly for agricultural use. With rapid population growth and the pressing need to provide the necessary infrastructure, the colonial government enacted the Land Acquisition Ordinance in 1920. This provided the government with general powers

S.-Y. Phang, *Policy Innovations for Affordable Housing In Singapore*,
Palgrave Advances in Regional and Urban Economics,
https://doi.org/10.1007/978-3-319-75349-2_2

to acquire private land for public purposes. The Ordinance was amended in 1946, 1955 and 1961. However, the government's powers to acquire private land remained limited, with the process cumbersome and slow. The LAA repealed the 1920 Ordinance in 1966. It granted the government increased powers for compulsory land acquisition, expedited the process for taking possession of land and regulated the compensation to be paid. There is therefore no constitutional right to ownership of private property in Singapore and, indeed, this is reflected in the Constitution of the Republic of Singapore—a point which is elaborated upon below. However, the government also implemented measures to mitigate the harsh effects of land acquisition, a point that will also be dealt with below.

Justification for Legislative Reform

Land in Singapore is extremely scarce. In 1965, the newly independent country with a population of 1.9 million occupied a total land area of 582 sq km. Through expensive and extensive coastal reclamation, the land area has increased steadily over the years and was about 720 sq km in 2017. With a population of 5.6 million in 2017, Singapore's population density is the third highest in the world after Monaco and Macau. It is this extreme land scarcity that has provided and continues to provide justification for the high degree of government intervention and optimization of land use through careful planning.

Recognizing that the prerequisite for building development infrastructure and a viable public housing programme was the availability of inexpensive land, Parliament paid much attention to reforming legislation on land reclamation and acquisition from the early 1960s. In 1961, after the huge Bukit Ho Swee fire, the government passed the fire-site provision for land acquisition. This allowed the state to acquire land occupied by squatters that was recently cleared by fire (or by natural disasters) on an encumbered basis, as though it were still occupied by squatters.

The Foreshores Act was amended in 1964 so that owners of prime seafront land would not be needed to be compensated if they lost seafront as a result of reclamation. This revision paved the way for the eventual reclamation of almost the entire coastline of Singapore for infrastructure, recreation and housing, including the Marina Bay (Centre for Liveable Cities 2016).

In 1964, Parliament also amended the Planning Ordinance to provide for a Development Charge. In moving the bill, the Minister for National Development Mr. Lim Kim San noted that with the rapidly increasing population, which was estimated to reach 4 million in 1990, the Master Plan that was originally designed for a population of 2 million would have to undergo radical changes. Approved planning permission for changes in land use and for increase in land density would cause an increase in the land price benefiting landowners through "no additional effort on their part, except that they are fortunate enough to own land near areas developed by the State".[4] Although the government was considering various other measures, including "the acquisition of development rights in land, the acquisition of the freehold in land, and even the freezing of land prices", the development charge was deemed the most practical and immediate measure that could be implemented.

The Development Charge remains an important aspect of land use control in Singapore up to the present day. The development charge as a betterment tax is levied when planning permission is granted for development projects that increase the value of the land—by the lifting of State title restrictions involving change of use and/or increase in intensity. The current development charge payable is 70% of the land enhancement value.

Since 2000, the land enhancement value or differential premium has been computed using the Development Charge Table of Rates as a reference. The Development Charge Table is updated and published by the government every half-year (on September 1 and March 1). The Table provides greater transparency and certainty in the determination of differential premiums payable for eight land use groups across 118 geographical sectors in Singapore.[5] In cases where the tenure of the land is leasehold, the rates are adjusted to reflect the residual tenure of the land using the Leasehold Table, which expresses the value of the residual tenure as a percentage of freehold value.

In 1964, the Land Acquisition Bill was also extensively debated in the legislative assembly while Singapore was a part of the Federation of Malaysia. The then Prime Minister Lee Kuan Yew explained that the approach to determining compensation for land acquired by the government should be the prevention of economic windfalls to landowners:

> *First, that no private landowner should benefit from development which had taken place at public expense; and secondly, the price paid on the acquisition for public purposes should not be higher than what the land would have been worth had the Government not contemplated development generally in the area.*[6]

Insofar as the matter of land acquisition was concerned, the views expounded by the Prime Minister were, however, inconsistent with Article 13 of the Malaysian Constitution, which provides for the right to adequate compensation in the event of compulsory acquisition. Upon independence in August 1965, the Singapore Parliament adopted all the provisions of the Malaysian Constitution regarding fundamental rights, with the exception of Article 13.

The LAA was enacted in 1966 and was a critical step in Singapore's housing policies and economic development and has had major redistribution effects (Phang 1996). The Act gives the state broad powers to acquire land:

(a) for any public purpose;
(b) by any person, corporation, or statutory board for any work or an undertaking which, in the opinion of the Minister, is of public benefit or of public utility or in the public interest; or
(c) for any residential, commercial, or industrial purposes.

Landowners cannot object to the decision, and appeals on compensation can only be made to an Appeals Board and not to the courts. Initially, almost all legal owners appealed the compensation awards and, in 1973, the concept of a statutory date was introduced. In the words of the Prime Minister (see Lee (2000, 118–119)):

> *Later, I further amended the law to give the government the power to acquire land for public purposes at its value on a date fixed at 30 November 1973. I saw no reason why private landowners should profit from an increase in land value brought about by economic development and the infrastructure paid for with public funds.*

Between 1975 and 1990, the annual GDP growth rate averaged 8%. The private housing price index grew at an average real rate of 10% per year. Land prices would have increased by much more than housing prices. Many private landowners were, however, unable to avail themselves of this high rate of return as the government acquired land not at market prices but at compensation fixed at the lower of 1973 prices or market values for most of that period. Compensation was capped at 1973 levels for some 14 years between 1973 and 1987, with no allowance being made for market valuation or the landowner's purchase price. Exceptions were made on a case-by-case basis.

Singapore has since moved to a more market-based approach for compensation of acquired land. Subsequent amendments to the Act changed the statutory date for purposes of valuation for compensation to January 1 of 1986, 1992, and 1995, respectively (Chew et al. 2010). In 2007, the use of a historical statutory date was removed by Parliament, and compensation has since been pegged to full market value.

The Land Acquisition Interface with Rent Control and Decontrol

A related piece of legislation that further depressed land prices for acquired land was the Control of Rent Act.[7] Rent control was introduced in Singapore in 1947 by the British colonial government in the aftermath of World War II to protect tenants at a time when there was a severe housing shortage. Premises built on or before September 7, 1947, except those owned by the government and statutory boards, were affected by rent control, which pegged rents to August 1, 1939 levels, or when premises built later were first let. A tenant of a rent control premise was protected from eviction by the landlord, which inhibited the release of the land for urban renewal. Rent control remained generally in effect for the next 40 years. The depressed land values caused by rent control, however, enabled the government to acquire controlled premises under the LAA for public sector projects at low compensation rates.

In 1968, with the impending withdrawal of British forces from Singapore in view, the government made the decision to establish the Asian Dollar Market in Singapore and to attract foreign financial institutions to set up operations in Singapore. This provided the impetus to develop modern commercial space within a central financial district. Legislation for block rent decontrol in the central business district was introduced in 1969.

The Controlled Premises (Special Provisions) Act of 1969 encouraged private owners of properties to redevelop their properties. The Act permitted rent-controlled premises situated in a "designated development area" to be recovered by the owners for development purposes. Under this form of decontrol, known as block decontrol, the owners of controlled premises in the designated area could apply to the Tenants Compensation Board to recover possession of their properties. They also had to demonstrate that funds were available for development. The Act provided for the compulsory acquisition of these properties if the owner failed to begin improvements within 6 months of recovery of possession of the premises.

Thirty-five hectares of commercial land in the heart of the CBD involving 770 properties were designated for block decontrol in 1970. This tract of land became known as "The Golden Shoe" area due to its high value and shape. It was selected for decontrol because of its proximity to vacant reclaimed state land that was immediately available for development (Shenton Way) and because of its location in the traditional commercial district of Raffles Place. The Tenants Compensation Board received a total of 209 applications for development of premises in the Golden Shoe area between 1970 and 1989. Of these applications, 112 were filed by the end of 1972. By 1975, 13 projects were completed, 14 were under construction and 9 were approved and waiting for work to begin (Dale 1999).

The government, however, felt that development was moving at too slow a pace. There were too many landowners each having small plots (Dale 1999). Where redevelopment did not occur, the government acquired, amalgamated and sold the land. A total of 215 lots of fragmented ownership (amounting to 31,700 square metres), which were considered unsuitable for private independent development, were acquired by the government in 1975. Despite the threat of compulsory acquisition, some owners remained reluctant to amalgamate; others were absentee landlords living in India, Sri Lanka, or Arabia (Dale 1999).

In July 1979, the Ministry for National Development warned that if owners of private properties failed to respond to the government's encouragement, the URA might have to step in to ensure redevelopment. In December 1979, the Ministry issued policy guidelines on the size of development to achieve bigger and more comprehensive development, as follows:

- Proposed development smaller than 8000 sq ft (748 sq m) would not be approved unless the adjoining site had already been developed and there was no possibility of enlarging the site.
- For any proposed development with adjoining state land of a smaller size, the developer would be asked to purchase the state land for a larger development.
- If the proposed development was smaller than 8000 sq ft and adjoining another piece of private land, both parties would be advised to combine their land. If the agreement could not be reached, then the government would acquire both pieces of land.
- If there was any private land smaller than 8000 sq ft adjoining a larger piece of state land, then the private land would be acquired to be amalgamated with the state land for future development.

As documented by Dale (1999), the government issued a second warning in January 1980 to the effect that compulsory acquisition would be considered if plans were not submitted within 3 months. In March 1980, all lots belonging to owners who did not comply or whose proposals were refused were compulsorily acquired. In 1982, after the decision was made to build Singapore's first Mass Rapid Transit lines, another round of acquisition was implemented to facilitate redevelopment of properties at Raffles Place MRT station. Between 1970 and 1985, more than 60 projects were completed, of which 80% were by the private sector and the remainder on sites sold by the URD/URA on behalf of the state (Dale 1999, 147).

Vacant rent decontrol was introduced in 1980. Block rent decontrol for designated conservation areas was implemented in 1988 and rent control was completely abolished by 2001.

Overcoming Public Resistance to Government Land Acquisition

State land, as a proportion of total land, grew from 44% in 1960 to 76% by 1985, and the ratio was approximately 90% by 2005.[8] A significant portion of the increase in state land can be attributed to land reclamation because about one-fifth of Singapore's land is reclaimed land, which automatically becomes state land. Land acquisition was an important step in Singapore's housing policies. However, it meant that existing owners had to be expropriated. In most other countries, such clearance would have encountered strong resistance by dwellers. This was also the case in 1960s Singapore, when resettlement was initially viewed with hostility and suspicion (Centre for Liveable Cities 2014, 21).

To overcome such resistance, the government's policy was to provide suitable alternative accommodation for *all* businesses and persons affected by its land acquisition programmes. Planners at that time estimated that for every slum structure demolished then, seven new flats were required to relocate families affected (Choe 1975). This meant that the processes for public housing construction, land acquisition, slum clearance and resettlement, and urban renewal in Singapore were closely interrelated. Chua (1997, 132) shows how commitment to universal provision of housing "allowed the PAP government to take the strong moral high ground on acquisition of land for public housing".

A detailed study of land acquisition and resettlement can be found in Centre for Liveable Cities (2014); the study highlights several reasons for the relative success of land acquisition and resettlement in Singapore as compared with obstacles and resistance in other countries. These included the following factors:

(i) Legal and constitutional mandate as well as clear processes in the form of the Land Acquisition Act that established legitimacy and the rule of law in the conduct of public officials carrying out these duties;
(ii) Meticulous and detailed processes for record keeping and calculation of compensation for squatters' assets at market value;

(iii) The superiority of alternative accommodation, business premises, and environments offered by the government to affected people to replace the land or property that had been taken from them—although squatters had no legal interest in the affected land, they were compensated for improvements (such as shacks, vegetable plots, and livestock) and were also given priority allocation of new land (in the case of farmers) or Housing and Development Board (HDB) flats. Displaced small traditional businesses in the central area were assigned shop units in modern complexes built be the Urban Redevelopment Authority, with subsidized rent.

(iv) Effective forward planning and coordination to ensure smooth resettlement due largely to the integrated housing, resettlement, and estate planning functions of the HDB as the Resettlement Department was housed within the HDB from 1963.

These nuanced and meticulously coordinated measures to minimize disruptions, combined with tangible growth and employment opportunities, led to greater popular support for land acquisition efforts.

Subsidiary legislation in the form of State Land Rules 1968 provided that titles for state-owned land would be for terms not exceeding 99 years. Through the Land Acquisition Act, the government cleared low-density housing, slums, villages, and squatter areas, and assembled land parcels in their stead. State land was leased to government agencies for the development of high-rise "public" housing that were sold on a 99-year leasehold basis to eligible households as well as for the development of industrial estates, educational institutions, and other urban public amenities.

From the 1960s to 1980s, the government was able to carry out its land acquisition activities as affected households and businesses were resettled into improved affordable HDB housing and commercial shop units. The benefits of the state land acquisition and land rents redistribution programme were very apparent as HDB housing estates and industrial and commercial developments were built—these also contributed to the creation of jobs and rapid economic development. To have acquired sites from private owners and then to release the same sites for sale via tender for *housing* would have been difficult for the government to justify then, although this did take place for *commercial* developments in the context of central area redevelopment.

A Quiet Revolution

Singapore's land policies can be described as land reform in an urban setting. In the 40 years after the LAA was enacted, over 15,000 land parcels were acquired (Centre for Liveable Cities 2014, 45). This involved a massive and steady transfer of land resources from private landowners to the state—a large-scale selective nationalization of land that was managed peacefully. The fact that large plots of land in Singapore were owned by a small number of wealthy landowners during the 1960s helped explain why acquiring land from this group was regarded as fair by Parliament.[9] When the LAA was passed, fewer than 10% of people owned property. Chua (1997, 134) writes that "the popularity of the government's action among the overwhelming property-less electorate enabled it to bear the rejection of this very small minority". This quiet revolution in land ownership contributed to the development of industrial estates, the financial district, commercial developments, the large public housing programme, as well as public sector infrastructure development.

Public land leasing for private sector development generally goes under the term "Government Land Sales" in Singapore.[10] Much urban redevelopment in Singapore has been achieved through this land sales programme administered mainly by the Urban Redevelopment Authority and, to a lesser extent, the Singapore Land Authority, the Jurong Town Corporation, and the HDB. Under the programme, the government amalgamated or reclaimed land, built infrastructure, provided planning and urban design guidelines, and released the land for sale to private (including foreign) developers (Phang 2005 and Chap. 5). Sites are usually sold on 99-year leases for commercial, hotel, and private residential development whereas leases for industrial sites are usually for 60 years or less. The lease tenure for other types of sites varies depending on the uses. The usual sale method is through public tender.

Proceeds from land sales do not constitute part of the government's operating revenue, but are instead channelled into government reserves. Singapore's public wealth is estimated to be more than 2.5 times its GDP. These are the net assets of the two sovereign wealth funds (Temasek Holdings and the Government Investment Corporation) and the Monetary Authority of Singapore. Investment income from these institutions contribute to the government's annual operating revenue.

The success of Singapore in capturing land rents for development and redistribution resonates with the ideas of the nineteenth century American economist Henry George (1879). Henry George made a strong case for 100% taxation of rents from land, which he regarded as common property. George claimed that such taxation would abolish poverty and economic crisis, as the latter, he said, resulted from speculation in land values. In its approach to land, Singapore has embraced a large dose of George's prescription (Phang 1996).

There is, however, no hint of Henry George's tax proposals if one is to examine the property tax system in Singapore. The Singapore government has, instead, relied on the process of nationalization of land on a selective basis in order to effect the process of land value capture. The determination of compensation for land acquired by the government, from 1960s to as recently as 2007, was consistent with Henry George's philosophy that landowners should not enjoy a windfall from development that had taken place at public expense. Rent flows directly to the state through leases instead of being paid by owners in the form of taxes. According to Andelson (2000, xxxv), "George had considered this approach and found it acceptable enough on moral grounds, but regarded the use of tax method as more efficient administratively and preferable where private ownership of land is well entrenched".

However, there are clear differences. First, George did not advocate nationalization of land, simply the taxation of the site or location value of land. The developmental objectives of the state in Singapore (coupled with severe land scarcity), however, necessitated the nationalization of large parcels of land for industrial and housing estates—land which was previously often under individual and fragmented ownership. Second, nationalization was enforced on a selective basis, thus violating the principle of horizontal equity resulting in wipeouts for some property owners and windfalls for others. Third, the process involved a one-time capture of land rents on a selective basis. A system for the perpetual capture of all land rents was not instituted. Since 2007, compensation for acquired land has been pegged to full current market value.

However, despite what (to George and many others) would have been considered shortcomings of this partial land value capture process, the Singapore government managed to capture a significant amount of land rents via its imperfect system, relative to the situations of governments elsewhere. The broad control over a critical resource effectively gave the state the capacity to extensively control and plan land use, enabling coordinated planning and a large public housing programme, as well as the flexibility to shift allocations among competing needs for economic development.

Notes

1. The 90% state land ownership figure is from the Singapore Land Authority website http://sla.gov.sg. Accessed 25 Oct 2005. The Singapore Land Authority was established as a statutory board on 1 June 2001 when the Land Office, Singapore Land Registry, Survey Department and Land Systems Support Unit were merged.
2. This chapter draws on my previously published writings on this topic in Phang (1992, 1996, 2001, 2007, 2013), and Phang and Helbe (2016).
3. For a succinct account of Singapore's land law, see Chew et al. (2010) and Chapter 29 of Singapore Academy of Law (2017).
4. Planning (Amendment Bill), Singapore Parliamentary Debates, November 2, 1964.
5. See the website of the Urban Redevelopment Authority at https://www.ura.gov.sg/uol/guidelines/development-control/development-charge. Accessed 1 Nov 2017.
6. Singapore Parliamentary Debates, June 10, 1964. See also Centre for Liveable Cities (2014, 12–18).
7. This section draws from Phang (2005).
8. Phang (1992, 24) and Singapore Land Authority, see note 1.

9. Large agricultural plots outside the city were owned by wealthy individuals and British private companies and less than 10% of the population owned property (Centre for Liveable Cities 2014, 46–47).
10. See the website of the Urban Redevelopment Authority at https://www.ura.gov.sg/uol/land-sales.aspx. Accessed 1 Nov 2017.

References

Andelson, Robert V. 2000. Introduction. Special supplement: Land Value Taxation Around the World. *The American Journal of Economics and Sociology* 59 (5), xix–xlii.

Centre for Liveable Cities. 2014. *Land Acquisition and Resettlement: Securing Resources for Development*. Singapore: Centre for Liveable Cities.

———. 2016. *A Chance of a Lifetime: Lee Kuan Yew and the Physical Transformation of Singapore*. Singapore: Centre for Liveable Cities and Lee Kuan Yew Centre for Innovative Cities.

Chew, Bryan, Vincent Hoong, Lee Koon Tay, and Manimegalia Vellasamy. 2010. Compulsory Acquisition of Land in Singapore: A Fair Regime. *Singapore Academy of Law Journal* 22: 166–188.

Choe, Alan F.C. 1975. Urban Renewal. In *Public Housing in Singapore: A Multi-Disciplinary Study*, ed. Stephen H.K. Yeh, 97–116. Singapore: Singapore University Press for Housing and Development Board.

Chua, Beng Huat. 1997. *Political Legitimacy and Housing: Stakeholding in Singapore*. London/New York: Routledge.

Dale, Ole Johan. 1999. *Urban Planning in Singapore: The Transformation of a City*. Shah Alam: Oxford University Press.

George, Henry. 1879. *Progress and Poverty: An Inquiry into the Cause of Industrial Depressions and of the Increase of Want with Increase of Wealth … The Remedy*. San Francisco: Author's Proof Edition. Edition referred to: 1971, New York: Robert Schalkenbach Foundation.

Lee, Kuan Yew. 2000. *From Third World to First: The Singapore Story 1965–2000*. Singapore: Singapore Press Holdings.

Phang, Sock-Yong. 1992. *Housing Markets and Urban Transportation: Economic Theory, Econometrics and Policy Analysis for Singapore*. Singapore: McGraw Hill.

———. 1996. Economic Development and the Distribution of Land Rents in Singapore: A Georgist Implementation. *American Journal of Economics and Sociology* 55: 489–501.

———. 2001. Housing Policy, Wealth Formation and the Singapore Economy. *Housing Studies* 16 (4): 443–459.

———. 2005. *Government and Private Sector Roles in Inner City Redevelopment: The Case of Singapore*. Paper Presented at Seoul International Seminar on Real Estate, December 7–8, 2005. Seoul: Korea Housing Association and Ministry of Construction and Transportation.

———. 2007. The Singapore Model of Housing and the Welfare State. In *Housing and the New Welfare State*, ed. Richard Groves, Alan Murie, and Christopher Watson. Aldershot: Ashgate.

———. 2013. *Housing Finance Systems: Market Failures and Government Failures*. Basingstoke: Palgrave Macmillan.

Phang, Sock-Yong, and Matthias Helbe. 2016. Housing Policies in Singapore. In *The Housing Challenge in Emerging Asia: Options and Solutions*, ed. Naoyuki Yoshino and Matthias Helbe, 174–209. Tokyo: Asian Development Bank Institute.

Singapore Academy of Law, Laws of Singapore, Chapter 29 at: http://www.singaporelaw.sg/sglaw/laws-of-singapore/commercial-law/chapter-29. Accessed 1 Nov 2017.

Singapore Parliamentary Debates. Official Reports. https://www.parliament.gov.sg/parliamentary-business/official-reports-(parl-debates). Accessed 1 Nov 2017.

3

Public Housing for Sale

The Orgins of Public Housing in Singapore

In almost all developed countries, the term "public housing" is commonly understood to refer to subsidized rental housing provided by the government to low-income households who are unable to afford minimum standard housing at market rental rates. This was the form of public housing also adopted in Singapore during the colonial period, which was characterized by chronic housing shortages. The Singapore Improvement Trust (SIT), a statutory board created by the colonial government in 1927, had been established as a town planning authority and also undertook road construction as well as general improvement of the city. In 1932, the housing shortage led the government to expand the SIT's responsibilities to include the provision of houses and flats for the lower-income groups. By 1941, on the eve of World War II, the SIT had completed construction of only 2000 dwellings.[1] The war and subsequent Japanese Occupation from 1942 to 1945 brought the SIT building programme to a halt.

During the post-war period, the immediate housing shortage was acute. In response, the colonial government implemented rent control in 1947 to protect tenants. The SIT stepped up public housing construction,

S.-Y. Phang, *Policy Innovations for Affordable Housing In Singapore*,
Palgrave Advances in Regional and Urban Economics,
https://doi.org/10.1007/978-3-319-75349-2_3

building an estimated 20,907 units between 1947 and 1959. However, the pace of construction was unable to deal adequately with the housing shortage, which had been exacerbated by rapid post-war population growth. SIT dwellings housed 8.8% of the population by 1959, with the majority of the population living either in overly congested shophouses, slums, or squatter settlements without piped water and modern sanitation (Latif 2009, 78)—housing that was of a very inferior quality when compared to SIT public housing.

Given the appalling overcrowding as well as accompanying conditions, the newly elected government made the provision of homes on a large scale a priority area of policy concern. The Planning Bill as well as the Housing and Development Board (HDB) Bill were passed by Parliament in 1959. In 1960, the SIT was dissolved and the HDB was set up as a new statutory board, with a mandate in order to provide "decent homes equipped with modern amenities for all those who needed them" (Teh 1975, 6). The SIT's planning and development control functions were taken over by the Planning Department under the Prime Minister's Office.

In its initial years of operation, the HDB followed the British public housing model of the SIT in providing only rental units. A target of completing 110,000 dwelling units was set for the period between 1960 and 1970. The effectiveness of the HDB was very soon put to the test. On May 25, 1961, a huge fire broke out in the Bukit Ho Swee squatter district, which rendered about 16,000 people homeless. Housing the victims of the fire became the HDB's first major challenge. The government compulsorily acquired the burned-out land as a site for 12,000 low-cost flats and promised to complete the first blocks of flats within 9 months. The first five blocks of flats were completed by February 1962 and all 16,000 people who had lost their homes in the fire had been rehoused on the same site by the end of 1964 (Latif 2009, 81–84).[2] Some of these were one-room "Emergency" flats (23 square metres) that had been hastily built. From these beginnings, the HDB went on to rapidly improve the quality and size of its flats and to exceed its building targets, building 54,430 units by 1965 and 120,669 units by 1970 (Yeh 1975, 9).

HDB Flats for Sale

An important housing policy innovation was launched in 1964: the HDB would build and offer public housing flats for sale on 99-year leases under a Home Ownership Scheme (HOS).[3] The HDB priced housing units affordably for households with incomes not exceeding S$800 a month, and offered loans such that owners paid less in monthly mortgage payments than they would have done in rents. The political and social motivations for the HOS are perhaps best understood in the words of the then Prime Minister, Mr Lee Kuan Yew, as follows:

> *My primary preoccupation was to give every citizen a stake in the country and its future. I wanted a home-owning society. I had seen the contrast between the blocks of low-cost rental flats, badly misused and poorly maintained, and those of house-proud owners, and was convinced that if every family owned its home, the country would be more stable (page 116)… I had seen how voters in capital cities always tended to vote against the government of the day and was determined that our householders should become homeowners, otherwise we would not have political stability. My other important motive was to give all parents whose sons would have to do national service a stake in the Singapore their sons had to defend. If the soldier's family did not own their home, he would soon conclude he would be fighting to protect the properties of the wealthy. I believed this sense of ownership was vital for our new society which had no deep roots in a common historical experience.* (Lee 2000, 117)

Policies were therefore introduced in order to achieve the goal of homeownership. Housing institutions were developed systematically and comprehensively in order to solve the housing crisis and to advance social development and economic growth.[4] HDB flats were priced affordably and the HDB itself also served as a mortgage lender—providing mortgage loans and mortgage insurance to purchasers of its leasehold flats. The current loan quantum is 90% of the price of the new flat and the maximum repayment period is 25 years. The government is the source of loans to the HDB to finance its mortgage lending. The switch to affordable homeownership also made economic sense. While subsidized rental public housing would be a permanent drain on the government's budget and would also be a less acceptable housing tenure to the middle class, homeownership allowed the government to recover the full construction costs of each project from sale revenues and to scale up the HDB programme in a sustainable way.

The Central Provident Fund was transformed to mobilize domestic savings for down payment and mortgage payments for homeownership (see the next chapter). This led to the HDB building housing estates for not just the lower-income group, but, over time, also for the middle- and upper-middle households. Singapore's large public housing sector is therefore, in ownership terms, a largely privatized sector. However, ownership tenure of an HDB dwelling differs in many aspects from ownership of a private dwelling. Ownership rights are limited by numerous regulations concerning eligibility conditions for purchase, resale, subletting, rental, and housing loans.

The HDB brought about a complete transformation of the housing supply side. Table 3.1 shows the rate of increase in population and the stock of housing from 1970 to 2017. The number of HDB dwellings increased dramatically from 120,138 units in 1970 to 337,198 units in 1980, an increase of 181%. This was in contrast to a population increase of 16% and a decline in the private housing stock of 30%, as low-density shophouses and squatter settlements were demolished. As the housing shortage eased, the HDB kept up with changes in household incomes, introducing the 4-room, 5-room, and Executive flats in the 1970s, which were priced affordably. The monthly household income ceiling to be eligible to purchase a HDB flat was raised from $1000 in 1964 to $2500 by 1979 and $5000 by 1989. The homeownership rate doubled from 29.4% in 1970 to 58.8% in 1980, and reached 87.5% by 1990. HDB dwellings as a proportion of the housing stock increased from 39% in 1970 to 83% by 1990—the housing shortage had been solved and the vision of a property-*owning* democracy had become a reality.

In 2017, the HDB housing stock of about 1 million flats housed 3.2 million (82%) of Singapore's resident population of 4.0 million in 2017. Figure 3.1 shows the distribution of dwelling types in Singapore with HDB flats accounting for 73% of the available housing stock.

These flats are located in 23 HDB towns and 3 estates extending outwards from the central area. Housing units increased by about 50% in

Table 3.1 Housing stock, housing supply, and homeownership rate, 1970–2017

	Population ('000)	Total housing stock	HDB housing	Private housing	Persons per dwelling unit	HDB dwellings as proportion of housing stock	Resident home-ownership rate
1970	2075	305,833	120,138	185,695	6.8	39%	29.4%
1980	2414	467,142	337,198	129,944	5.2	72%	58.8%
1990	3047	690,561	574,443	116,118	4.4	83%	87.5%
2000	4017	1,039,677	846,649	193,028	3.9	81%	92.0%
2010	5076	1,156,732	898,532	258,200	4.4	78%	87.2%
2017	5612	1,385,497	1,017,335	368,162	4.1	73%	90.9%
% Change							
1970–1980	16%	53%	181%	−30%	−24%	84%	100%
1980–1990	26%	48%	70%	−11%	−15%	15%	49%
1990–2000	32%	51%	47%	66%	−12%	−2%	5%
2000–2010	26%	11%	6%	34%	14%	−3%	−5%
2010–2017	11%	20%	13%	43%	−8%	−6%	4%

Sources: Data from Singapore government publications and websites

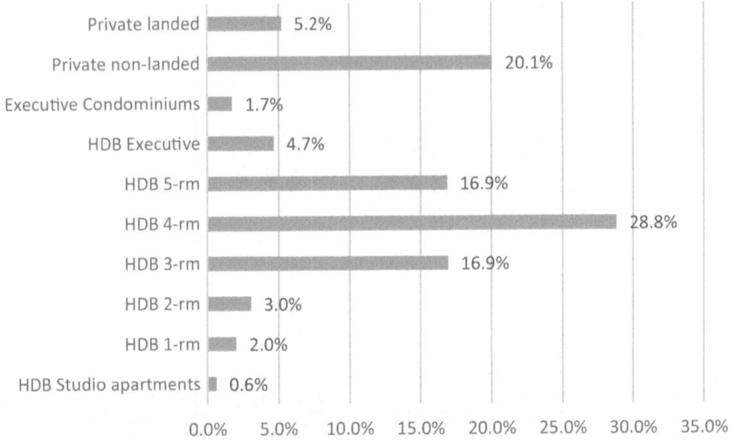

Fig. 3.1 Stock of available housing in Singapore by dwelling type, 2017 (Source: HDB and Singapore Department of Statistics websites)

each decade from 1970 to 2000, outstripping population growth. In particular, HDB housing displaced private housing as low-density shophouses, squatter settlements, and villages were acquired by the government and demolished, and affected residents resettled in high-rise flats.

To discourage rentals, the HDB limited rental flats available under its Public Rental Scheme to mainly 1- and 2-room flat types. The eligible criteria to rent a flat from the HDB were very stringent with the income ceiling first set at $800 in 1960 and remaining unchanged for more than four decades. This was finally raised to $1500 only in 2003 and has remained unchanged since. However, households earning more than $800 per month receive a lower subsidy on their flat rentals than those earning less than $800. Tenants were encouraged to become homeowners with those in selected locations given the option to purchase their existing flat from the HDB. Only 5.7% of HDB flats in 2017 were allocated for the Public Rental Scheme.

In the 1990s, the focus of housing policy *shifted* from resettlement to "upgrading" as well as demand-side housing policies. HDB provided larger and better-quality flats and facilitated upgrading for existing HDB and upper-middle-income households. An active secondary HDB housing market enabled a household that had purchased another property (either HDB or private housing) to sell the HDB flat at market prices after a minimum of 5 years of occupancy. Resale HDB prices are higher than prices for new HDB flats as, unlike new flats, there is no need to wait 3 to 4 years for the new projects to be completed. Moreover, permanent resident households as well as those who are ineligible for HDB subsidized flats are permitted to purchase resale flats instead. In order to encourage first-time homeowners who are otherwise eligible to buy HDB new flats to buy a resale flat instead, Central Provident Fund housing grants for resale HDB flats were introduced (see Chap. 8 for details). Chapter 6 describes the deregulation of the HDB resale market from the late 1980s. Programmes were also launched for the redevelopment of older estates, and retrofitting of existing flats (see below). During this period, the government frequently referred to HDB homes as an asset with value enhancement potential, as well as a source of security for retirement (Centre for Liveable Cities and HDB 2013, 15).

HDB Estate Improvements and Redevelopment

In the HDB sector, a spatial age gradient for HDB estates as well as households had become evident by the late 1980s. As the city expanded outward from the central business district (CBD), while older HDB estates had been built closer to the CBD, new towns were built at distances further away. Also evident was the trend of younger families moving out of older HDB towns because they were allocated new flats in outlying new towns. In 1989, HDB upgrading programmes to improve existing estates were announced by the government. The upgrading programmes vary in nature and scale and are substantially subsidized by the government (see Table 3.2; Tay 2008; and Centre for Liveable Cities and HDB 2013).

The government also introduced the Selective En bloc Redevelopment Scheme (SERS) in 1995. Under this scheme, old HDB estates with high redevelopment potential are identified. The government acquires the flats by compensating flat owners at the prevailing market price plus removal expenses. Affected households have the option to be resettled in new and higher-density replacement flats located within the same neighbourhood

Table 3.2 Programmes under HDB's estate renewal strategy

Main Upgrading Programme (MUP)
Launched in 1989 to enhance overall living environment of estate
Residents offered "standard package" comprising improvements to precinct, block, and within flat
Option of space adding item, that is, extra bathroom, balcony, or kitchen extension
Proceed only if 75% of Singapore Citizen-eligible households vote in favour of upgrading works
Lift Upgrading Programme (LUP)
Launched in 2001 to provide direct lift access, where feasible, to existing HDB blocks without 100% direct lift access
Proceed only if 75% of Singapore Citizen-eligible households in a block vote in favour of it
Home Improvement Programme
Replaced the MUP since August 2007
Focus is on improvements within the flats
Essential improvements include replacement of waste pipes, repair of structural cracks, spalling concrete and ceiling leaks, as well as upgrading of electrical supply, which are fully funded by the government
Residents may opt for *improvements works* such as replacement of entrance door, grille gate, and refuse hopper, as well as upgrading of toilets/bathrooms, at highly subsidized costs (Singapore citizens residing in 3-room flats pay 5% of the cost, while those in 5-room flat contribute 10% of the costs)
Interim Upgrading Programme (IUP) and IUP Plus
Launched in 1993
Provides pedestrian covered linkways, repainting of blocks, and new letter boxes
Fully funded by the government
Combined with LUP as "IUP Plus" in May 2002
Neighbourhood Renewal Programme
Replaced the IUP Plus in August 2007
Focus on block and neighbourhood improvements and can be implemented on a larger area basis of two or more contiguous precincts
All costs borne by government and implemented by town councils
Examples of improvements include residents' corners and lift lobby tiling, drop-off porch, linkways, soccer pitch, fitness corners, and jogging track at neighbourhood level
Proceed if at least 75% of eligible flat owners in the neighbourhood indicate their support

(*continued*)

Table 3.2 (continued)

Selective En Bloc Redevelopment Scheme (SERS)
Introduced in 1995 to rejuvenate and intensify development in older estates
Precincts are selected based on criteria of clear economic benefits to the country; this is assessed by considering the redevelopment potential of the site, taking into account the cost of acquisition and reconstruction, and other related costs
Remaking Our Heartland
Launched in 2007 as a new comprehensive blueprint to renew and further develop existing HDB towns and estates
To ensure sustainability and vibrancy of the HDB heartlands and to make Singapore a distinctive and endearing home for all

Sources: HDB website; Centre for Liveable Cities and HDB (2013, Appendix B); and Tay (2008)

(termed as designated replacement sites). These are priced below market values and come with fresh 99-year leases. From 1995 to 2016, 80 sites were selected for redevelopment through the SERS. As of 2017, redevelopment at 73 sites has been completed, and 6 are currently in progress.[5]

Middle-Income Housing Schemes

The success of the HDB in resettling households and providing affordable homeownership led to increased requests for assistance from the "sandwiched" middle-income households. These constituted young professionals whose incomes were too high to qualify for HDB housing, but which were too low for them to afford owning private apartments. The supply gap between HDB new flats and private sector housing options therefore needed to be filled. Over the past few decades, the government has experimented with different schemes in response to these concerns, with varying degrees of success.

The first such scheme, launched between 1974 and 1982, was middle-income housing to be provided by a government-owned company—the Housing and Urban Development Company (HUDC). The household ceiling for HUDC in 1974 was set at $4000 per month as compared to the HDB's then $1500 income ceiling for 5-room flats. The HUDC was established as a joint venture company by the HDB and the Urban

Redevelopment Authority. HUDC flats were larger than HDB flats and constructed in exclusive estates, similar to private sector condominiums. Purchasers of HUDC were allowed to use their savings in the Central Provident Fund (CPF) in the same manner as HDB homebuyers (see Chap. 4). Between 1976 and 1982, the HUDC sold 2732 units of housing.

The HUDC was absorbed into the HDB in 1982, after which the HDB built an additional 5275 units of middle-income housing between 1982 and 1987. The sale prices of HUDC units were not subsidized after 1983, and were priced to recover total development costs (Phang 1992, 65–66). The relaxation of CPF regulations in order to allow the purchase of private housing with CPF savings, followed by the property downturn in the mid-1980s, led to a situation where the HDB was unable to sell over 1000 HUDC units in 1986. This was despite an increase in the HUDC income ceiling to $6000 and the HDB's to $4000 in 1985. The HUDC middle-income housing scheme was then discontinued.

Commencing in 1979, the HDB began offering larger Executive flats as part of its Home Ownership Scheme. The sizes of these flats at 145 sq metres are comparable to, if not larger than, most private housing apartments. The growing demand for this category of housing and their resale premiums in the 1990s caused a rethink of the role of the HDB in providing such apartments at subsidized prices. In 1995, in response to concern over the affordability of private housing, the government introduced the Executive Condominium (EC) scheme, a hybrid public-private house type. ECs are of comparable quality to suburban private sector condominium projects. The EC scheme also facilitated the HDB's withdrawal from the upper-middle-income housing market, allowing it to discontinue its building of Executive Flats.

The government auctions land for the development of EC units to housing developers (private as well as government-linked companies) who are responsible for design, construction, and pricing. Applicant households have to satisfy eligibility conditions and abide by resale and other regulations governing these units. Executive Condominiums (EC) are classified as private housing, but purchasers face many of the restrictions that apply to HDB homeowners. The sector is regulated in the following ways: prices are set by the developer; supply is determined by the government land sales programme; applicant households have to satisfy eligibility conditions (such as household income ceiling) and abide by occupancy, resale and other regulations governing these units; first-time homeowners are eligible for the CPF housing grant which can be used towards the down payment; the units can be sold only after 5 years to Singaporeans and permanent residents, and can be sold after 10 years to foreigners. The EC's similarity with 99-year leasehold private condominiums provided the government with another instrument on the supply side to impact private housing prices.

In June 2005, the HDB launched a Design, Build and Sell Scheme (DBSS) under which the government tendered out land for public housing development to private developers. The developer who is awarded the tender will undertake the entire development from planning, design, and construction to the sale of flats at prices to be determined by the developer. However, the flats remain as HDB flats with 99-year leaseholds and are subject to all HDB eligibility criteria, rules, and conditions. First-time homeowners were eligible to receive a demand-side subsidy in the form of the $30,000 (or $40,000) CPF housing grant similar to first-time buyers of HDB resale flats. In 2010, the DBSS income ceiling was raised to $10,000 and further increased to $12,000 in 2015 (the same as the HDB's). However, land sales for DBSS projects have been halted since 2011 due to public unhappiness over high prices as well as complaints by flat owners about design and quality.

Exporting HDB's Expertise

The HDB plays a major role as master planner of its estates and towns: it acquires and clears sites for development or redevelopment, resettles and/or compensates affected households and businesses, and coordinates with other government agencies for provision of infrastructure as well as local and social amenities. HDB planners and architects provide detailed building designs for private sector construction companies that tender for HDB projects. Over the decades, its Building and Development Division had built up rich and deep expertise in urban planning, design, and construction of high-density new towns.

After the Asian Financial Crisis of 1998, both the private and public housing sectors were faced with a situation of declining prices and unsold units. A study in 2001 estimated unsold housing stock of approximately 19,800 units for the private sector (Monetary Authority of Singapore 2001). With more than 17,500 unsold new flats in early 2002, the HDB suspended its Registration for Flat or queuing system, diverting remaining and new applicants to a Build-To-Order (BTO) programme, under which flats are built only when there is sufficient demand for them. In July 2003, in a major restructuring exercise, the HDB's 3000-strong Building and Development Division was reorganized and the HDB Corporation Private Limited (HDB Corp) set up as a fully owned subsidiary of HDB. At the time of restructuring HDB's staff strength was 8000, including 3000 in the Building and Development Division. The new HDB Corp took in about 800–1000 staff.

In November 2004, HDB divested its 100% shareholding in HDB Corp to the government's investment holding company, Temasek Holdings. Under Temasek, HDB Corp evolved into the Surbana group of companies, which continues to provide town planning services to the HDB and which also ventured into several housing development projects overseas. In 2015, in a merger involving two Jurong Town Corporation subsidiaries and two Temasek urban development companies, Surbana became part of Surbana Jurong Private Limited. The merged integrated company has a combined aggregate value of S$5 billion and is involved in large scale and complex urban development projects in several Asian countries. The HDB's experience in sustainable high-density housing provision on a large scale has thus become an exportable expertise.

HDB's Supply Responses to Changes in Demand

As is generally the case for all real estate markets, the property markets in Singapore exhibit cyclical behaviour (Phang 2013, Chapter 9). As the housing stock comprises mainly high-density apartments, which are capital intensive and come with longer approval processes and completion

Fig. 3.2 HDB and private housing price indices, 1975–2017 (Source: Singapore government websites)

times, the supply lag can be up to 5 years. Moreover, projects are generally irreversible once begun. The HDB, as the dominant supplier of housing in Singapore as well as the provider of subsidized homes, has had to adjust its supply policies in response to booming and waning demand. Figure 3.2 shows the cyclical behaviour of housing prices in the private housing and HDB resale housing sectors (nominal values). HDB began tracking resale prices only from 1990 when the resale market become more active, while the private housing index became available from 1975.

From Fig. 3.2, it can be seen that, since 1975, consistent with growth in incomes, population, and wealth, the property market has been on a long-term upward trend. There were, however, five periods of price declines for private housing prices:

(i) 1984–1986, when Singapore experienced its first recession since independence;
(ii) 1996–1998, after anti-speculation measures were introduced and which were then followed by the Asian financial crisis;
(iii) 2000–2003, when recovery was anaemic during a period when the economy was affected by global uncertainties following 9–11, the Bali bombings, and the SARS crisis;

(iv) 2008–2009, when the US subprime crisis evolved into a global financial crisis;
(v) 2013–2016, when several rounds of macroprudential measures to deflate property prices took effect.

During the contrasting periods of housing booms in the first half of the 1980s and 1990s, the HDB was faced with long and growing waiting lists for its flats. There were more than 100,000 households on the waiting list in some of the boom years. However, during the housing bust period, the waiting list "evaporated" and the HDB found difficulty in selling its flats. In the late 1980s, the HDB's stock of unsold housing was location specific and coexisted with a general waiting list of over 40,000 households. The HDB subsequently converted the smaller 3- and 4-room flats in Yishun into larger 7-room or Jumbo-Executive flats in order to clear the stock of unsold flats in Yishun.

In the late 1990s, the housing bust during the Asian crisis led to a situation of more than 17,500 unsold new HDB flats. The HDB, however, maintained the prices of its new flats despite the unsold flats and thus helped to cushion price declines in the HDB resale market. In 2002, the HDB suspended its Registration for Flat or queuing system, diverting remaining and new applicants to its BTO programme, under which flats are built only when there is sufficient demand for them. After successfully balloting and confirming their booking for a flat in a particular project, the household would then have to wait for 3 to 4 years for the project to be completed. For the entire decade 2000–2010, the number of HDB dwelling units increased by only 6%, or around 50,000 units (see Table 3.1)—one of the slowest growth periods for housing stock in HDB's history. This was during a period when the population increased by 1 million or 26% (from 4.0 to 5.1 million), as compared to an overall increase in housing stock of 117,000 units (11%).

The combination of conservative housing supply policy, population increases, and US' quantitative easing monetary policies contributed to rapid increase in prices for both new and resale HDB flats from 2007 to 2011. The 2011 election served to reveal the deep unhappiness of the electorate over various municipal issues—the influx of new immigrants, overcrowding on trains, escalating house prices, and, for first-time homebuyers, repeated failure to secure a HDB BTO flat at ballots. The PAP managed to win only 60% of the popular vote and lost six parliamentary seats.[6]

To address the housing affordability issue, the government introduced a slew of stringent market "cooling" measures in rapid succession to curb house price increases (see Chap. 6). The income ceiling for HDB and ECs were raised and CPF housing grants made more generous. On the supply side, the government ramped up HDB's building programmes and government land sales significantly. Between 2010 and 2016, the number of HDB flats increased by 10% or 94,000 units, with another 86,307 units under construction as at March 2016 (HDB Annual Report 2015/2016). In 2013, the Minister for National Development announced that prices of new HDB flats would be delinked from resale prices, which began to decline from mid-2013. A "soft-landing" rather than a crash had been achieved and the PAP government went on to regain 70% of the electoral vote in the 2015 election.

A Successful State-Owned Housing Developer

The HDB is undoubtedly one of the most important government agencies in Singapore. The organization itself as well as its leaders have won numerous international awards and accolades for successfully housing an entire nation. That a 100% state-owned enterprise (SOE) has been able to achieve this may come as a surprise to those who hold a negative view of SOEs. Housing provision and real estate development are, after all, best performed by the private sector in almost all capitalist economies. In the 1950s and 1960s, however, it was recognized by development economists and the World Bank that SOEs can be a strategic investor in new industries, help fill a market gap, or reduce the concentration ratio and potential abuse of dominance by real estate oligarchs. After World War II and right up to the 1970s, SOEs in fact played an enormous role in production throughout the world even in market economies. Government ownership was more restrained in the US, Japan, and Germany, and was significant in countries such as UK, Italy, France, Austria, as well as in former colonies in Africa and Asia. In the socialist economies, the state owned and controlled everything.[7]

In practice, SOEs were often "highly inefficient, inflexible, poorly performing employment agencies, politically pressured to maintain and expand employment far beyond what was needed" (Yergin and Stanislaw 1998, 97). The stagflation of the 1970s led to a serious rethink of failings of SOEs and the mixed economy, beginning in Chile and the UK. After the Conservative Party election victory in 1979, the then Prime Minister Margaret Thatcher subsequently moved to get the government out of running businesses—a policy that became known as privatization. The wave of privatization was to spread around the world, to the rest of Europe, Latin American, and India, accelerating after the collapse of communism in the USSR and in Eastern Europe.

The HDB is thus unique amongst large housing developers in having resisted being privatized, and continues to be run as a statutory board. How is one to understand the factors behind the HDB's resilience and continued sustainability as an SOE for more than five decades? In order to address this question, we consider both the wider context within which the HDB operates as well as its organizational practices.

The Wider Context

By delivering on the government's promises to make homeownership affordable, the HDB brought about the physical and social transformation of the country. This was in the context of rapid growth in incomes and standards of living, and low unemployment. To perform its task, the HDB enjoyed the unstinting support of the government on all fronts. The Land Acquisition Act of 1966 conferred powers on the HDB to acquire land, resettle affected households, and redevelop the city from the central area outwards. The long-term land use plans made provisions for the development of comprehensive HDB towns. With one unitary level of government, planning and infrastructure provision for HDB towns was efficiently coordinated across multiple agencies (Liu 2017).

The government supported the HDB financially in the form of annual grants to fully cover its deficits incurred for development, maintenance, and upgrading of estates. It also provided loans to the HDB in order that it could offer mortgage loans to homebuyers. In the next chapter, we will discuss how domestic savings since 1968 have been compulsorily mobilized in order to support the HDB's homeownership programme, and which constitutes the other important pillar of the housing framework in Singapore. Since 2005, the government has also provided housing grants in a targeted manner to households in order to ensure housing affordability even as housing prices increased.

The HDB's housing policy "innovation" of providing homes for sale and eventually catering to the housing needs of more than 80% of the population have also helped to sustain the social stability of the HDB housing sector. With the majority of the population residing in comprehensive HDB towns that define the Singaporean way of life, there is little social stigma attached to living in HDB homes. This provided social stability to HDB neighbourhoods that is often not the case in public housing estates in other countries.

The HDB's performance is also attributable to the fact that it belongs to a government network of competent, non-corrupt institutions that together provide rich, public sector capacity. The public sector in Singapore consistently ranks high on the World Bank's governance scores for "government effectiveness" and "control of corruption". On a percentile rank basis, Singapore's score for 2016 was 100.0 for government effectiveness and 97.1 for control of corruption.[8] The government has developed a rigorous recruitment system: it sponsors the nation's "best and brightest" to attend the top universities in the UK and US, who then return to become public officials. Senior civil servants earn perhaps the highest salaries among bureaucrats in the world, their pay benchmarked against private sector salaries (Phang 2000).

This system helps the government to minimize corruption as well as to recruit and retain talent. Recruitment and promotion are based on merit rather than seniority, kinship, and ethnic ties. Supervisors assess employees' ultimate potential and promote high flyers quickly so they will reach the top ranks by age 45. The civil service has developed a culture where corruption is viewed as a "high risk, low reward" activity (Quah 1996, 76). The powers of the Corrupt Practices Investigation Bureau are defined under the Prevention of Corruption Act (which was originally enacted in 1960). The Corruption (Confiscation of Benefits) Act of 1989 provides for the confiscation of benefits derived from corruption. Whether the Singapore style of public administration is transferable elsewhere is debatable because of the high salaries involved (Quah 1996).

HDB's Organizational Practices

The organizational practices of the HDB have also helped it to reduce the inefficiencies commonly associated with state-owned enterprises in general, and public housing in particular. These practices are similar to private sector corporate best practices, and include the following:

(i) *Outsourcing*: Despite the scale of the work the HDB performs to "house a nation", its staff strength of 5744 in 2015/2016 is not particularly large. This is because the HDB does not undertake any construction work but contracts out all its infrastructure and building projects to private sector contractors through an open tender system. The HDB has a long-standing reputation for exercising stringent building and quality control checks on its contractors (Wong and Yeh 1985, Chapter 6).

(ii) *Developing in-house and contractors' capacity*: Despite outsourcing of construction, the HDB developed in-house technical design and management capabilities for its large building programme. In the 1960s, it also sourced for and produced construction materials such as steel rods, tiles, bricks, sand, granite, and concrete, as well as provided heavy duty construction equipment for lease to smaller contractors. In the 1970s, the role of ensuring adequate supply of building materials was transferred to the Resources Development Corporation, a wholly state-owned company. When the local construction industry was lagging in construction best practices such as prefabrication technology, the HDB took the lead in R&D and investments to help grow private sector capacity and expertise (Centre for Liveable Cities 2017). In 2009, the HDB established an in-house dedicated building research centre that focuses efforts on R&D in building and environmental sustainability, and "nurturing new technologies for future generations of public housing".[9]

(iii) *Corporate downsizing and restructuring*: During the post-Asian crisis period, Singapore was faced with a situation of excess housing stock. Until then, HDB planners and architects in its 3000 strong Building and Development Division had planned and designed all HDB estates. In 2003, HDB undertook a major downsizing exercise. The division was corporatized and eventually devolved from HDB. It is now known as Surbana Jurong, a private company that is 100% owned by the Singapore government's investment holding company, Temasek Holdings. Surbana Jurong claims HDB's history and record of housing achievements as its own and provides urban planning and project management services to the HDB as well as to cities across Asia and the Middle East.[10]

(iv) *Product improvement and customization*: The HDB started with building low-cost, low-quality "Emergency" flats in the early 1960s, during a period of extreme housing shortage. Over the decades, as household incomes rose, HDB expanded its market coverage and built increasingly larger flats of better quality, with Executive and Multi-Generation flats offered for sale. In recent years, in response to changes in demographic structure, it has provided 30-year-leasehold studio apartments for the elderly and, since 2015, flexi-leases for 2-room flats.

(v) *Pricing for affordability*: The strong support of the government for land, financial subsidies, and loans has enabled HDB to price flats affordably and to offer mortgage loans to flat buyers. Similar to other firms with monopoly power, the HDB practices discriminatory pricing for its flats according to ability to pay. Per square metre prices are higher for larger flat types purchased by higher-income households (see Chap. 5). The same HDB flat could be sold at different prices depending on household income and other characteristics of the buyer through differentiating housing grants for new flats (see Chap. 8).

(vi) *Ascertaining demand and preferences of potential customers*: The HDB previously used a queuing system for flat allocation. When queues vanished during the market downturn, the HDB adopted a BTO system from 2002, under which flats are built only when there is sufficient demand for them. In 2011, in response to a backlog of unfilled demand, the government instructed the HDB to "build ahead of demand".

(vii) *Aftersales surveys of customers*: The HDB conducts regular surveys of households (once every 5 years) to gather feedback on preferences and lifestyles, identify emerging trends, and measure satisfaction. For example, findings from the HDB's Sample Household Survey in 2013 showed that 90% of HDB households were satisfied with their flat, neighbourhood, and estate facilities and 91% were satisfied with their flat. These surveys provide information to the HDB on areas that are in need of improvement and/or policy attention.

(viii) *Aftersales maintenance and upgrades*: The state remains very involved in the maintenance and upgrading of the HDB estates even after the HDB flats are sold, albeit not in a direct controlling way. The administration and maintenance of HDB estates are the responsibilities of the estate's Town Council, which is chaired by the Member of Parliament for the constituency. The HDB's upgrading programmes to improve existing estates help preserve asset values and selective en bloc redevelopment projects are considered a windfall for affected households.

(ix) *Facilitating resale and upgrading*: Homeownership is the most important investment decision of the majority of young households. The HDB has facilitated the development of an active resale market that enables the returns on homeownership to be realized and households to move up the "housing ladder". This has been effected through careful market segmentation and regulations that tread the balance between affordability for first-time homeowners and asset values for existing homeowners (see Chap. 6).

(x) *Focusing on core competencies*: The HDB has attempted various ways of reducing its role in providing housing for upper-middle-income households, preferring the demand to be met by private sector developers instead. Previous middle-income housing initiatives such as the HUDC and DBSS schemes, however, did not work well and were discontinued. The EC scheme has been relatively successful and has helped to fill the gap between HDB housing and private sector-built condominiums.

The organizational practices of the HDB and other SOEs in Singapore have much in common with private corporations rather than those of the 1970s SOEs of western countries, the former Soviet Union, and China. Singapore was certainly ahead of the curve in how SOEs were established for strategic purposes, as well as how they could be operated profitably and be partially rather than fully privatized (Chua 2017, Chapter 5). Such mixed public-private ownership structures are now increasingly common and have been described as new and growing forms of state capitalism that have developed on a global scale.[11] Today, Singapore's SOEs in the real estate space have leveraged their domestic experience and expertise and are, in fact, involved in numerous urban development projects in cities across the world.

Notes

1. See Phang (1992, Chapter 3) for a description of the SIT and other public sector agencies involved in housing development in the 1960s and 1970s.
2. As a consequence of the fire, an amendment to the Land Acquisition Ordinance was passed to allow land that had been devastated by fire to be acquired at not more than one-third of the value of the vacant site, unless the minister specified otherwise. The one-third figure was to ensure that landowners did not benefit from an appreciation in the value of their land that would then be free from encumbrances (see Chap. 2).
3. See HDB website at http://www.hdb.gov.sg.
4. There exists a vast body of literature on various aspects of the housing sector in Singapore spanning five decades, in particular, by sociologists. See, for example, books by Yeh (1975), Chua (1997), Phang (1992), Wong and Yeh (1985), and Chua (2017), as well as numerous articles. This chapter draws extensively from my previous writings on the topic, the more recent being Phang (2001, 2007, 2013, 2015), Kim and Phang (2013), and Phang and Helbe (2016).
5. HDB Annual Report, 2015/2016. See the HDB web page on SERS and SERS projects at http://www.hdb.gov.sg/cs/infoweb/residential/living-in-an-hdb-flat/sers-and-upgrading-programmes/overview-of-sers. Accessed 1 Nov 2017.
6. See Chua (2017), Chapter 4 for a comprehensive review of the socio-political context of HDB policies.
7. This section draws from Phang (2013) Chapter 7 on housing institutions. See also Shleifer (1998).
8. See the World Bank website at http://info.worldbank.org/governance/wgi/#reports. Accessed 1 Nov 2017.
9. See a more detailed description of HDB's R&D activities at: http://www.hdb.gov.sg/cs/infoweb/about-us/our-role/centre-of-building-research-page. Accessed 1 Nov 2017.

10. See Surbana Jurong's corporate website at https://surbanajurong.com/about-us/#history. Accessed 1 Nov 2017.
11. Musacchio and Lazzarini (2014) present a book length study of leviathan in business and reinventing state capitalism on a global scale.

References

Centre for Liveable Cities. 2017. *Working with Markets: Harnessing Market Forces and Private Sector for Development*. Singapore: Centre for Liveable Cities.

Centre for Liveable Cities and Housing and Development Board. 2013. *Housing: Turning Squatters into Stakeholders*. Singapore: Cengage Learning.

Chua, Beng Huat. 1997. *Political Legitimacy and Housing: Stakeholding in Singapore*. London/New York: Routledge.

———. 2017. *Liberalism Disavowed: Communitarianism and State-Capitalism in Singapore*. Singapore: National University of Singapore Press.

Housing and Development Board. 2016. *Annual Report, 2015/2016*. Singapore: Housing and Development Board.

Kim, Kyung-Hwan, and Sock-Yong Phang. 2013. Singapore's Housing Policies: 1960–2013. In *Frontiers in Development Policy: Innovative Development Case Studies*. Seoul: KDI School and World Bank Institute.

Latif, Asad-ul Iqbal. 2009. *Lim Kim San: A Builder of Singapore*. Singapore: Institute of Southeast Asian Studies.

Lee, Kuan Yew. 2000. *From Third World to First: The Singapore Story 1965–2000*. Singapore: Singapore Press Holdings.

Liu, Thai Ker. 2017. Planning and Urbanization in Singapore: A 50-Year Journey. In *50 Years of Urban Planning in Singapore*, ed. Chye Kiang Heng, 23–44. Singapore: World-Scientific.

Monetary Authority of Singapore. 2001. *Quarterly Bulletin* III (1, March).

Musacchio, Aldo, and Sergio G. Lazzarini. 2014. *Reinventing State Capitalism: Leviathan in Business, Brazil and Beyond*. Cambridge: Harvard University Press.

Phang, Sock-Yong. 1992. *Housing Markets and Urban Transportation: Economic Theory, Econometrics and Policy Analysis for Singapore*. Singapore: McGraw Hill.

———. 2000. How Singapore Regulates Urban Transportation and Land Use. In *Local Dynamics in an Era of Globalization*, ed. Shahid Yusuf, Weiping Wu, and Simon Evenett, 159–163. New York: Oxford University Press for The World Bank.

———. 2001. Housing Policy, Wealth Formation and the Singapore Economy. *Housing Studies* 16 (4): 443–459.

———. 2007. The Singapore Model of Housing and the Welfare State. In *Housing and the New Welfare State*, ed. Richard Groves, Alan Murie, and Christopher Watson. Aldershot: Ashgate.

———. 2013. *Housing Finance Systems: Market Failures and Government Failures*. Basingstoke: Palgrave Macmillan.

———. 2015. Singapore's Housing Policies: Responding to the Challenges of Economic Transitions. *The Singapore Economic Review* 60 (3): 1550036 (25 pages). Reprinted in *Singapore's Economic Development: Retrospection and Reflections*, ed. Linda Y.C. Lim. Singapore: World Scientific.

Phang, Sock-Yong, and Matthias Helbe. 2016. Housing Policies in Singapore. In *The Housing Challenge in Emerging Asia: Options and Solutions*, ed. Naoyuki Yoshino and Matthias Helbe, 174–209. Tokyo: Asian Development Bank Institute.

Quah, Jon S.T. 1996. Public Administration in Singapore: Managing Success in a Multi-Racial City State. In *Public Administration in the NICs: Challenges and Accomplishments*, ed. A.S. Huque, J.T.M. Lam, and J.C.Y. Lee, 59–89. Basingstoke: Macmillan Press.

Shleifer, Andrei. 1998. State Versus Private Ownership. *Journal of Economic Perspectives* 12 (4): 133–150.

Tay, K.P. 2008. *The Twin Pillars of Estate Rejuvenation*. https://www.cscollege.gov.sg/Knowledge/Ethos/World%20Cities%20Summit/Pages/05The%20Twin%20Pillars%20of%20Estate%20Rejuvenation.aspx. Accessed 1 Nov 2017.

Teh, Cheang Wan. 1975. Public Housing in Singapore: An Overview. In *Public Housing in Singapore: A Multi-Disciplinary Study*, ed. Stephen H.K. Yeh, 1–21. Singapore: Singapore University Press for Housing & Development Board.

Wong, Aline, and Stephen H.K. Yeh, eds. 1985. *Housing a Nation: 25 Years of Public Housing in Singapore*. Singapore: Maruzen Asia for Housing & Development Board.

Yeh, Stephen H.K., ed. 1975. *Public Housing in Singapore: A Multi-Disciplinary Study*. Singapore: Singapore University Press for Housing & Development Board.
Yergin, Daniel, and Joseph Stanislaw. 1998. *The Commanding Heights*. New York: Simon & Schuster.

4

Provident Fund Savings for Housing Finance

How does a country finance affordable housing for its low- and middle-income groups? This is a question for which the answers as well as the outcomes differ markedly across countries. Without government intervention, private sector developers are unlikely build housing for low-income tenants who are unable to afford market rents. Commercial banks and investors are unlikely to provide mortgage loans to low-income households at affordable interest rates due to higher default risks. Phang (2013) provides a comprehensive review of the housing finance systems used in different countries that have been established to deal with these challenges.

Singapore's policy innovation in 1968 was to transform the then existing Central Provident Fund (CPF) into a source of domestic savings for housing finance. In the process, it introduced a new method of housing finance through the use of housing provident funds that has subsequently been adopted by a number of other countries. This chapter explains the origins of the CPF during the colonial period, the context under which changes were made in 1968, the evolution of the CPF system since as well as some of the unintended consequences of the scheme.

S.-Y. Phang, *Policy Innovations for Affordable Housing In Singapore*,
Palgrave Advances in Regional and Urban Economics,
https://doi.org/10.1007/978-3-319-75349-2_4

The Colonial Origins of the CPF

Prior to 1955, except for those working in the civil service or in some of the larger companies, most workers were not provided with retirement benefits by their employers. The concern was that most would not have adequate resources to support themselves in retirement. As a result, the government felt that some form of social security arrangement was needed. The merits of alternative social security systems were studied and debated in Singapore's Legislative Council from 1951. Rather than a pay-as-you-go defined benefits pension plan, the decision was made to adopt a defined-contributions individual accounts system and the CPF Ordinance was thus enacted in 1953.

In 1955, the CPF was established as a statutory board to manage compulsory savings which were to be deposited in the fund. Contributions were required by both employers and employees of a certain percentage of the individual employee's monthly salary towards the employee's personal and portable account in the fund. The contribution rates at the inception of the CPF in 1955 were 5% of the monthly salary for employees and 5% for employers. These rates remained unchanged until 1968. CPF savings could be fully withdrawn at age 55—the then retirement age. It was not mandatory for employers, the self-employed and unpaid family workers to make contributions to the scheme.

The 1968 Transformation of the CPF into a Housing Provident Fund

In 1964, the Housing and Development Board (HDB) launched the Home Ownership Scheme, and offered housing loans of 80% of the selling price, at a low interest rate, with a repayment period of up to 15 years. However, demand was limited as prospective buyers could not afford the 20% down payment. After a few years, the government decided to provide a boost to homeownership by expanding the CPF scheme "into a fund that would enable every worker to own his home" (Lee 2000, 117). In September 1968, an amendment to the CPF Act introduced the Public

Housing Scheme and transformed the CPF into an institution for financing homeownership. The amendment allowed members to withdraw their deposits from the fund to finance the down payment and mortgage payments for HDB flats, with mortgage loans also offered by the HDB.

CPF Contribution Rates

From 1968, the CPF contribution rates were adjusted steadily upwards and peaked at a total of 50% (25% of wages for both employers and employees from 1984 to 1986). The current contribution rates (in 2017) for Singaporean citizen and permanent residents are 17% of wages for employers, and 20% of wages for employees. As CPF contributions are not subject to income taxes, there are caps on contributions, with maximum monthly contributions currently set at $1200 for employee's contribution and $2200 for total contribution (for age 55 and below). Contribution rates are lower for workers above 55 years of age.

Contribution rates have varied depending on economic conditions and adjustments to rates (Fig. 4.1), with their impact on inflation and wage costs, have been useful as a supply side macroeconomic stabilization instrument for a very open economy. During the economic recessions in

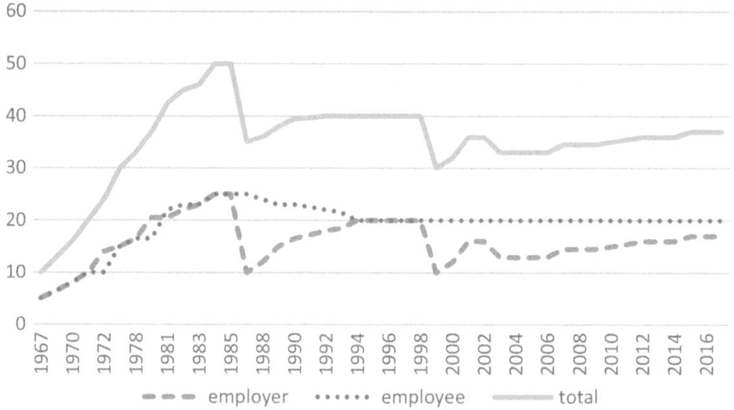

Fig. 4.1 Central Provident Fund contribution rates (% of employee wages), 1967–2017 (Source: Data from Central Provident Fund)

1985 and 1998, employers' contributions rates were adjusted sharply downwards (by 15 and 10 percentage points, respectively), effectively cutting wage costs. As the economy recovered, the contribution rate for employers was restored gradually in stages.

In 2003, given its concern over a weak economy following the burst of the dot.com bubble, 9/11 terrorist attacks, and outbreak of SARS earlier that year, the government reduced the employer's contribution rate by 3 percentage points, from 16% to 13%, to address concerns over cost competitiveness (Wilson 2016). In the midst of the global financial crisis in 2009, the government implemented a major fiscal stimulus package. However, instead of employees suffering a wage cut through CPF rate cuts as in previous recessions, employers received a 12% cash grant from the government on the first $2500 of each month's wages for each employee on their CPF payroll. This temporary Job Credit Scheme was funded from Singapore's reserves. When the economy rebounded in 2010, the scheme was stepped down and phased out by mid-2010.

Fulfilling Multiple Objectives

From its relatively simple beginnings as a savings scheme for retirement, the CPF has evolved into a macroeconomic stabilization tool as well as complex social security scheme encompassing homeownership and medical and retirement financing, with differentiated interest rates and specific grants for different purposes that vary in amounts by income and age groups.[1] In 2016, the CPF had 3.8 million members with 2.0 million active members. Contributions are allocated into 3 accounts—Ordinary, Special, and Medisave Accounts, respectively. The proportion of contributions allocated to each account varies with age.[2] Instead of allowing members to withdraw the full amount of savings at age 55, the government has, since 1987, required members to retain a minimum sum that is withdrawn over the retirement years.

From 2009, on a member's 55th birthday, a fourth account—the Retirement Account—is created, in which savings from the Special Account and Ordinary Account, up to a specified minimum retirement sum are transferred. The amount in the Retirement Account can then be used for the purchase of an annuity (CPF LIFE) that provides the member with monthly payouts for life. The interest rate on CPF Ordinary Account savings is the legislated minimum of 2.5% or a 3-month average of major local banks' interest rates, whichever is higher. Savings in the Special, Medisave, and Retirement accounts currently earn 4% interest.[3] From January 2008, an extra 1% interest per year (up to 5%) has been paid on the first S$60,000 of a member's combined balances. From January 2016, CPF members aged 55 and above also earn an additional 1% interest on the first $30,000 (that is, up to 6%) of their combined balances.

The bulk of contributions can only be withdrawn for specific purposes, of which housing dominates. Contributions can also be withdrawn partially at age 55, subject to a minimum sum to be retained in the CPF account, on permanent incapacitation of the contributor concerned, or upon death by the estate. Between 1968 and 1981, CPF savings could only be withdrawn for payments related to the purchase of public-sector-built housing, including middle-income housing built by the Housing and Urban Development Company. In 1981, the scheme was extended to permit withdrawals for mortgage payments for the purchase of private housing. In 1981, a mortgage insurance scheme for HDB homeowners using CPF savings for home purchase was implemented and administered by the CPF. From 1984, rules governing the use of CPF savings have been gradually liberalized to permit withdrawals for medical expenses and education loans (1984), medical insurance (1990), as well as investments in various financial assets (1986). Table 4.1 shows CPF

Table 4.1 CPF contributions and withdrawals by purpose, 2016 ($ millions)

Total contributions	$35,851.7	
Total withdrawals (net of refunds) by members	$18,527.0	100.0%
Housing schemes—public housing	$6971.9	37.6%
Housing schemes—private housing	$3905.5	21.1%
Reached 55 years of age and above	$3343.7	18.0%
Leaving Singapore & Malaysia permanently	$753.6	4.1%
Death	$756.2	4.1%
Medisave scheme	$931.3	5.0%
Private medical insurance scheme	$674.4	3.6%
Others	$1190.4	6.4%

Source: Singapore Department of Statistics

contributions and withdrawals (net of refunds) by purpose for 2016. Of the total CPF net withdrawals by members of $18.5 billion, 59% were for housing, with 37.6% for HDB housing and 21.1% for private housing.

CPF's Housing Finance Function

Figure 4.2 shows a schematic view of the mobilization of domestic savings for housing finance through the CPF. CPF collects member contributions and invests these in special non-tradable government securities that earn the same interest that it pays out to its members. HDB's annual deficit is fully covered by government expenditure grants from the government's current budget. The government also provides the HDB with housing development, mortgage financing, and upgrading financing loans—the latter two types of loans are at interest rates pegged to the CPF savings interest rate. The HDB also issues bonds and borrows from commercial banks for its housing development and operational requirements. The mortgage lending rate charged by the HDB to homeowners is 0.1 percentage point higher than the rate at which it borrows from the government, and this ensures the sustainability of the financing arrangement (see Fig. 4.2). The HDB currently offers mortgage loans of tenure up to 25 years, and up to 90% of the purchase price or value, whichever is lower.

The CPF itself does not make housing loans to its own members due to potentially conflicting objectives. The HDB provides loans to purchasers of both new and resale flats, with the CPF previously having first claim on a property if a borrower defaults on his loan, thus protecting the CPF savings of the purchaser. The low interest rate environment, however, has given rise to the anomaly where interest rates for commercial bank housing loans have been lower than HDB's "concessionary" loan rate of 2.6% (as there is a 2.5% floor on the CPF ordinary account savings rate). From 2003, in a significant privatization of the mortgage market, commercial banks were allowed to compete for a slice of the HDB mortgage loan market. Banks, instead of the CPF, would be given first

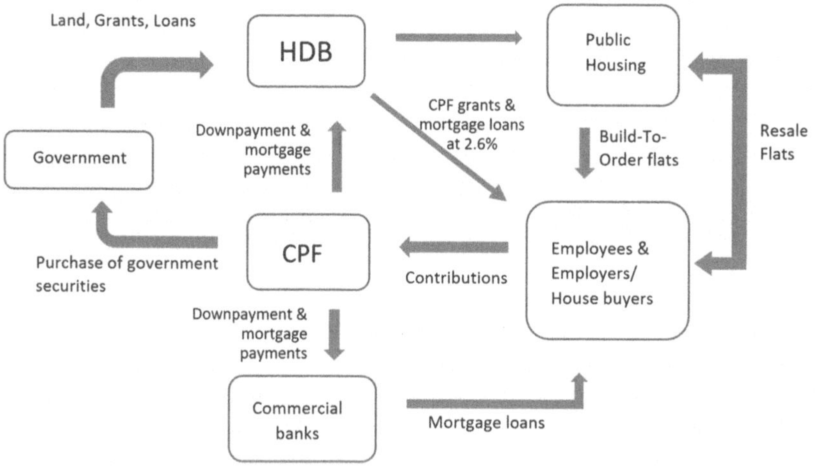

Fig. 4.2 Central Provident Fund mobilization of domestic savings for housing (Source: Phang (2013, modified))

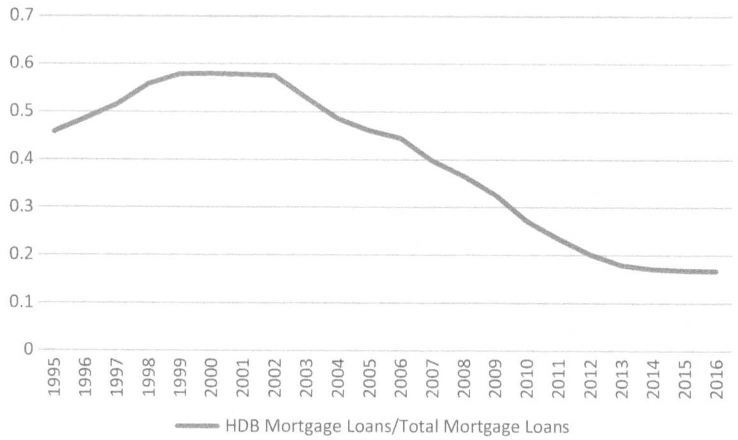

Fig. 4.3 HDB share of mortgage loans outstanding, 1995–2016 (Source: Data from Singapore Department of Statistics)

claim for such HDB housing loans. Competition amongst banks to provide financing for HDB flats has been keen. This has reduced the HDB's share of the residential mortgage market over time from 59% in 2000 to 17% by 2015 (see Fig. 4.3).

Table 4.2 provides the statistics that show the flow of resources for housing in 2016, as illustrated by the HDB-CPF framework in Fig. 4.2. The HDB's staff strength was 5744 in 2015/2016. It received \$1.64 billion in government grants that year in order to fully finance its deficit, which was 0.4% of the GDP. HDB, however, spent \$4.35 billion to purchase land from the government. HDB loans payable to the government, bondholders, and banks stood at \$69.23 billion (or 17% of GDP).

Table 4.2 The HDB-CPF framework (2016 statistics)

GDP at current market prices	\$410.27 b	
Total housing stock (HS)	1,331,200	
HDB housing stock (HHS)	992,472	
Resident households (RH)	1.26 m	
Resident labour force (LF)	2.26 m	
Total housing mortgage loans (ML)	\$225.76 b (55% of GDP)	
HDB statistics 2015/2016		
Government grant to HDB to cover deficit	\$1.64 b	0.4% of GDP
HDB purchase of land from the Singapore Land Authority	\$4.35 b	
HDB loans payable (to government, banks, and bondholders)	\$69.23 b	16.9% of GDP
HDB residential units under construction	86,307	6.5% of HS
Bookings for new HDB flats	22,432	1.8% of RH
Number of HDB flats with keys issued	21,621	Average \$311,000
Gross sale proceeds from HDB flats	\$6.73 b	per unit
CPF housing grants netted off against sale proceeds	\$208 m	Average of \$15,310 per
Number of Additional and Special CPF housing grants disbursed for new flat buyers[a]	13,587	grant[a]
Applications registered for resale HDB flats	19,620	2.0% of HHS
CPF housing grants for resale flats and ECs	\$212 m	Average of
Number of CPF housing grants disbursed for resale flat buyers (Family, Singles, Joint Singles, Proximity)[a]	8565	\$24,750 per grant[a]
Mortgage loans granted to households in 2015/2016	\$5.34 b	1.3% of GDP
HDB's mortgage loans receivable	\$38.21 b	16.9% of ML
CPF statistics 2016		
CPF member balances	\$328.90 b	80.2% of GDP
Amount of CPF contributions	\$35.85 b	8.7% of GDP
CPF net acquisition of government securities	\$27.65 b	6.7% of GDP

(continued)

Table 4.2 (continued)

Number of members making withdrawals for HDB flat financed with loans from HDB	519,210	CPF members who made withdrawals for housing loans comprised 42% of resident labour force
Number of members making withdrawals for HDB flat financed with loans from banks	220,754	
Number of members making withdrawals for private housing (including EC) financed with loans from banks	201,763	
Withdrawals for HDB flat financed with loans from HDB[b]	$7.87 b	Total amount withdrawn for housing comprised 4% of GDP, and 45.8% of CPF contributions
Withdrawals for HDB flat financed with loans from banks[b]	$2.92 b	
Withdrawals for private housing (including EC) financed with loans from banks[b]	$5.63 b	

Notes: Figures for HBD are for fiscal year April 1, 2015 to March 31, 2016. Figures for CPF are for calendar year January to December 2016

Sources: HDB Annual Report 2015/2016 and CPF Annual Report 2016

[a]One family can benefit from more than one type of CPF housing grant

[b]Gross withdrawals not taking into account refunds from members who sell their properties or who make voluntary refunds

HDB's loan portfolio comprised 63% government loans, 29% bonds, and 8% bank loans. It had 86,307 housing units under construction, which comprised 6.5% of the total housing stock in 2016. 22,432 households or 1.8% of resident households made bookings for new HDB flats that year, while another 21,621 households received keys to their completed flats.

The HDB received $6.73 billion in gross sale receipts and disbursed $208 million in Special and Additional Housing grants to new flat buyers. There were 19,620 resale market transactions, which was approximately 2% of the HDB's housing stock. 6173 CPF grants amounting to $212 million were disbursed for resale transactions. The HDB provided $5.34 billion in mortgage loans to HDB flat buyers and had $38.21 billion in mortgage loans payable that was entirely financed by loans provided by the government. This was 17% of total mortgage loans outstanding. The ratio of total housing mortgage loans outstanding (HDB and financial institutions) for both HDB and private housing was about 55% of GDP.

The CPF forms the other pillar of the housing framework. In 2016, CPF members' contributions were $35.85 billion or 8.7% of GDP. The total CPF balances amounted to 80% of the GDP. The CPF placed $27.65 billion into government securities. 942,000 CPF members, comprising 43% of the resident labour force, made withdrawals for housing down payments and to finance loans for HDB and private properties. CPF members who sell their properties purchased with CPF savings are required to refund the amount withdrawn together with accrued interest back into their respective CPF accounts. CPF members who had previously withdrawn savings for housing may also refund cash into their CPF accounts. Gross withdrawals for housing payments totalled $16.4 billion, while withdrawals net of refunds amounted to $10.88 billion (see Table 4.1).

The CPF system has thus been restructured to mobilize domestic savings in order to finance HDB's building programme in a sustainable way, without housing becoming a drain on fiscal resources. Features that contribute to the success of the HDB-CPF homeownership framework include the following factors:

i) Both employee and employer CPF contributions are made by employers to the CPF. The CPF makes mortgage payments directly to lenders, from the savings accounts, on behalf of its members. This process reduces the default risks for mortgage loans, thus keeping interest rates for residential mortgages low. This has been particularly important for low-income households that are otherwise unable to obtain loans from commercial banks. They have been able to access mortgage loans at 2.6% interest from the HDB, a rate that commercial banks would not have offered for subprime loans.

ii) Through the HDB's housing policies, homeownership has been made affordable for 90% of the population, including low-income households. The savings of low-income households are thus not helping to subsidize homeownership for households that are better off.

iii) CPF savings rates are pegged to commercial rates with a minimum rate of 2.5%, while government loans to HDB are pegged at the CPF savings rate, with HDB mortgage loans at CPF rate + 0.1%. The government is thus not providing a subsidy for mortgage loans.

iv) The macroeconomic environment has been one of high savings and income growth, low unemployment, inflation and interest rates, and government budgetary surpluses, as well as exchange rate appreciation.

v) Cycles aside, there has been a long-term trend of housing price appreciation (due, in large part, to the scarcity of land in Singapore) which has increased the value of CPF funds invested in housing.
vi) There is strong legislation and a proper fund-governance structure in order to ensure that the interests of CPF members are adequately protected. The CPF operates within the context of a political system and public sector known for its efficiency as well as zero tolerance for corruption. These last-mentioned factors behind the successful operation of the CPF cannot be overemphasized.

Unintended Consequences and Policy Adjustments

Singapore's housing provident fund innovation has demonstrated that retirement savings can be effectively mobilized for housing finance. The system is not, however, without its critics and/or weaknesses. The mandatory nature of the CPF, together with the dominance of the HDB, resulted in an allocation to the housing sector that was much higher than that for other economies at comparable stages of development. The CPF collects from members more than what is required for housing. This could have crowded out consumption and, as CPF savings and HDB housing equity are both illiquid, this has been cited as a reason behind a weak domestic start-up sector.

The share of HDB-originated mortgage loans at over 50% of the mortgage market prior to 2003 crowded out commercial mortgage lending for housing (Phang 2001). The affordable rental segment of Singapore's housing market has been marginalized by the homeownership bias of the HDB-CPF system. HDB rental flats under the social housing scheme are limited in size (mostly 1- and 2-room units) in order to encourage homeownership. Current high market rental yields for HDB flats indicate that there is a need to expand the affordable rental sector. In Phang (2013) and Phang et al. (2014), I have proposed increasing the availability of rental housing and the establishment of housing Real Estate Investment Trusts in order to meet the rental housing needs of an increasingly diverse population.

Moreover, the large allocation of CPF savings for housing poses the risk of housing bubbles, with adverse consequences to the economy and households that result from the bursting of such bubbles. In the initial period of CPF for housing (1968–1981) when CPF savings were directed only towards public housing, administered prices, stringent eligibility criteria, and long waiting lists were used to allocate the HDB's supply of new flats. Further, in the absence of a secondary market for HDB flats during that period, the housing asset inflationary impact of the CPF was not immediately apparent. However, such mechanisms could not be used when CPF savings were similarly directed to private housing beginning in 1981. The 1981 liberalization as well as the 1993 liberalization of HDB and CPF regulations for HDB resale flat housing loans had significant impacts on housing prices, contributing to the development of speculative bubbles that subsequently burst (Phang and Wong 1997).

The price declines were especially pronounced during the Asian Financial crisis, when private housing prices fell by 45% (from their peak in 1996 to the trough in 1998), while HDB resale prices fell by 28%. The cut in employer's CPF contribution rates by 10 percentage points in the midst of the crisis also posed difficulties for households who were using CPF contributions for housing mortgage payments. In the absence of other measures, the CPF cuts would have increased the mortgage default rate and possibly affected the stability of lending institutions.

Adjustments were, however, concurrently made by the CPF to allow automatic withdrawal of funds from a member's CPF Special Account (meant for old age) to service mortgage payments, should there be a shortfall (Phang 2007). The CPF Board also made bridging loans available for those who had depleted savings in both their Ordinary and Special Accounts. The HDB, as the largest player in the housing loans market, made available various aid schemes for those affected by the recession and/or CPF cut. These included a 5-year reduction in monthly mortgage payments (payments to be reassessed from the sixth year), payment of mortgage loan arrears by instalments over 6 months to a year, deferment of payment, extension of loan repayment period, and including more family members as joint owners. Such measures undoubtedly reduced the default rate on mortgage loans, thus contributing to the overall stability of the financial sector in the midst of the Asian Financial Crisis.

Turning to another issue, present concerns for Singapore's rapidly ageing population include the lack of unemployment safety nets as well as the possible inadequacy of personal resources for both retirement and healthcare in the future. The phrase "asset rich and cash poor" neatly encapsulates the basic problem (McCarthy et al. 2002) and raises the problematic issue of over concentration of household assets in housing resulting in a risky under-diversified portfolio upon retirement. A government appointed Economic Review Committee in 2002 made recommendations to limit the use of CPF for housing (Economic Review Committee 2002).

From 2002, the government implemented a cap on CPF withdrawals for housing at 150% of the value of the property, with the cap moving down gradually to 120% over 5 years for new private housing loans. (From 1993, the CPF Board had permitted withdrawals of CPF savings to be used to meet interest payments on mortgage loans for resale HDB and private housing purchases. Before 1993, CPF members were allowed to withdraw only up to 100% of the value of these properties at the time of purchase). An exception to the 120% withdrawal limit is made for new HDB flats financed with HDB loans, where there is no limit on the amount of CPF funds that can be used, as these flats are sold at subsidized prices. This withdrawal limit as well as numerous other market-cooling measures (see Chap. 6) have helped to bring the ratio of mortgage loans to GDP down from 71% in 2003 to 55% in 2016.

Similar to HDB policies, CPF policies in Singapore are constantly being reviewed and changed. The allocation of a very high rate of compulsory savings to be used for housing purchases has been a key pillar of homeownership, housing price appreciation, and housing wealth formation in Singapore. The concerns over distortionary effects, however, are well founded, as are concerns over adequacy of retirement financing despite one of the highest national savings rates in the world (averaging about 46% of GDP over 2012–2016). In this regard, in Chap. 9, we will examine the issues surrounding the need for housing equity extraction for retirement financing in Singapore.

Notes

1. The CPF website provides details of its history, evolution, contribution rates, interest rates, and different schemes.
2. For details as to how contribution and account allocation rates differ by income and age of contributor, see CPF website at: http://mycpf.cpf.gov.sg/Members/Gen-Info/Con-Rates/ContriRa.htm. Accessed 1 Nov 2017.
3. The Ordinary Account interest rate is calculated based on a weightage of 80% of the 12-month fixed deposit rates and 20% of the savings rates of the major local banks, subject to a minimum of 2.5% per annum. It is reviewed quarterly to keep up with prevailing market interest rates. See the CPF web page on details of interest rates payable for various accounts at https://www.cpf.gov.sg/Members/AboutUs/about-us-info/cpf-interest-rates. Historical interest rates can be found at https://mycpf.cpf.gov.sg/Assets/common/Documents/InterestRate.pdf. Accessed 1 Nov 2017.

References

Central Provident Fund. 2016. *Annual Report 2016*. Singapore: Central Provident Fund Board.

Economic Review Committee: Sub-Committee on Policies Related to Taxation, the CPF System, Wages and Land. 2002. *Refocusing the CPF System for Enhanced Security in Retirement and Economic Flexibility*. Singapore: Economic Review Committee.

Housing and Development Board. 2016. *Annual Report 2015/2016*. Singapore: Housing and Development Board.

Lee, Kuan Yew. 2000. *From Third World to First: The Singapore Story 1965–2000*. Singapore: Singapore Press Holdings.

McCarthy, David, Olivia S. Mitchell, and John Piggott. 2002. Asset Rich and Cash Poor: Retirement Provision and Housing Policy in Singapore. *Journal of Pension Economics and Finance* 1: 197–222.

Phang, Sock-Yong. 2001. Housing Policy, Wealth Formation and the Singapore Economy. *Housing Studies* 16 (4): 443–459.

———. 2007. The Singapore Model of Housing and the Welfare State. In *Housing and the New Welfare State*, ed. Richard Groves, Alan Murie, and Christopher Watson. Aldershot: Ashgate.

———. 2013. *Housing Finance Systems: Market Failures and Government Failures*. Basingstoke: Palgrave Macmillan.

Phang, Sock-Yong, and Wing-Keung Wong. 1997. Government Policies and Private Housing Prices in Singapore. *Urban Studies* 34: 1819–1829.

Phang, Sock Yong, David Lee, Alan Cheong, Kok-Fai Phoon, and Karol Wee. 2014. Housing Policies in Singapore: Evaluation of Recent Proposals and Recommendations for Reform. *Singapore Economic Review* 59 (3): 1450025.

Wilson, Peter. 2016. Monetary Policy and Financial Sector Development. *The Singapore Economic Review* 60 (3): 1550031 (25 pages).

5

Facilitating Higher Housing Densities Through Land Use Planning

Economic growth is uneven around the world and uneven across cities within a country (Moretti 2013). Many global cities that are financial and innovation hubs, with strong labour markets and attractive amenities, face fundamental problems of persistent housing shortages and high housing prices. Housing supply generally lags behind growth in population, incomes, and investor demand. Studies have shown that housing supply elasticities vary tremendously internationally, and from city to city within a country (Kim et al. 2012). With increasing demand and housing supply constraints, the residents of these cities face higher than average increases in house prices, reduction in housing space per capita, and longer commutes over time. Gyourko et al. (2013) refers to these cities as the "superstar cities".

The impact of land use regulations on housing supply and prices in US and European cities has been extensively studied by urban economists (*e.g.*, Glaeser et al. 2005; Quigley and Raphael 2005; Glaeser and Ward 2009; Gyourko and Molloy 2015; Hilber and Vermeulen 2016). Although land supply constraints and geographical restrictions are contributory explanatory factors, land use regulations on redevelopment and permitted densities, and policies such as green belts, urban growth boundaries, and rent control also contribute to inelasticity on the supply

S.-Y. Phang, *Policy Innovations for Affordable Housing In Singapore*,
Palgrave Advances in Regional and Urban Economics,
https://doi.org/10.1007/978-3-319-75349-2_5

side. These regulations can make it more difficult for developers to build at higher densities, thus constraining new housing supply where it is needed.

Land use regulations typically fall under the purview of local governments (which is not the case in Singapore). There is a remarkable variety in land use regulations, which include zoning plans to segregate land use, density, minimum lot sizes, subdivision rules, building setbacks, height restrictions, green belts, and urban growth boundaries. Theoretically, land use regulations can be beneficial and can be justified as policies to minimize negative externalities such as pollution from industries, traffic congestion, and noise, as well as to provide or preserve amenities with local public good characteristics, such as parks and beaches. However, land use regulation is a powerful instrument that can also be used to either facilitate or obstruct real estate development, determine local housing supply and prices, and consequently, affect housing affordability and wealth distribution.

This chapter begins with a brief review of the literature on land use regulations and housing prices in the US and UK. It then describes how Singapore reformed its land use planning legislation in the 1990s from a passive regime to a growth-oriented one that facilitated high-density housing to meet the demands of a growing population and rising incomes. Amendments to the strata title legislation were also made to facilitate collective private sales for urban redevelopment. Although the Housing and Development Board (HDB) was and remains the primary driver of housing supply (see Chap. 3), government land sales have played an increasingly important complementary role in meeting the demand for private housing.

Restrictive Land Use Regulations in the US and Europe

Land use regulations that attempt to oppose rather than re-channel market forces can generate inefficiency, lead to activities to circumvent regulation, result in wide disparities in market values for adjacent plots, and contribute to higher housing prices by imposing limits on supply. Gyourko and Molloy (2015) provide a comprehensive review of the literature on the causes and effects of local government regulations. Although many forms of regulations are designed to generate local amenities and mitigate negative externalities, many recent studies for the US and Europe found that the costs of regulation outweigh the benefits by a substantial margin. This section elaborates on a few of such studies for US cities and England.

In a study comparing the adoption of 15 growth control measures across 407 Californian cities, Quigley and Raphael (2005) developed a city level index of regulatory stringency and related this index to housing prices at the city level. The growth control measures for California included growth management elements and urban limit lines, urban service boundaries or growth moratorium, minimum quality standards, large lot zoning, fiscal zoning, and specific residential and commercial restrictions. They found housing price levels as well as changes in housing prices to be higher in cities with more stringent regulation of development and land use. Studies such as Quigley and Raphael (2005) require much effort to collect accurate data on the wide variety of land use regulations in different cities and to arrive at a measure of regulatory stringency. However, complex local land use regulations can be extremely challenging to quantify accurately for comparative purposes.

An innovative indirect measure of regulatory stringency was proposed by Glaeser et al. (2005). Using simple economic analysis, they argued that in the market for high-density condominiums, theory predicts that, with or without regulation, competition among builders would keep price equal to average cost. In an unregulated condominium market, building heights would therefore be expected to rise to the point where the marginal cost of adding an additional floor equals the average cost. However, in a supply restricted market, under the standard assumption of an increasing marginal cost function, prices and average costs would be above marginal costs. The difference between the market price and marginal cost of building an additional floor, referred to by the authors as "the regulatory tax", could then be used as a proxy for the extent of supply restrictions. Using this approach, Glaeser et al. (2005) concluded that, for Manhattan, the ratio of price to construction cost was over 1.5

between 1984 and 2002 and above 2 since 2001 (i.e. the regulatory tax was at least 50% of price).

Glaeser et al. (2005) acknowledged that this regulatory tax is not necessarily inefficient as one purpose of land use controls is to contain or limit negative externalities. Density controls could possibly be justified on the basis of elimination of views from existing apartments, extra crowding, and the fiscal burden of new residents. Using Manhattan data, the authors suggest that lost views from new construction could justify approximately a 12.5% tax on new housing values. They propose an additional 5% zoning tax on new apartments owing to their contribution to congestion. They argued that new residents in Manhattan condominiums would likely be a fiscal boon and not a fiscal drain on the city. From these estimates, they found no externality associated with new housing units that was remotely large enough to justify the gap between construction costs and apartment prices. They attribute the increasing tax to a reassignment of property rights from developers to local homeowners who attempt to reduce supply in order to boost the value of their own homes.

For many European cities with historic buildings and architecture, the challenge has been to balance the desire for preservation with the need for growth. In Britain, the 1947 Town and Country Planning Act introduced a comprehensive and compulsory planning and development control system covering the entire country. The Act required all landowners to obtain planning permission from the local planning authority for any land development.

When compared to US cities, Cheshire and Hilber (2008) consider the UK situation for land use regulation as more restrictive by several orders of magnitude. Greenbelts surrounding cities, growth controls as well as a raft of preservation designations, and height controls on buildings have been in place since 1947. Geographically fragmented decision making as well as fiscal disincentives to local communities to allow commercial development contribute to the level of regulatory restrictions in Britain. Adopting the regulatory tax approach proposed by Glaeser et al. (2005), Cheshire and Hilber (2008) estimated the regulatory tax for 14 British and 8 continental European office locations. They show that the tax is substantially higher in Britain than it is in comparable continental European cities.

Hilber and Vermeulen (2016) describe the English planning system as rigid, inflexible, and unresponsive to market signals and as failing to cope with changing socio economic conditions. As a result, real house prices have grown faster in the UK over the past 40 years than in any other OECD country, with negative consequences for housing affordability and inequality. Using a panel dataset of 353 local planning authorities in England from 1974 to 2008, they find that a similar labour demand shock leads to larger increases in house prices in more regulated areas.

Growth-Oriented Land Use Planning

Modern comprehensive land use planning and development control were introduced into the colony of Singapore soon after the UK Parliament enacted the Town and Country Planning Act in 1947. The origins of planning are to be found in the 1951 amendment to the Singapore Improvement Trust (SIT) Ordinance, when the colonial government charged the SIT to carry out a diagnostic survey of Singapore and to prepare a Master Plan. This was the first formal land use plan since a town plan was prepared in 1822, a few years after the arrival of Sir Stamford Raffles in 1819 (Choe 2017). The intervening 130-plus years included a period of war and Japanese occupation before a return to British colonial rule. Population explosion and practically no legal control over the development of land[1] had led to slums and chronic overcrowding in the central city area. The objective of introducing statutory land use planning and development control in the 1950s was to better enforce government control over private land use and development.

The first Master Plan, which was formally approved and given legal effect in 1958, was prepared by colonial officers and modelled on the Greater London Plan of 1944 (Khoo and Guo 2017). The 1958 Master Plan is the single statutory plan delineating land use for the whole of Singapore. In line with British planning practices, the plan was detailed and precise, regulating land use through zoning, density, and plot ratio controls. It was similarly predicated on the assumptions of slow managed growth, reliance on the private sector for physical development of the city, and the preservation of past institutions.

Recognizing that the needs of the city were not well served by the preservation mode of the 1958 Master Plan (Khoo and Guo 2017), the newly elected government enacted the Planning Ordinance (now known as the Planning Act) in 1959 that provided for the revision of the Master Plan at least once every 5 years. This was in recognition of the rapid changes to land use that were expected to follow the attainment of self-government status in 1959.

Following British planning practices, development controls regulated for all landowners or developers to obtain written permission before subdividing their holdings or making any alterations to land use. In 1964, an amendment to the Planning Ordinance had provided for higher densities and zoning alterations to the Master Plan to incur a surcharge known as the development charge (see Chap. 2).[2]

Although the 1958 Master Plan allowed for a legal process of public advertisement and inquiry for changes in the plan, this was found to be too limiting and too cumbersome to deal effectively with the many large-scale development programmes of the new government that departed from the Master Plan. This led to the exemption of the physical development projects of the government and statutory boards from the constraints of the statutory Master Plan. Within the HDB, the Urban Renewal Unit performed the task of planning housing projects to facilitate resettlement and urban renewal for the central area. The unit was renamed the Urban Renewal Department in 1966. The Economic Development Board (and later, the Jurong Town Corporation) took charge of planning and developing industrial estates. Rapid development of housing and industrial estates in the 1960s led the government to see the drawbacks of an ad hoc approach and the need for an integrated long-term land use and transport plan instead.

In 1967, work began on an island-wide plan with assistance from the United Nations Development Program (Choe 2017). Known as the State and City Planning Project, the project team comprised HDB planners, the Planning Department, the Public Works Department, as well as United Nations consultants. The Concept Plan, a strategic long-term blueprint for land use and urban transportation for the entire city-state, was completed in 1971. The Ring Concept Plan was selected from several alternative strategies; the plan envisaged the development of a ring-cum-linear urban form, with the water catchment area located at the centre of the ring. The Plan mapped out the strategic location of new towns, industrial estates, an island-wide expressway system, a Mass Rapid Transit (MRT) network, and Changi Airport. Government agencies had the powers to initiate development in accordance with the Concept Plan, and the plan guided agencies in the location and development of public housing, industrial estates, and major transport infrastructure projects throughout the 1970s and 1980s.

The Planning Act confers upon the Minister (for National Development) the authority for planning and development control matters. The Minister may appoint a "competent authority" to be responsible for the operation of the Act. Prior to 1989, the Planning Department within the Ministry of National Development was the government agency responsible for land use planning for the country, while responsibility for urban redevelopment of the central area rested with the HDB from 1960 to 1974. In 1974, an independent Urban Redevelopment Authority (URA) was created to take over the functions performed by the HDB Urban Renewal Department, and to plan and redevelop the central area in a comprehensive manner. In 1989, the different government agencies involved in research and data collection, land use planning, urban renewal, development control, sale of sites, and conservation functions were centralized under a new statutory board, which retained the URA name. The Chief Planner of the URA is the competent authority. The new URA became the only land use planning and conservation authority, which has allowed for effective centralized planning, development control, and coordination of land use matters.

Throughout the 1970s and 1980s, Singapore operated with these two plans for land use purposes: the Master Plan was statutory while the Concept Plan guided public sector agencies who were major players in developing new towns, urban redevelopment projects, and building industrial estates. Public sector development was coordinated through the Master Plan Committee, chaired by the Chief Planner, and comprising representatives from all relevant government agencies (Yuen 2007). Between 1965 and 1985, the Master Plan was reviewed every 5 years, with each review being essentially an update of the preceding plan that took into account approved developments and ad hoc re-zonings. The government also prepared various non-statutory plans to guide permissible forms of development that were not made public. Applications that varied from the Master Plan were evaluated by referencing these "bottom-drawer" plans and using "cumbersome decision-making processes" that lacked transparency (Khoo and Guo 2017).

This unsatisfactory situation was remedied in the late 1980s when a fundamental shift in land use planning practices and processes occurred. The planning, conservation, and urban redevelopment functions within the government were merged under the new URA. The land use planning regime was radically changed from a static approach to one where land use planners provided transparent guidance for permitted future development to existing landowners (Dale 1999, 85). Instead of updating the Master Plan 1985, the URA (as the new planning authority from 1989) undertook a comprehensive review of the 1971 Concept Plan.

This review was timely as, by the late 1980s, the housing shortage had been solved, and several expressways in the 1971 Concept Plan had been completed and opened. The MRT project proposed in the 1971 Concept Plan had been approved by the government in 1982 and began operations in stages from 1987. The initial 67 km MRT system linked key HDB towns to the CBD, and allowed for significant increases in commercial land use density in the central area as well as in residential densities around stations.[3] Land use restrictions that were previously needed to alleviate traffic congestion could be liberalized. The update of the 1985 Master Plan, expected in 1990, was put on hold in anticipation of the changes expected to be made to the Concept Plan.

The review of the Concept Plan was completed in 1991. Instead of "business as usual", a radical change in the preparation process of the Master Plan was made. The broad "macro" visions of the 1991 Concept Plan were translated by URA planners into detailed proposals through 55 "micro-level" plans, known as Development Guide Plans (DGPs), between 1993 and 1998.[4] Private consultants were engaged to assist the planners in the preparation of the DGPs. Each DGP represented the planning vision for its area, and set out the control parameters such as land use, plot ratio, building height, as well as the provision of facilities and amenities. Zoning and plot ratio prescriptions contained within each DGP could deviate from the then existing land use with the objective of guiding the future physical development in a specific planning area and "unlocking" the redevelopment potential of privately held land parcels.

As each DGP was completed, public feedback was sought in the form of comments and general evaluation before the DGP concerned was gazetted, whereupon it would replace the corresponding part of the 1985 Master Plan. When all 55 DGPs were completed, they were collectively gazetted in 1999 as the Master Plan 1998. The Master Plan, instead of primarily being a document that recorded the changes that had taken place since the preceding plan was published, had become a policy instrument for guiding and facilitating changes in land use in a manner consistent with the visions of the land use planners.

Planners also implemented the "white zone" concept for the Government Land Sales (GLS) programme in 1995 to provide developers the flexibility to propose a mix of commercial, residential and hotel uses. For land parcels zoned as "white sites", developers have the discretion to choose the mix of uses and quantum of floor space of each use within the total permissible gross floor area for the site. This discretion extends for the life of the project and changes can be made without the need for payment of a differential premium. This built-in flexibility enables the private developers to optimize valuable space in response to changing market conditions (Yu and Sing 2017).

In 2000, to complement the objective of the revised DGPs, the URA announced that storey height limits for flats and condominiums housing developments in many areas would be increased to allow more flexibility in design and to free up more space for communal use (see Table 5.1).

In Master Plan 2003, a new impact-based zoning system was introduced that gave businesses greater flexibility and choice of location.

Table 5.1 Standard gross plot ratio / storey height typologies

	Storey height control	
Gross plot ratio	Existing	Revised
1.4	4	5
1.6	10	12
2.1	20	24
2.8	30	36
>2.8	>30	>36

Source: URA Circular No: URA/PB/2000/08-DCD (April 24, 2000)

New zone specifications, Business 1 (B1) and Business 2 (B2) zones, depending on their environmental impact, replaced Warehouse, Light Industry and General Industry zones in the 1998 Master Plan, while the Telecommunication and Utility zones were merged into a single Utility zone. Additional flexibility was allowed for parcels zoned as B1-White and B2-White to allow for a wider mix of land uses on these parcels.

The Concept Plan has been revised every 10 years since, in 2001 and 2011, to guide land use development over the next 40–50 years. The 2011 land use Concept Plan outlines strategies to provide for a projected population of 6.5–6.9 million by 2030. The strategies have been translated into the 2014 Master Plan, which will guide land use of the next 10–15 years. The Master Plan is reviewed every 5 years. The regular reviews and amendments to both Plans have allowed the government to make changes in response to population growth and local and global trends. For example, Table 5.2 shows the upward revisions to the long-term population scenarios that each review of the Concept Plan had made. These changes were necessary in order to ensure that land use plans and densities remained relevant to address future challenges and meet the needs of Singaporeans.[5] Khoo and Guo (2017) view this built-in flexibility to change or adapt land use plans as a critical factor behind Singapore's urban development success.

Table 5.2 Concept Plan population projections

Concept Plan year	Resident population	Total population	Population scenarios for Concept Plan
1971	2.0 million	2.1 million	3.4 million by Year 1992
1991	2.8 million	3.1 million	Resident population projections of: 3.2 million by Year 2000 3.5 million by Year 2010 3.7 million by Year 2030 Population of 4 million by Year X
2001	3.3 million	4.1 million	5.5 million within the next 40–50 years
2011	3.8 million	5.2 million	6.5–6.9 million by 2030

Sources: Singapore government official statistics; URA website

Land Use Planning and Private Housing Supply

Forward land use planning has facilitated increases in the stock of private housing. Private housing units doubled from approximately 100,000 units in 1990 to 200,000 units by 2000. Growth was slower between 2000 and 2010, when the increase was approximately 60,000 units. An additional 120,000 private housing units have been added to the private housing stock between 2010 and 2017 (see Fig. 5.1). In mid-2017, the private housing stock comprised 382,413 units, of which 26,297 (7%) had been built under the Executive Condominium (EC) Scheme (see Chap. 6). In addition to public housing supply by the HDB (see Chap. 2), two important sources of private housing supply are collective sales and government land sales. The details of these two sources are described below.

Facilitating Private Collective Sales for New Housing Developments

Urban redevelopment at higher densities was further facilitated by changes to legislation that removed gridlock in properties co-owned by multiple parties.

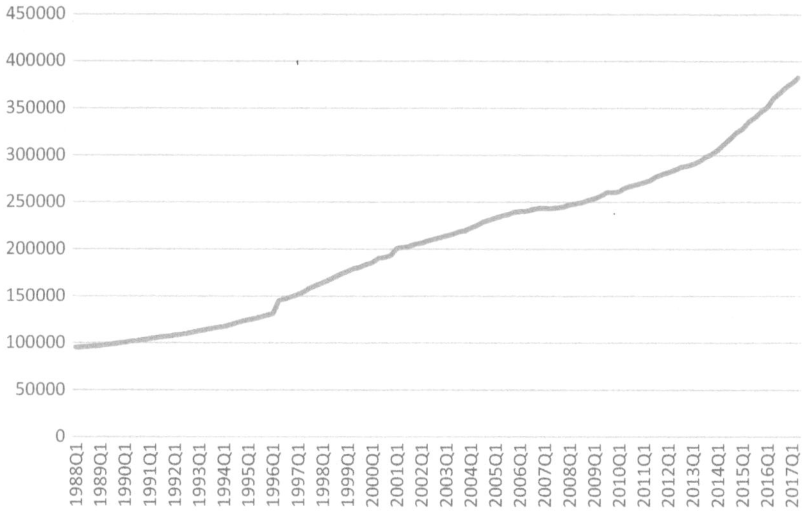

Fig. 5.1 Stock of available private housing units, 1988–2017 (Note: Includes Executive Condominiums; Source: URA REALIS Database)

The Land Titles (Strata) Act in Singapore governs buildings that are divided both horizontally and vertically in accordance with an approved strata title plan. Such subdivision facilitates dealings or disposition by the individual owners of their interests in the units that have been created by the subdivision. In addition, the Act contains provisions relating to a system of managing such buildings through the establishment of a Management Corporation (MC).

The DGPs released by the planning authorities from 1993 revised the density parameters for residential land upwards, particularly in areas that enjoyed new or improved public infrastructure, in particular, MRT stations. To redevelop a site to the density permitted by the 1990s changes in planning regulations, the developer would have to pay the development charge (DC).[6] As development charges payable were 50% of land value enhancement (from 1985 to 2007), developers were prepared to pay a premium for land with high redevelopment potential. The 1990–1996 period was also a period of rapidly escalating real estate prices.

However, many of these sites were held under residential strata title which, prior to 1999, required that all the strata titled property owners must unanimously agree to a sale. Many sales had to be aborted when a minority (in some cases, just one) of the owners refused to participate in the sale. Frustrated owners appealed to the government and, in 1999, the Land Titles (Strata) Act was amended to facilitate collective sales. The concerns of the majority were accepted by Parliament as legitimate and the actions of dissenting minority owners were described as "impeding efforts to maximize the development potential of en bloc sale sites and preventing the rejuvenation of older estates".[7]

To make it easier for en bloc sales to succeed if the majority of homeowners in a development wanted it so that more prime land for higher-intensity development could become available, Parliament passed amendments to the Act that abolished the 100% requirement. The new provisions applied to only strata developments with more than 10 units. (En bloc sales have included developments that have as few as 2 units to those with as many as 618 units.) Where a development is fewer than 10 years old, there must be at least 90% agreement; for developments 10 years old or more, at least 80% agreement will suffice for a collective sale (both figures are based on share values). The Strata Title Board would review applications for collective sales. The Land Titles (Strata) (Titles Boards) Regulations 1999 sets out the procedure for applications to the Board, the proceedings of the Board, and other matters such as appeals to the Board and the High Court (Christudason 2004, 2009).

Christudason (2004) has described the amendments as "radical in nature" and "an abrogation of fundamental property rights" as, unlike compulsory acquisition by the state, there is no self-evident "public interest/benefit /utility", nor is the state involved in the "taking". The amendments, however, were effective in facilitating en bloc sales as a source of new private housing supply. Between 1995 and 2017, there were more than 500 en bloc transactions, exceeding $36 billion in value.[8] Table 5.3 shows a list of ten of the largest en bloc transactions in terms of total sales proceeds. What is notable within the list are the number of leasehold properties as well as privatized Housing and Urban Development Company (HUDC) leasehold developments (see Chap. 3). Several developments were fewer than 35 years old at the time of sale, with remaining leases of between 66 and 77 years.

For leasehold redevelopments, the developer typically applies for planning approval for intensification of land use and an extension of the existing lease (lease top-up) to 99 years for the new development. The land premiums payable will thus comprise two components. The first component is a Differential Premium based on the Development Charge (DC) Table for intensification of land use. Where the tenure of the land is leasehold, the DC rates are adjusted to reflect the residual tenure of the land based on a Leasehold Table. The Leasehold Table expresses the value of the residual tenure as a percentage of freehold value. The second component for lease extension is the land premium for topping up the lease, which is determined by the Chief Valuer on a case-by-case basis.

Government Land Sales for Private Housing Supply

The government is the largest landowner in Singapore (see Chap. 2). Through its vacant land sales programme, the government works with the private sector to implement the land use plans formulated by the

Table 5.3 Ten largest en bloc sales between 1995 and July 2017 (by sales proceeds)

En bloc sale details						
Year	Project	Number of units	Remaining lease at time of sale (years)	Transacted price ($'000)	Average proceeds per unit ($)	New project (number of units)
2007	Farrer Court[a]	618	69	$1,338,800	$2,166,343	D' Leedon (1715 units)
2007	Leedon Heights	314	Freehold (Built 1986)	$835,000	$2,659,236	Leedon Residences (381 units)
2017	Eunosville[a]	330	71	$765,782	$2,320,551	
2016	Shufu Ville[a]	358	69	$638,000	$1,782,123	
2007	Grangeford Apartment	192	66	$625,000	$3,255,208	Twin Peaks (462 units)
2017	Rio Casa[a]	286	73	$575,000	$2,010,490	
2007	Gillman Heights[a]	607	77	$548,000	$902,801	The Interlace (1040 units)
2017	Serangoon Ville[a]	244	69	$499,000	$2,045,082	
2007	Anderson 18	71	Freehold (Built 1992)	$477,700	$6,728,169	Nouvel 18 (156 units)
2007	Westwood Apartments	48	Freehold (Built 1975)	$435,000	$9,062,500	3 Orchard By-the-Park (80 units)

Note: [a]Denotes privatized housing estates that were built and sold by a government agency, the Housing and Urban Development Company
Data sources: URA, and Square Foot Research at: https://www.squarefoot.com.sg/market-watch/enbloc market; and Teoalida website at: http://www.teoalida.com/singapore/hudclist/. Accessed 1 Nov 2017

planners for each locality. Much urban redevelopment to support the growth of the Singapore economy has been achieved through the Sale of Sites programmes first launched in 1967. Later known as Government Land Sales (GLS), these sales are administered mainly by the URA and the HDB as agents on behalf of the Singapore Land Authority. Under the programme, the government clears slums, assembles land parcels, inserts comprehensive infrastructure and services to the site, provides planning, plot ratio, and urban design specifications, and releases the land for sale by tender, typically on a 99-year leasehold basis to private developers. The agents use a variety of sales mechanisms, of which the sealed-bid tender is most commonly deployed for large sites. The site is awarded to the highest bidder unless the highest bid is below the reserve price set by the government. As of 2016, a total of 1624 parcels have been sold through the GLS programme, contributing 53% of hotel rooms, 38% of private housing, 40% of office space, and 48% of retail space in Singapore (Centre for Liveable Cities 2017).

The purpose and locations of GLS sites are strategically chosen to achieve economic and land use objectives. The first sale in 1967 featured 14 sites in the central area for hotel, shopping and entertainment developments with the stated objective of developing the tourism industry. Sales in the late 1960s and early 1970s focused on the creation of a new financial district at Shenton Way and the redevelopment of the CBD area within the Golden Shoe and its fringe. The 1974 sale featured sites for private condominium housing as well as Orchard Road shopping malls. 1987 witnessed the sale of a site for Suntec City at Marina Centre with the objective of developing convention facilities, as well as parcels of conservation shophouses and the Raffles Hotel extension, reflecting the new focus on heritage and cultural aspects of the built environment (Choo 2002).

The supply of sites has also been responsive to market conditions. In the 1990s, the rising demand for private housing and rapidly rising home prices brought about a period of accelerated residential site sales, including plots for Executive Condominiums (see Chap. 6). To provide greater predictability of supply in order to help curb speculation and rapidly rising prices, the government announced that it would provide yearly disclosure of impending sales. When the Asian Financial Crisis occurred in 1997, the government changed the frequency of reviews to half yearly reviews and halted land sales altogether in 1998 and 1999 as the crisis deepened.

When GLS resumed in 2000, developers who were still hurting appealed to the government to reconsider its sales programme. This brought about the introduction of the Reserve List system in June 2001, where sites are placed by the government on a Reserve List. These sites are put up for tender only if there are developers indicating interest. A developer must propose and commit to a minimum acceptable bid price to trigger the sale. This price would be publicized prior to the public tender to be held within six weeks thereafter (Choo 2002). The Reserve List system serves to make GLS more flexible and responsive to market conditions.

During the housing boom periods in 1994–1997 and 2009–2014, the URA and HDB jointly sold 66 and 97 land parcels respectively, for private housing, including Executive Condominium housing (these numbers do not include sales for landed housing). Sing (2017) estimates that these sites resulted in a total supply of 23,884 units for the 1994–1997 sales and 41,941 units for the 2009–2014 sales.

GLS has been used strategically for the comprehensive development of reclaimed land. These developments include the Marina Square area in the 1980s and the Marina Bay area from 2003. The Marina Bay site sits entirely on 360 hectares of reclaimed land and is significant for the extent of its forward and integrated planning. In this project, the URA assumed the role of "master developer" for the phased coordinated development of the entire precinct over long project completion periods. GLS in Marina Bay expanded the financial centre from the Raffles Place-Shenton Way CBD to include a New Downtown. This heralded an era of more integrated and larger-scale projects, including the iconic Marina Bay Sands integrated resort and the Marina Bay Financial Centre.[9]

From the beginning of the GLS programme, the government has put in place measures to prevent the use of these sites for land speculation and hoarding. The successful tenderer is required to maintain at least a 50% controlling stake in the project before its completion. A project completion period (PCP) is also specified as part of the tender conditions. Failure to meet the PCP timelines would invite financial penalties, which were in the form of liquidated damages prior to May 2000, and are currently in the form of premiums required to be paid to extend the PCP. The government has also exercised discretion in the PCP, extending it during past periods of recession and shortening it during periods of market boom (Centre for Liveable Cities 2017, 66–67).

Land Cost as a Proportion of Housing Price

The regulatory tax proposed by Glaeser et al. (2005) discussed earlier in this chapter (where regulatory tax = market price of the housing unit – marginal cost of that unit) is an innovative idea to capture the restrictive impact of land density regulations on condominium supply. However, it requires a number of conditions to be met before the price-cost gap can be considered a regulatory tax. If these conditions are not met, the gap may actually exaggerate the role of regulation. These conditions relate to the neo-classical assumptions of competitive markets, profit maximizing firms, increasing marginal costs, as well as the absence of externalities that may justify regulation. Negative externalities that were discussed in Glaeser et al. (2005) included congestion, elimination of views, and fiscal burden. Moreover, when comparing price to construction costs, price includes those of existing older units while construction costs are for new products. Glaeser et al. (2005) acknowledged that as prices are not adjusted upwards to account for economic depreciation for older units, the estimate of the regulatory tax is a conservative one. Data on average construction costs for condominiums are also more easily available as compared with marginal costs of adding another floor. Specifically, average costs tend to rise with building height, although Glaeser et al. (2005) reports that the cost schedule does not rise steeply with building height. The implied marginal costs for the 25th floor of average or good-quality apartments are about 6% higher than average construction costs.

Bearing the above limitations in mind, I attempt an estimate of the land value tax, defined as the land cost as a proportion of price for (i) a GLS residential project; and (ii) new flats sold at a HDB town. Due to the extreme scarcity of land in Singapore and the need to allocate land for the current and long-term needs of a country (and not simply a city), one can expect the land cost component to be high.

GLS for private residential (non-landed) developments in 2016–2017 have witnessed winning bids in excess of $10,000 per square metre per gross floor area for sites in suburban location and $13,336 for a central area location.[10] In comparison with 2017 construction cost estimates for private condominiums that range from $2600 to $5900 per square

Table 5.4 Government land sale for residential development: Waterfront@Faber

Year of GLS launch and award	2013
Site area	15,125.4 sq m
Gross floor area	21,176 sq m
Successful tender price for land	$156,688,000
Land price psm per GFA	$7400
Number of units	210
Area of units	77–129 sq m (median 99 sq m)
Price range of units at launch in 2016	$890,000 to $1,750,000 (median $1,288,000)
Price range of units in per square metres	$11,717 to $13,701 psm (median $13,010 psm)

Sources: URA databank for GLS and REALIS

metre per gross floor area (depending on quality of developments),[11] land cost comprises a significant proportion of total development cost for private housing developments—certainly in excess of 50%. In the example of a fully sold suburban development (about 25 minutes' drive and 40 minutes by public transport from the CBD), Waterfront@Faber provided in Table 5.4 below, the average land cost ($7400 psm) is estimated to be 57% of the median sale price ($13,010 psm). If construction costs of $4000 per square metre is assumed for the development, the gap between price and construction cost is estimated to be about $9010, giving a price to construction cost ratio of 3.25.

Table 5.5 shows a list of building works contracts (comprising 1000 or more dwelling units) that were awarded by the HDB via competitive tendering to contractors in 2017. Using the successful tender price and the number of units for each award, the average construction cost per dwelling unit for these contracts range from $110,800 to $126,000. Assuming the size of an average unit is 90 square metre (the size of a HDB 4-room flat), the average construction cost per square metre of residential space is estimated to be in the range of $1230–$1400. As these are construction cost estimates based on gross building areas, a 20% provision for carparks, walls, common areas, and facilities is made to arrive at a range of $1540–$1750 (dividing by 0.8). Adding another 20% for costs of professional services, infrastructure development and development financing brings the average construction cost estimates to between $1850 and $2100 psm. In Table 5.6, construction cost (CC) of $2000 psm for net floor area is assumed.

Table 5.5 HDB residential building works contracts, 2017

Location of project	Number of dwelling units for contract	Successful tender price $	Average cost per unit $	Average construction cost per square metre[a] $
Tampines	2022	246,600,000	121,958	1355
Punggol	1295	143,743,803	110,828	1231
Bidahari	1000	110,800,000	110,800	1231
Clementi	1179	148,529,000	125,979	1400
Clementi	1104	125,000,000	113,225	1258
Punggol	1014	126,968,000	125,215	1391

Note: [a]I have assumed an average of 90 sq metre per unit, which is the typical size of a 4-room HDB flat

Source: Estimated from tender award information from HDB webpage on "List of Tender Awards by Date" at http://www20.hdb.gov.sg/isoa035p.nsf/FI10FList OfTenderAwards?OpenForm. Accessed 1 Nov 2017

Table 5.6 provides comparison of the above average cost estimate with market prices of HDB flats, subsidized new flat prices, and new flat prices after housing grants that are dependent on household incomes. I calculate the mark-up of price over average construction cost as the land cost component in the case of new HDB flats. Table 5.6 shows the estimates of the range of prices on a per square metre basis (columns A, B, C) for each HDB flat type at Sengkang new town (about 30 minutes' drive and 45 minutes by public transport from the CBD) in August 2017. Column A shows the median resale prices in Sengkang new town. Consistent with current market norms, smaller units sell at a higher per square metre price. The resale prices are 2.0–2.6 times the average construction costs (Column D) for 3- to 5-room flats, and the price over construction cost mark-ups based on resale market prices (50–62%, Column G) are broadly in the range of the land value tax rate obtained for the private sector condominium example in Table 5.4 (57%).

HDB resale prices, however, represent asset prices of older units that are not adjusted for depreciation while the construction costs are for new products. As such, I do not refer to the resale prices over construction cost as a land value tax. In the case of HDB resale flats, the price difference between the resale price and the price paid at the time of purchase accrues to the first owners of the flats as a form of capital gains.

Table 5.6 HDB flats: resale prices and new flat prices, 2017

	Price per square metre			Price to CC ratio			(Price-CC)/Price		
HDB flat type	Resale market price (A)	New flat price (B)	New flat price with grants (C)	Resale market price (D)	New flat price (E)	New flat price with grants (F)	Resale market price (G) (%)	New flat price (H) (%)	New flat price with grants (I) (%)
3-rm	$5262	$2769	$1692	2.6	1.4	0.8	62	28	−18
4-rm	$4611	$3222	$2667	2.3	1.6	1.3	57	38	25
5-rm	$3982	$3273	$3273	2.0	1.6	1.6	50	39	39

Notes: Estimated using Construction Cost (CC) of $2000 psm for net floor area. Data on new flat prices and new flat prices with grants are from Rivervale Shores at Sengkang new town launched for sale in August 2017. See Table 1.1 and HDB website at http://esales.hdb.gov.sg/hdbvsf/eampu09p.nsf/0/17AUGBTO_page_8557/$file/about0.html. Accessed 1 Nov 2017

The HDB does not price its new flats on a profit maximizing basis but rather, on a household's ability to pay. HDB new flat prices are thus "regulated" policy-driven prices and not competitive market prices. On the one hand, these prices represent discounted prices from the market resale prices. On the other hand, they may also be regarded as a lower land value tax as compared to the land value component of the price paid by buyers of resale HDB and private housing. The pattern of HDB new flat pricing is the reverse for resale flats—larger units are priced at a higher per square metre price (Columns B and C). The increasing average price per square metre for larger flat types, from $2769 to $3273 per square metre (column B), and $1692 to $3273 with housing grants (column C) provides clear evidence that HDB's pricing of its flats is based on affordability rather than costs.

Prior to 2013, as noted by Phang (2010), the HDB had determined the prices of its new flats by "first looking at the recently transacted prices of resale units nearby. Adjustments are then made to account for factors like location, finishes of the flat, and other attributes. The price reflects the flat's value at the point of purchase and is what people are willing to pay on the open market for such a unit. The HDB then sells it at a significant discount, which is the subsidy given by the Government" (Toh 2009). This approach, however, led to new HDB prices moving upwards at the same rate as resale prices from 2008, as population growth outpaced new housing supply.

This approach of referencing the resale market for setting new flat prices was modified in 2013, when the Minister for National Development announced that prices for flats in the HDB's BTO launches would be delinked from market prices to make homeownership more affordable for first-time homeowners (Chang 2013).

Using HDB's new flat prices (Column E), the price to construction cost ratio falls to 1.4 for 3-room flats and to 1.6 for 5-room flats. When targeted housing grants that are available to first-time homeowners are considered (Column F), the ratio drops to 0.8 for 3-room flats that are sold at below construction costs. Land value tax estimated based on new HDB flat prices are 28% for 3-room flats (Column H) and higher, at around 39%, for 4- and 5-room flats. With housing grants, land value tax estimates are negative for 3-room flats (−18%), 25% for 4-room flats, and 39% for 5-room flats.

These land value tax estimates are fairly consistent with HDB's capital expenditures on buildings and land. The HDB pays market rates for state land and receives an annual government grant, which can be considered a land premium subsidy. In 2015/2016, HDB's expenditure on buildings was $5.1 billion and its expenditure on land was $4.9 billion. It received a government grant of $1.6 billion to finance its deficit for the year (HDB Annual Report 2015/2016). If these figures are broadly typical, the HDB's effective land cost component of $3.3 billion ($4.9 billion minus $1.6 billion) is 39% of its overall net capital expenditure of $8.4 billion ($3.3 billion + $5.1 billion).

In summary, the land value tax based on 2017 sale prices and GLS premium paid is estimated at 57% for a suburban condominium, Waterfront@ Faber. At Sengkang HDB town, the land value tax was 39% and 25% for new HDB 5- and 4-room flats, respectively, while buyers of new HDB 3-room (and 2-room flats) benefit from housing prices that were below construction costs. As these are suburban locations, the land value tax can be expected to be higher for locations closer to the central area.[12]

This chapter concludes with the following observations on the impact of land use planning and regulations in Singapore. First, despite the extreme land constraint, the land cost component of prices for high-density housing (in particular for HDB new flats), are lower than that in several cities with higher house price-to-income ratios (see Chap. 1). This can be attributed to land use policy that facilitates rather than restricts housing supply as well as non-market pricing for HDB flats. Second, a significant portion of the land cost for housing is captured by the government through the HDB, GLS, as well as differential premiums/development charges. Third, the mark-up of price over construction costs for unsubsidized resale HDB housing is within the same range as the land value tax for private condominiums for suburban locations, evidence of the efficiency of HDB resale markets despite various restrictions on ownership. The benefits of the difference between the price of a resale HDB flat and the price at the time of purchase accrue to the first owner of the HDB flat. Finally, as the HDB is the developer of affordable housing for low- and middle-income households, regulated housing prices are used as a redistributive mechanism, such that buyers of new smaller flat types (3-room or smaller) pay prices that are below average construction costs, that is, the land value tax is progressive and negative for lower-income households in suburban locations.

Notes

1. Yuen (2007) contains a detailed account of institutional framework, legislative basis, development objectives, plans, and policy instruments for Singapore's land use planning.
2. Fixed rates were payable for DCs levied between 1965 and 1980. From 1980 to 1985, developers were required to pay 70% of the land enhancement value, and from 1985 to 2007, 50% of the land enhancement value. In 2007, the DC rate was revised to 70% of the appreciation in land value. See note 6.
3. See Singh (2017) for a comprehensive account of land transport planning in Singapore.
4. Liu Thai Ker was the CEO of the URA from 1989 to 1992 and led the major revision of the Concept Plan. Liu (2017) provides a detailed account of the major shift in land use planning policy.
5. Refer to the URA website for the latest Concept Plan and Master Plan https://www.ura.gov.sg/uol/master-plan.aspx?p1=View-Master-Plan. Accessed 1 Nov 17.
6. From 1989, charges have been based on prescribed rates with the quantum computed using a published Development Charge Table, which

greatly improved transparency. The DC Table is updated by the Ministry of National Development in consultation with the Chief Valuer every half year (on 1 Sep and 1 Mar). The prescribed average land rates are currently based on 70% of estimated land values by 8 land use groups in 118 geographical sectors (see note 2). These published rates allowed developers to estimate the DC payable.

7. Report of the Select Committee on the Land Titles (Strata) (Amendment) Bill, presented to Parliament on 19 Apr 1999. As cited in Christudason (2009).
8. Sing (2017) for 1995–2013 figures, updated for 2014–2017 from data available at https://www.squarefoot.com.sg/market-watch/enbloc-market. Accessed 1 Nov 2017.
9. In 2013, another large-scale redevelopment project was announced by the Prime Minister that involves the relocation of port terminals near the city and at Pasir Panjang to the west by 2027. This massive relocation is expected to free up 1000 hectares of land, and the URA has since unveiled preliminary conceptual plans for the Greater Southern Waterfront site at: www.ura.gov.sg/uol/master-plan/view-master-plan/master-plan-2014/master-plan/Regional-highlights/central-area/central-area/Greater-southern-waterfront. Accessed 1 Nov 2017.
10. From GLS databank available at the URA website.
11. I use data from RLB (2017) for construction cost ranges for median, good and luxury quality condominiums.
12. Ideally, a more complete study would be based on a larger sample of both private sector and HDB projects as well as estimates of the regulatory tax based on marginal construction costs. I hope to undertake this study in the future.

References

Centre for Liveable Cities. 2017. *Working with Markets: Harnessing Market Forces and Private Sector for Development*. Singapore: Centre for Liveable Cities.

Chang, Rachel. 2013. BTO Prices Will Not Rise with Resale Market: Khaw. *The Straits Times*, 31 Jan.

Cheshire, Paul, and Christian A.C. Hilber. 2008. Office Space Supply Restrictions in Britain: The Political Economy of Market Revenge. *Economic Journal* 118: 185–221.

Choe, Alan. 2017. The Early Years of Nation-Building: Reflections on Singapore's Urban History. In *50 Years of Urban Planning in Singapore*, ed. Chye Kiang Heng. Singapore: World Scientific.

Choo, Steven. 2002. Government Land Sales Through the Years—Remaking Singapore's Landscape. In *Skyline 20th Anniversary Commemorative Edition*. Singapore: Urban Redevelopment Authority.

Christudason, Alice. 2004. *Private Sector Housing Redevelopment in Singapore: A Review of the Effectiveness of Radical Strata Title Legislation*. Paper Presented at the ENHR Conference, July, Cambridge, UK.

———. 2009. Property Rights: Achieving a Fine Balance in Collective Sales of Strata Developments in Singapore. *International Journal of Law in the Built Environment* 1 (1): 26–41.

Dale, Ole Johan. 1999. *Urban Planning in Singapore: The Transformation of a City*. Shah Alam: Oxford University Press.

Glaeser, Edward L., and Bryce Ward. 2009. The Causes and Consequences of Land Use Regulation: Evidence from Greater Boston. *Journal of Urban Economics* 65: 265–278.

Glaeser, Edward L., Joseph Gyourko, and Raven E. Saks. 2005. Why Is Manhattan so Expensive? Regulation and the Rise in Housing Prices. *Journal of Law and Economics* 48 (October): 331–369.

Gyourko, Joseph, and Raven Molloy. 2015. Regulation and Housing Supply. In *Handbook of Regional and Urban Economics*, ed. G. Duranton, V. Henderson, and W. Strange, vol. 5B. Amsterdam: Elsevier.

Gyourko, Joseph, Christopher Mayer, and Todd Sinai. 2013. Superstar Cities. *American Economic Journal—Economic Policy* 5 (4): 167–199.

Hilber, Christian A.L., and Wouter Vermeulen. 2016. The Impact of Supply Constraints on House Prices in England. *The Economic Journal* 126: 358–405.

Khoo, Teng Chye, and Remy Guo. 2017. Making Singapore a Liveable and Sustainable City: Our Urban Systems Approach. In *50 Years of Urban Planning in Singapore*, ed. Chye Kiang Heng, 81–100. Singapore: World Scientific.

Kim, Kyung-Hwan, Sock-Yong Phang, and Susan Wachter. 2012. Supply Elasticity of Housing. In *International Encyclopaedia of Housing and Home*, ed. Susan J. Smith, 66–74. Oxford: Elsevier.

Liu, Thai Ker. 2017. Planning and Urbanization in Singapore: A 50-Year Journey. In *50 Years of Urban Planning in Singapore*, ed. Chye Kiang Heng, 23–44. Singapore: World Scientific.

Moretti, Enrico. 2013. *The New Geography of Jobs*. New York: Houghton Mifflin Harcourt.

Phang, Sock-Yong. 2010. Affordable Homeownership Policy. *International Journal of Housing Markets and Analysis* 3 (1): 38–52.

Quigley, John M., and Steven Raphael. 2005. Regulation and the High Cost of Housing in California. *AEA Papers and Proceedings* 95 (2): 323–328.

Rider Levett Bucknall (RLB). 2017. *Singapore Construction Market Update*, June. http://assets.rlb.com/production/2017/09/08062907/RLB-Singapore-Construction-Market-Update-June-2017.pdf. Accessed 1 Nov 2017.

Sing, Tien Foo. 2017. Changing Skyline: Real Estate Development Industry. In *Singapore's Real Estate: 50 Years of Transformation*, ed. Ngee-Huat Seek, Tien Foo Sing, and Shi Ming Yu. Singapore: World Scientific.

Singh, Mohinder. 2017. Transportation: Mobility, Accessibility, and Connectivity. In *50 Years of Urban Planning in Singapore*, ed. Chye Kiang Heng, 127–152. Singapore: World Scientific.

Toh, Mavis. 2009. Are Flats Too Pricey or Buyers Too Choosy? *Sunday Times*, 20 Sep.

Yu, Shi Ming, and Tien Foo Sing. 2017. Transforming a Nation: Role of Government Agencies. In *Singapore's Real Estate: 50 Years of Transformation*, ed. Ngee Huat Seek, Tien Foo Sing, and Shi Ming Yu, 19–54. Singapore: World Scientific.

Yuen, Belinda. 2007. *Guiding Spatial Changes: Singapore Urban Planning*. Paper Presented at 4th Urban Research Symposium on Urban Land Use and Land Markets, May 14. Washington, DC: The World Bank.

6

Market-Responsive Housing Regulations

Regulation is the use of government's power to restrict or constrain the decisions of economic agents. Regulation of markets has been justified to promote competitive outcomes, to curb monopoly power, as well as where externalities justify government intervention. In the traditional regulatory literature, housing markets are generally regarded as competitive markets, with little need for economic regulation. However, in high-density urban environments, social regulations of housing, which include environmental and planning regulations, are, in fact, well accepted. The positive externalities of providing affordable minimum standard housing for the lower-income group have also been long recognized by governments of developed countries. This merit good characteristic of housing has been used to justify rent control regulations and public housing provision. Newer regulations governing consumer protection and controlling the build-up of systemic risk have become an increasingly prominent part of the regulatory mix.

The housing market, however, is one of the most challenging markets to regulate well. Housing market regulations can exist at both the national and sub-national levels and can form a complex bureaucratic web. Rent control, public housing, privatization, and gentrification are

S.-Y. Phang, *Policy Innovations for Affordable Housing In Singapore*,
Palgrave Advances in Regional and Urban Economics,
https://doi.org/10.1007/978-3-319-75349-2_6

examples of policies that have come under heavy criticism in several cities around the world for their unexpected negative consequences. More specifically, the US subprime crisis of 2007–2008 can be considered a regulatory failure of immense proportion. In the aftermath of the Global Financial Crisis (GFC), macro-prudential regulation for financial stability has become a new regulatory area for international financial regulators and central bankers.

Since the 1960s, the Singapore government has devised and experimented with a wide range of housing market regulations in order to enhance housing affordability across the income spectrum. Singapore's housing tenure forms are thus incredibly complex, with public-private hybrids defined by ownership or rental as well as by Housing and Development Board (HDB) or private housing developer. Property ownership is also further defined by freehold, leasehold (and number of years of remaining leasehold), fully owned or part-owned (strata-title) status. The HDB and private housing segments are regulated differently, with regulations that have been changed frequently in response to market conditions.

In this chapter,[1] we consider three categories of housing market regulations that have contributed to housing affordability in Singapore: (i) market segmentation, (ii) resale regulations, and (iii) macro-prudential regulation. This chapter concludes with justifications for housing regulations for housing affordability that are responsive to changes in social and economic conditions, including housing bubbles.

Housing Market Segmentation for Housing Affordability

The housing market in Singapore is highly segmented by regulations on the eligibility of households based on their residency status (citizen/permanent resident/foreigner), household type (single, couple, extended family), household incomes, and house types (see Table 6.1). This market segmentation disqualifies higher-income, foreign buyers, speculators, and investors from purchasing housing in a large segment of the housing

Table 6.1 Housing market segmentation for housing affordability

Housing segment	Citizens	Permanent residents	Foreigners
HDB Public Rental Scheme[a]	Income ceiling of $1500	Not eligible	Not eligible
Purchase a new HDB flat[a]	Income ceiling of $12,000	Not eligible	Not eligible
Purchase a new Executive Condominium[a]	Income ceiling of $14,000	Not eligible	Not eligible
Purchase of resale HDB flats[a] After the initial 5 years, owners are allowed to sell their units to Singaporeans and PRs	No income ceiling	PR status for at least 3 years	Not eligible
Purchase of resale Executive Condominiums	After the initial 5 years, owners are allowed to sell their units to Singaporeans	Foreigners and PRs can only buy an Executive Condominium 10 years after it was first sold	
Rental and purchase of private strata-title condominiums and apartments	Yes	Yes, ABDS of 5% for first property	Yes, ABDS of 15% for first property
Rental of private landed properties	Yes	Yes	Yes
Purchase of private landed properties including strata-title landed and cluster housing	Yes	Not eligible, except at Sentosa Cove (one home, not to be rented out); foreigners with PR status for at least 5 years can apply to the Minister for Law for approval	Not eligible, except at Sentosa Cove (one home, not to be rented out)

Note: [a]At any point in time, each eligible household can only own or rent one HDB unit

Sources: Author's compilation from Singapore government websites

market and has, as a result, contributed to making homeownership affordable for lower- and middle-income households.

The private housing sector caters largely to higher-income Singapore citizens, permanent residents, expatriates, and foreign investors. Foreign ownership of property, land, and housing has been regulated by the Residential Property Act since 1973. Under the Residential Property Act, foreigners who are not permanent residents (PRs) are not permitted to own landed housing.[2] Those with PR status of at least five years and who wish to purchase landed housing have to obtain prior approval from the Singapore Land Authority's Land Dealings Approval Unit. Approval is granted on a case-by-case basis for PRs with "exceptional economic contributions to Singapore" as one of the criteria for approval. If approval is granted, the PR is required to use the property for residence only, and not for rental or other income-generating purposes. A minimum occupation period of five years (after which they can sell) and limitation of ownership to one landed house applies. From 2004, foreigners have been permitted to purchase landed homes located at Sentosa Cove—a luxurious seafront housing enclave located on Sentosa island. As a result of the Residential Property Act, foreigners' purchase is largely confined to private flats and condominiums, and is also subject to additional buyer's stamp duty of 15%.

Only citizens are eligible for the HDB public rental scheme and to purchase a new flat directly from the HDB or under the Executive Condominium scheme. Housing subsidies are means-tested, and the gross monthly household income is one of the eligibility criteria for housing subsidies. The household income ceiling for HDB 1- and 2-room rental flats was $800 in the 1960s and was only raised to $1500 in 2003. It has remained at $1500 since, reflecting the strong housing policy bias towards homeownership.

The monthly gross household income cap in order to be eligible to purchase a HDB flat for couples was $1200 for 3- and 4-room HDB flats, and $2000 for 5-room flats in the 1970s (Phang 1992). Over the years, as household incomes increased, the income ceiling for purchase of a HDB flat was raised periodically and more targeted market segments introduced for lower-income households (Table 6.2 and Phang 2010). Figure 6.1 shows the adjustments to income ceilings in relation to increases in the median household income from 2000 to 2016.

Table 6.2 Household income ceiling revisions for HDB and middle-income housing

Year of revision	HDB 2-room	HDB 3-room	HDB 4-room	HDB 5-room	HDB Executive	DBSS	HUDC	EC
1964		$1000						
1970								
1971		$1200		$1500				
1974							$4000	
1979		$1500		$2000	$2500			
1980							$6000	
1981		$1500	$3500					
1985			$4000					
1989			$5000					
1994			$8000					
1997								$10,000
2004			$8000					
2005		$3000				$8000		
2006	$2,000							
2010								
2011		$5000/ $10000*	$10,000			$10000		
2012	$2000/ $5000*							$12,000
2013	$5000							
2015	$6000	$6000/ $12000*	$12,000			$12000		$14,000

Note: [a]Depending on project, lower cap for non-mature estates, higher cap for mature estates

Sources: Phang (1992, 2010) and author's compilation from HDB Annual Reports and HDB website

The income ceilings to purchase new subsidized 4- and 5-room HDB flats are currently $12,000 for families and $18,000 if the applicant household is a multi-generational one or comprises parents and adult working children. For 2-room and 3-room HDB flats, the income ceilings for families are lower at $6000 (see Table 6.2).

A separate housing scheme for middle-income households existed between 1974 and 1987 in the form of the Housing and Urban Development Company (HUDC) scheme, and this was reintroduced in 1997 in a different form as the Executive Condominium (EC) Scheme. The income ceiling for ECs is currently set at $14,000. Table 6.2 shows the income ceiling changes for homeownership subsidies for families from the 1964 to 2017.

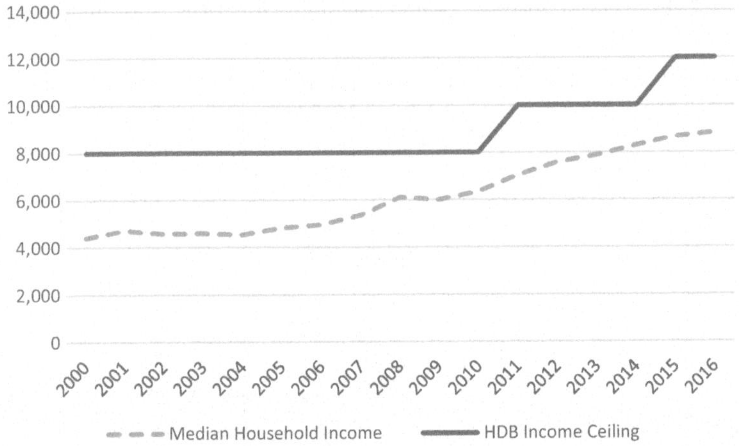

Fig. 6.1 HDB income ceiling and median household income ($), 2000–2016 (Note: Median Household Income refers to monthly household income from work (including employer CPF contributions) among resident employed households; Source: Data from Singapore government statistics)

To allow for greater private sector participation in design, the HDB launched a Design, Build and Sell Scheme (DBSS) in 2005, where private sector developers were invited to undertake the entire development process for HDB flats—from tendering for the land to designing, building, and selling the flats. Sale prices were set by the developer instead of the HDB, with the household income ceiling similar to that for HDB at $8000. In addition, first-time buyers for DBSS were eligible to receive the Central Provident Fund (CPF) grant similar to first-time buyers of HDB resale flats. In 2010, the DBSS income ceiling was raised to $10,000, and was further increased to $12,000 in 2015. However, land sales for DBSS projects have been halted since 2011 due to public unhappiness over high prices as well as complaints by flat owners about design and quality.

Market segmentation also applies to household composition, marital status, and age. The housing needs of married couples and families were accorded priority during the earlier period of housing shortage. Singles aged 35 and above were only allowed to purchase resale HDB flats from 1991, and have been eligible for CPF housing grants from 1998. From 2013, those earning below $5000 per month also became eligible to purchase 2-room flats in a non-mature estate directly from the HDB. In 1998, a 30-year leasehold studio apartment scheme for the elderly was introduced to facilitate downsizing from larger flats. A 2-room Flexi leasehold scheme was introduced by the HDB in 2015. It replaced the 2-room flat and studio apartment scheme for the elderly and offers flexible shorter leases to applicants aged 55 years and above. Instead of a 99-year lease for a new flat, the lease period for the 2-room Flexi ranges from 15 to 45 years.[3]

Resale Market Regulations and Housing Prices

Rules governing the resale of HDB flats have undergone numerous changes over time, as the market share of the segment increased. In the 1960s and 1970s, resale regulations for subsidized HDB apartments were extremely onerous when there were long waiting lists for HDB flats. The HDB allocated flats, with priority given to households affected by resettlement and on a first-come-first-served basis for other households. Separate waiting lists were maintained for rental and sale flats, and applicants could state their preferred zone and type of flat desired. The waiting lists averaged 70,000 households per year between 1971 and 1985 (Phang 1992, 166). During this period of housing shortage, there was concern that HDB dwellings should not become a vehicle for speculation by allowing the price subsidies to be capitalized on a secondary market.

Restrictions on resale of HDB flats took the following forms:

(i) Ban on market transactions prior to 1971: The HDB required owners who wished to sell their flats to return them to the HDB at the original purchase price plus the depreciated cost of improvements.
(ii) Minimum occupancy period: In 1971, HDB allowed owners who had resided in their flats for a minimum of 3 years to sell their flats at market prices to buyers of their choice who satisfied the eligibility requirements for HDB homeownership. The minimum occupancy period before resale was increased to 5 years in 1973 and has remained in place since. There is therefore no market for HDB apartments that are fewer than 5 years in age.
(iii) Debarment period: In 1971, when resale became permitted, those who sold their flat were debarred from buying another HDB flat for

a year. The debarment period was increased to 2.5 years in 1975. The debarment period did not allow for household mobility within the HDB sector and was a great deterrent to any household considering sale of its dwelling. This was abolished in 1979, thereby greatly facilitating transactions within the public housing sector.

(iv) Resale levies: In 1979, in place of the debarment period, a 5% levy on the transacted price of the first flat purchased from the HDB was imposed on the seller to "reduce windfall profits". A system of graded resale levies (10–25% of the resale price), based on flat type, was introduced in 1982. Rules regarding circumstances under which levies could be waived were fine-tuned in the 1980s to facilitate upgrading to private housing or via the HDB resale market. This led to the resale levy being payable only by households that purchased a second subsidized HDB flat. The resale levy became a means of reducing the amount of housing subsidy enjoyed by the second-time HDB flat buyer as compared to the first-time HDB flat buyer. From 2006, rather than a percentage of the resale price, fixed resale levy amounts based on flat type were introduced. The resale levy amounts vary from $15,000 for a 2-room flat to $55,000 for Executive Condominiums (ECs).[4]

Only citizens, non-owners of any other residential property—households with a minimum size of two persons with household incomes below the income ceiling set by the HDB—were eligible to purchase new or resale HDB flats prior to 1989. These rules restricted mobility even as household incomes increased. Phang (1992) found that, in 1981, 31% of multiple worker HDB households with length of tenure longer than 5 years were no longer eligible to purchase HDB flats. The consequence for commuting time was that, on average, workers residing in HDB housing commuted greater distances by 2.2 minutes of auto time or 5.6 minutes of transit time, as compared to those residing in private apartments.

As the housing shortage eased and households sought to upgrade their housing or change their location, there was a need to amend resale regulations on the eligibility of buyers in order to facilitate household mobility within the HDB sector, as well as from the HDB to the private sector and vice versa. Facilitating the development of an HDB resale market through deregulation speeded up in the late 1980s and early 1990s. This could also be considered as in line with the then-worldwide trend towards privatization and deregulation.

From 1989, the income ceiling restriction was removed for HDB resale flats; the resale market was opened to permanent residents as well as private property owners who had to owner-occupy their HDB flat. HDB flat owners who could not own any other residential property before could also invest in private sector-built dwellings. From 1991, single citizens above the age of 35 have been allowed to purchase HDB resale flats for owner-occupancy.

The HDB also provides loans to buyers of resale HDB flats. Loan financing prior to 1993 was based on 80% of 1984 HDB new flat (posted) prices. As both new and resale prices rose (see Fig. 3.1), households purchasing resale flats had to pay an increasingly larger proportion of the price in cash. In 1993 HDB moved its mortgage financing terms closer to market practice by granting loan financing of up to 80% of current valuation or the declared resale price of the flat, whichever is lower. In 1993, the CPF Board also began to allow withdrawals of CPF savings to be used to meet interest payments on mortgage loans for resale HDB and private housing purchases. Before this, CPF members were allowed to withdraw only up to 100% of the value of these properties at the time of purchase.

Deregulation of the HDB resale market was accompanied by an increase in the number of resale HDB transactions and helped fuel a housing boom. Financial liberalization as well as positive macroeconomic factors resulted in rapidly rising housing prices in the early 1990s (see Fig. 3.1). In response to growing concern over the affordability of private housing, the government introduced the Executive Condominium (EC) scheme, a hybrid public-private house type in 1995. The EC scheme also facilitated the HDB's withdrawal from the upper-middle-income housing market, allowing it to discontinue its building of Executive Flats. Its similarity with 99-year leasehold private condominiums house type provided the government with another instrument on the supply side to impact private housing prices. The government auctions land for the development of EC units to housing developers (private as well as government-linked companies) who are responsible for design, construction, pricing, as well as arrangements for financing and estate management. Applicant households have to satisfy eligibility conditions and abide by resale and other regulations governing these units.

Despite an increase in HDB's supply of new housing, the introduction of the EC scheme as well as the increase in government land sales for private housing development, housing prices continued to soar (with the private housing price index more than tripling between 1990 and 1996). On May 15, 1996, the government introduced a package of anti-speculation measures to curb real estate speculation. These included capital gains taxes on the sale of any property within three years of purchase, stamp duty on every sale and sub-sale of property, limitation of housing loans to 80% of property value, as well as limiting foreigners to non S$-denominated housing loans.

The HDB also tightened various regulations: in April 1997, HDB flat buyers were limited to two loans from the HDB, where there had been no limit before. In May 1997, the HDB implemented various measures to curb housing demand of upgraders (households applying for a second new subsidized flat from the HDB). These measures include lengthening the time period before flat lessees are eligible to purchase a second new flat from the HDB from five to ten years, and revising the graded resale levy system.

The immediate effect of these measures was to cool the property market, which, however, entered a slump with the unexpected onset of the Asian economic crisis in 1997 (see Fig. 3.1). In response to the fall in demand that was particularly pronounced in 1998, the government halted land sales and also ended its long-standing policy of not providing housing subsidies for singles by introducing a $15,000 CPF housing grant for eligible single persons to purchase resale 3-room or smaller flats. As housing prices declined further, the CPF housing grants was reduced in stages over 10 months from January to October 1999—$500 reduction per month for the Single Citizen housing grant, and $1000 reduction per month for the other housing grants.

From 2003, HDB also began to deregulate the rules on homeowners subletting of their HDB flats as a way of facilitating homeowners to earn rental income from their housing asset. Prior to this, HDB owners had to owner-occupy their flats and could not sublet their whole flats except under very exceptional circumstances. The rules were further eased in

2005. Homeowners who had met the 5-year minimum occupancy period and who had no outstanding housing loan were allowed to rent out their whole flat. Those who had occupied their flats for at least 10 years could rent out their flat, regardless of whether they had an outstanding housing loan. In 2005, the 1997 rule that required a 10-year waiting period between buying the first subsidized flat and applying for the second subsidized flat was reverted back to 5 years.

Macro-Prudential Regulations to Curb Housing Speculation

The years after the Asian Financial crisis up to 2007 was a period of economic uncertainty for Singapore which was reflected in both property prices and housing policies (see Fig. 3.1). In the post-Global Financial Crisis (GFC) period, limited new supply, rapid population increase, the low interest rate environment and high global liquidity resulting from the very accommodative monetary policies of Central Banks in developed economies led to accelerated price increases of Singapore property (see Fig. 3.1). The general upward trend in Singapore real estate prices caused housing to be viewed as an attractive investment class as compared to other asset classes. Leverage in real estate and Singapore Dollar appreciation further magnified the returns. The continuous upward trend in housing prices exerted pressure on policy makers to react with both macro-prudential and supply side measures to ensure housing affordability.

Macro-prudential policy became a buzzword in policy circles in the wake of the 2008 global financial crisis. Macro-prudential regulation concerns itself with the stability of the financial system as a whole, while micro-prudential regulation concerns itself with the risk of individual asset classes, the stability of individual entities, and the protection of individuals. Micro-prudential regulation ignores endogenous risks such as feedback effects, the interconnectedness of the system, as well as the systemic importance of individual institutions.

In the past decade, there is growing global consensus on the importance of macro-prudential regulation to safeguard against financial instability (Phang 2013). The reach of these reforms have extended to the whole of the financial sector, with several dealing directly with housing and housing credit booms (IMF/FSB/BIS 2016). Specific instruments of macro-prudential regulation to address the systemic risk of housing price changes include caps on loan-to-value (LTV) ratio and debt service-to-income (DTI) ratio. These limit mortgage loans to individuals, thus reducing pressure on housing prices and containing speculative demand. In some countries, caps on LTV and DTI have been fine-tuned to target housing booms by location as well as by market segments.

Between 2010 and 2013, the Singapore government announced several consecutive rounds of macro-prudential measures to curb demand for housing and mortgage loans (see Table 6.3). These measures took the form of additional stamp duties on sale and purchase of residential properties and the tightening of caps for LTV and DTI ratios. Rather than being implemented all at once, the measures were introduced incrementally, with the intention of not destabilizing or "crashing" the market, but to bring it to a "soft-landing" instead.

In addition to the numerous demand curbing measures, the government increased the supply of HDB flats substantially from 2011. While HDB dwelling units increased by a mere 23,000 units from 2006 to 2011,[5] approximately 25,000 HDB flats were launched for sale in 2011, followed by 27,000 units in 2012 and 25,000 new flats in 2013. With the increase in supply of both HDB and private housing, prices have declined and stabilized. In March 2017, with prices stabilizing, seller stamp duty rates were calibrated downwards by four percentage points for each tier, with the new rates ranging from 4% (for properties sold in the third year) to 12% for those sold within the first year.

A Market-Responsive Housing Regulatory Framework

Achieving the goal of decent and affordable homeownership for more than 90% of resident households in Singapore has required numerous housing market regulations. At different stages of economic develop-

Table 6.3 Measures to curb house price increase, 2010–2013

FEB 2010	In February 2010, seller stamp duty was re-introduced for sale of properties and land within 1 year of purchase and LTV ratio was lowered from 90% to 80%, except for HDB loans
AUG 2010	In August 2010, the holding period for imposition of seller stamp duty was increased to 3 years. For borrowers with existing housing loan(s), their LTV ratio was lowered from 80% to 70% and minimum cash-component down payment was raised to 10% from 5%
JAN 2011	In January 2011, the holding period for imposition of seller stamp duty was increased to 4 years. The seller stamp duty rate was increased to 16%, 12%, 8%, and 4% for properties sold within the first, second, third, and fourth years of purchase, respectively. For borrowers with existing housing loan(s), their LTV ratio was lowered from 70% to 60%
DEC 2011	In December 2011, additional buyer stamp duty was imposed; Singapore citizens buying their third and subsequent residential property paid 3%, Singapore permanent residents buying their second and subsequent residential property paid 3%, and foreigners buying their first and subsequent residential property paid 10%
OCT 2012	In October 2012, the Monetary Authority of Singapore (MAS) imposed a 35-year tenor restriction for housing loans on new residential properties. For borrowers without any existing housing loan(s) and where loan tenors exceed 30-year or extend beyond borrowers' retirement age of 65 years old, the LTV ratio was lowered to 60%. LTV ratio was lowered to 40% for borrowers with existing housing loan(s) where the loan tenors exceed 30 years or extend beyond borrowers' retirement age of 65 years
JAN 2013	In January 2013, additional buyer stamp duty was raised; Singapore citizens buying their second residential property pay 7% and those buying their third and subsequent residential property pay 10%, Singapore permanent residents buying their first residential property pay 5% and those buying their second and subsequent residential property pay 10%, and foreigners buying their first and subsequent residential property pay 15%
	LTV ratio was lowered to 50% and 40% for borrowers applying for their second and third or subsequent housing loans, respectively, where loan tenors do not exceed 30 years or do not extend beyond the borrowers' retirement age of 65 years. In cases where loan tenors exceed 30 years or extend beyond borrowers' retirement age of 65 years, LTV ratios of 30% and 20% apply for borrowers applying for their second and third or subsequent housing loans respectively. The minimum cash-component down payment was also raised to 25% from 10% for buyers taking their second or subsequent housing loan

(*continued*)

Table 6.3 (continued)

JUN 2013	The MAS introduced the Total Debt Servicing Ratio (TDSR) for homebuyers with the intention that the measure "...will help strengthen credit underwriting practices by [financial institutions, FIs] and encourage financial prudence among borrowers". The TDSR is the total monthly debt service as a percentage of the borrower's income and is capped at 60%. In computation of TDSR, FIs will need to take into account the monthly repayment on the property loan that the borrower is applying for plus the monthly repayments on all other outstanding property and non-property debt obligations of the borrower; apply a specified medium-term interest rate or the prevailing market interest rate, whichever is higher, to the property loan that the borrower is applying for when calculating the TDSR; apply a haircut of at least 30% to all variable income (e.g. bonuses) and rental income; and apply haircuts to and amortize the value of any eligible financial assets taken into consideration in assessing the borrower's debt servicing ability, in order to convert them into "income streams"
	MAS also required borrowers named on a property loan to be the mortgagors of the residential property for which the loan is taken; "guarantors" who are standing guarantee for borrowers otherwise assessed by the FI at the point of application for the housing loan not to meet the TDSR threshold for a property loan to be brought in as co-borrowers; and in the case of joint borrowers, that FIs use the income-weighted average age of borrowers when applying the rules on loan tenure
AUG 2013	Effective August 27, 2013, new Singapore Permanent residents have to wait for 3 years before they are eligible to purchase resale HDB flats. The maximum tenure for HDB housing loans was reduced from 30 years to 25 years. The mortgage servicing ratio limit was reduced from 35% to 30% of the borrower's gross monthly income. The maximum tenure of new housing loans and re-financing facilities granted by financial institutions for the purchase of HDB flats was reduced from 35 to 30 years
DEC 2013	From December 2013, the government required second-time applicants who bought Executive Condominium units directly from property developers to pay a resale levy, similar to second-time applicants who bought HDB BTO flats. The Mortgage Servicing Ratio for housing loans granted by financial institutions for EC units bought directly from property developers was capped at 30% of a borrower's gross monthly income

Sources: Government websites, Lee et al. (2013), and Phang (2015)

ment, the market failures in the housing sector were of a different nature, necessitating different types of regulations.

In the 1960s and 1970s, during a period of housing scarcity, rent control remained in place and the HDB sector was tightly regulated through a web of eligibility rules and restrictions on resale to curb house price increases and profiteering. Recognizing the diversity of households being served by "public housing", the government has responded to the needs, preferences, and purchasing power of target groups with different housing schemes. Housing segmentation has been by household characteristics, including nationality, income, marital status, life cycle, as well as ethnicity (the subject of the next chapter). Segmentation allowed the government to identify the different housing needs of various groups, prioritize the needs to be addressed, and to respond with appropriate housing policies to meet the different preferences of each sub-group. The income ceiling and other eligibility conditions defining each market segment have been responsive to changes in incomes, demography, and market conditions. The frequent reviews and changes to housing regulations reduced the risk of out-dated regulations that could have led to inefficiencies.

Market regulations have also been implemented to deter speculative activity that can lead to the development of housing bubbles and cause house prices to rise beyond the reach of consumer households. These regulations extended across the HDB sector from the early days of the programme in the form strict eligibility criteria, minimum occupation period, owner-occupancy requirement, financing restrictions, and resale levies. These regulations were eased as the housing shortage was solved, creating an asset market for HDB resale flats that facilitated household mobility within and across housing sectors. Deregulation, however, contributed to asset bubbles that were also developing across the region, which burst with the onset of the Asian financial crisis of 1997.

The impacts of the Global financial crisis of 2008 on housing prices in Singapore were the opposite of those of the Asian financial crisis. Policies adopted were radically different: zero interest rates and quantitative easing implemented by the developed countries inflated asset markets. In Singapore, demand pressures from immigration, foreign capital inflows, and limited housing supply led to a rapid increase in housing prices

(Phang 2012). From 2010, numerous macro-prudential measures were needed to contain mortgage debt and stem housing price increases.

As a small open city-state with only 720 sq km of land, higher housing prices arising from investment demand of foreigners create negative externalities in the form of higher house prices for residents. From a macro-prudential standpoint, there is a strong justification for sheltering the real estate sector from the large and potentially destabilizing foreign capital flows. Moreover, there is a clear domestic bias for real estate investment as compared to other asset classes due to the importance of local knowledge in real estate investment decisions. Singapore has not banned foreigners from purchasing housing—which would be detrimental to its status as a global financial centre. In order to achieve a balance, it has, however, subjected foreign purchasers to careful regulation, including revenue generating stamp duties. With careful and market-responsive regulation of the sector, housing in Singapore remains an attractive long-term investment, given the underlying framework and future economic prospects of Singapore.

Notes

1. This chapter draws from my previous published works (Phang 1992, 2005, 2007, 2010, 2012, 2013, 2015; Phang and Helbe 2016).
2. Foreigners are required to seek approval to purchase vacant residential land, private landed residential properties, strata landed house not within an approved condominium, shophouses for non-commercial use, and so on. See the Singapore Land Authority website at: http://www.sla.gov.sg/Services/Restriction-on-Foreign-Ownership-of-Landed-Property. Accessed 1 Nov 2017.
3. Flat applicants aged 55 and above can choose units with shorter leases ranging from 15 to 45 years, in five-year increments. The lease length chosen must last the applicant and his/her spouse until they are at least 95 years old. See HDB website for details of eligibility criteria and other conditions: http://www.hdb.gov.sg/cs/infoweb/residential/buying-a-flat/new/2room-flexi-flats. Accessed 1 Nov 2017.
4. See the HDB website at: http://www.hdb.gov.sg/cs/infoweb/residential/selling-a-flat/additional-information. Accessed 1 Nov 2017.
5. HDB Annual Reports 2005/2006 and 2010/11.

References

Housing and Development Board. *Annual Report*. Various years. Singapore.

International Monetary Fund, Financial Stability Board, and Bank for International Settlements. 2016. *Elements of Effective Macroprudential Policies: Lessons from International Experience*. https://www.imf.org/external/np/g20/pdf/2016/083116.pdf. Accessed 1 Nov 2017.

Lee, David, Sock-Yong Phang, Kok-Fai Phoon, and Karol Wee. 2013. *Evaluating the Effectiveness of Cooling Measures on Property Prices: An Exploration of Alternative Econometric Techniques*. Paper Presented at the Asian Meeting of the Econometric Society, Singapore, 2–4 August 2013.

Phang, Sock-Yong. 1992. *Housing Markets and Urban Transportation: Economic Theory, Econometrics and Policy Analysis for Singapore*. Singapore: McGraw Hill.

———. 2005. The Creation and Economic Regulation of Housing Markets: A Comparison of the Experiences of Singapore and Korea. In *Residential Welfare and Housing Policies: The Experience and Future of Korea*, ed. MoonJoong Tcha, 143–180. Seoul: Korea Development Institute.

———. 2007. The Singapore Model of Housing and the Welfare State. In *Housing and the New Welfare State*, ed. Richard Groves, Alan Murie, and Christopher Watson. Aldershot: Ashgate.

———. 2010. Affordable Homeownership Policy: Implications for Housing Markets. *International Journal of Housing Markets and Analysis* 3 (1): 38–52.

———. 2012. Public Housing: Appreciating Assets? In *Singapore Perspectives 2012*, ed. Soon Hock Kang and Chan-Hoong Leong, 81–88. Singapore: Institute of Policy Studies and World Scientific.

———. 2013. *Housing Finance Systems: Market Failures and Government Failures*. Basingstoke: Palgrave Macmillan.

———. 2015. Singapore's Housing Policies: Responding to the Challenges of Economic Transitions. *The Singapore Economic Review* 60 (3): 1550036 (25 pages).

Phang, Sock-Yong, and Matthias Helbe. 2016. Housing Policies in Singapore. In *The Housing Challenge in Emerging Asia: Options and Solutions*, ed. Naoyuki Yoshino and Matthias Helbe, 174–209. Tokyo: Asian Development Bank Institute.

7

Building Diverse Neighbourhoods Through Integration Policies

The Historical Context

The history of modern Singapore dates from 1819, when Sir Stamford Raffles established the island as a British free trading port. Raffles formed a Town Planning Committee in 1822, which prepared Singapore's first detailed town plan by 1823. The plan laid out street patterns for the coastal settlement around the gateway of the Singapore River to support mercantile trade along the river. Land was then divided into narrow lots which individuals could purchase on a freehold or leasehold term of up to 999 years. Parcels were carved out for businesses, the government precinct, educational, recreational, and religious activities.

Separate residential areas were identified for the different ethnic communities of settlers: Europeans, Bugis, Arabs, Chinese, Indians, and Malays. Chinatown was further sub-divided for different dialect-speaking groups from southern China: Cantonese, Hokkien, Teochew (Hodder 1953; Choe 2017; Yuen 2007). Colonial town planning practices thus established residential segregation in Singapore from the early nineteenth century. The dominant permitted structure type was the low-rise mixed-use shophouse, with commerce permitted on the ground floor and

S.-Y. Phang, *Policy Innovations for Affordable Housing In Singapore*,
Palgrave Advances in Regional and Urban Economics,
https://doi.org/10.1007/978-3-319-75349-2_7

residences on the upper floor(s). Apart from the implementation of the Raffles Town Plan in the 1820s, the colonial government adopted a laissez-faire attitude towards urban development throughout the nineteenth century.

Up to the eve of Japanese Occupation in 1942, Singapore remained largely an immigrant society. The growth of the trading port from 1818 to 1942 was dependent on immigrants of several nationalities, with men from the coastal provinces of southeast China by far the largest group. Increasing population densities within the town with new immigrant arrivals caused the European merchants and a few wealthy Chinese and Arab-Malays to move to the suburbs. The Tanglin-Claymore area to the north became the residential area of the wealthy. By the 1840s, the European Town was taken over by the rapidly growing Chinese immigrant population and was colloquially known as "little town", as distinct from the "big town", the original area allocated to the Chinese (Phang 1992, 266).

It was only in the 1930s, when immigration quotas favouring women were imposed, that the gender ratio became more balanced (Saw 1970). Data from the 1947 population census reveals that persons born in Singapore formed the majority of the population for the first time. By 1957, the population had increased to 1.4 million and comprised a clear Chinese majority; it was 75% Chinese, 14% Malay, 9% Indians and 2% others. Within the Southeast Asian region where the Chinese were often the market-dominant minority,[1] the large proportion of Chinese in Singapore's population caused Singapore to be regarded as a "city foreign to its hinterland" (Huff 1994, 25).

Within Singapore, the city began to spread outwards only in the interwar period, with wider adoption of the motor car, greater use of bus transport, and a growing Asian middle class (Huff 1994, 49). The majority of the population, however, continued to cluster in the congested central area where employment opportunities were confined. Within the urban area, immigrants remained geographically segregated along race, dialect, and occupational groups (Hodder 1953).

Huff (1994, 47) observed that before resettlement by the Housing and Development Board (HDB), "practically all Singapore's inhabitants lived in readily distinguishable racial and, in the case of the Chinese pang (dialect) groups, ethnic areas". Outside the central city area, there were several rural and coastal kampongs and village settlements that were exclusively either Chinese or Malay. An observer in 1940 described little racial mixing: "the races maintain their individual integrity and customs by tacit agreement without proselyting".[2] There were, however, numerous accounts of conflict over issues of race and religion during Singapore's pre-independence history. The 1950 Maria Hertogh riots involving Muslims and Christians are consistently evoked by the government to exemplify the need for vigilance over ethno-religious matters (Mathews and Khidzer 2015).

Mounting tensions and intense politicking between the political leaders of Singapore and Malaysia during the short-lived merger between 1963 and 1965 centred on race. Then Prime Minister Lee Kuan Yew described the relationship between Singapore and Malaysian leaders as one where "the race issue overshadowed everything else" (Lee 1998, 602). In 1964, there were two major episodes of ethnic violence between the Chinese and the Malays that resulted in several deaths and injuries. Continued hostile and intense disagreements over the issue of special privileges for the Malays eventually led to Singapore being expelled from Malaysia in 1965 (Lee 1998).

Soon after independence, the Singapore government worked on policies to safeguard racial and religious harmony, emphasizing equal rights and opportunities for all citizens. The National Pledge was approved by the Cabinet in 1966. It is a pledge "to be one united people, regardless of race, language, or religion".[3] However, communal riots broke out again in 1969. This was following the outbreak of Chinese-Malay racial riots in Malaysia after the General Election, which spilled over to Singapore. The situation was brought under control in Singapore by security forces but not before a final toll of 4 dead and 80 wounded.

Singapore's present policies on race and religion must be understood against the historical context of the communal tensions described above. As a global city, Singapore today is home to an even more racially diverse population. In 2017, the total population was 5.612 million, of which 3.439 million were citizens, 0.527 million were permanent residents, and 1.647 million comprised foreigners of diverse nationalities. The Chinese majority comprised 76.1% of the citizen population, the Malays 15.0%,

Indians 7.4%, with other races comprising 1.5% (Singapore Department of Statistics 2016).

The preservation of racial and religious harmony are fundamental goals of the government—to be achieved through adoption of continuously proactive, pre-emptive and interventionist measures (Matthews and Khidzer 2015). The national pledge is recited by students on every school day, by soldiers in the armed forces, and at the annual National Day Parade. Racial Harmony Day is observed in schools every year on July 21st—the date in 1964 when communal riots first broke out. In 1989, the Maintenance of Religious Harmony Act was passed and empowers the government to "make a restraining order" against persons or groups who cause feelings of enmity, hatred, ill will, or hostility between different religious groups.

Pre-emptive measures also extend to the protection of the rights of minority groups. From 1988, the Group Representation Constituency was introduced as an electoral division where teams of candidates, instead of individual candidates, compete to be elected as Members of Parliament. At least one member of the team has to be from a minority group in order to ensure minority representation in Parliament. More recently, in 2016, Parliament amended the Constitution to ensure that a minority president would be elected from time to time. This was done by reserving an election for a particular racial group if no one from that group had been president for five continuous terms. The 2017 presidential election was reserved for the Malays.

Matthews and Khidzer (2015) and Chua (2017) provide a comprehensive account of the multicultural policies, legal apparatus, and other "softer" programmes to ensure that Singapore society remains harmonious. In the remainder of this chapter, we focus on how HDB's housing mix and ethnic quota policies have been used to facilitate social and ethnic integration in Singapore.

HDB's Housing Mix Policy

The large HDB housing sector has played a defining role in the shaping of Singapore society. In 2016, 73% or 1,011,000 units of the housing stock in Singapore comprised HDB flats that housed 80% of the resident population. The physical plans of HDB new towns have been designed to integrate the various income groups served by the public housing programme, and this has prevented the development of low-income ghettos. There is a deliberate policy of providing for all flat types (generally ranging from 1-room to 5-rooms) in public housing estates and new towns.

HDB's public rental scheme is highly subsidized and comprises mainly 1- and 2-room flats which account for 5.6% of the HDB housing stock in 2016. Increasingly, HDB elderly studio and 2-room flexi flats are also meeting the housing needs of seniors who are downsizing and singles above the age of 35. In 2016, 4.2% of the resident population resided in HDB 1- and 2-room flats. When we consider the geographical distribution of residents of 1- and 2-room HDB flats across Singapore's 55 planning areas in 2016, there are only 3 planning areas where more than 10% of the population reside in 1- and 2-room HDB flats.[4] These are Bukit Merah (16.4%), Kallang (12.5%), and Outram (30.0%)—older HDB estates that are located within or close to the central area and which were constructed in the 1960s. In these 3 as well as all planning areas where 1- and 2-room HDB flats are located, other larger HDB flat types (3- to 5-room) are to be found as well. The population distribution by dwelling type in Bedok Planning Area, which includes Bedok HDB town, is shown in Table 7.1.

Table 7.1 Residents in Bedok by dwelling type, 2016

	Bedok Planning Area[a]		Bedok HDB town[b]	
House type	Resident population	% of residents	Resident population	% of residents
Total	**287,170**	**100.0**	**239,320**	**100.0**
HDB total	**189,240**	**65.9**	**189,200**	**79.1**
HDB 1 & 2-room flat	9890	3.4	9860	4.1
HDB 3-room flat	60,490	21.1	60,490	25.3
HDB 4-room flat	70,950	24.7	70,950	29.6
HDB 5-room flat	47,910	16.7	47,910	20.0
Condominium and other apartments	50,250	17.5	22,800	9.5
Landed properties	44,950	15.7	25,470	10.6
Others	2740	1.0	1880	0.8

Notes: [a]Bedok Planning Area includes Bedok HDB town and 3 subzones of private housing estates—Bayshore, Frankel, and Siglap

[b]Includes 5 subzones in the Bedok Planning Area—Bedok North, Bedok Reservoir, Bedok South, Kaki Bukit, and Kembangan

Data source: Singapore Department of Statistics

HDB planners used two methods in allocating housing mix for a neighbourhood. First, blocks of different room types are mixed together when planning a precinct of about 2.5–3.5 hectares, considered of sufficient scale for different house types. Within the blocks, there is also mixing of successive room types: 2- and 3-room, 3- and 4-room, and 4- and 5-room, that is, between "socio-economic levels that are likely to be compatible with each other" (Wong and Yeh 1985, 71–74 for block plans). According to Liu and Tuminez (2015), HDB planners considered it inadvisable to mix 1- and 3-room or 2- and 5-room flats within the same block as these larger socioeconomic disparities "could create divides or diminish natural social interaction and cohesion". Such a careful housing mix policy has facilitated integration of the majority of the population who reside in HDB housing. In addition, HDB planners consulted with sociologists, paying special attention to the design of communal spaces, sizes of precincts, common areas such as corridors, lift lobbies, and void decks (ground level empty spaces) in order to facilitate community interaction.

In the development of new towns, in addition to residential use, HDB planners prepare simultaneously for the provision of comprehensive facilities. The general land use allocation in a new town include provisions for playgrounds, car parks, shopping facilities, schools, parks and gardens, sports and recreational, public transportation, bus terminals, and MRT stations. Institutional facilities include the town's administrative office, clinics, community centres, and places of worship. In addition, land is allocated for fresh produce markets, cooked food centres, and commercial and industrial use in order to provide necessary amenities and employment for residents (Wong and Yeh 1985, 103; Cheong 2017). Chua (2017, 84) suggests that this comprehensive planning approach for all towns homogenizes the daily life experiences for 90% of the population and helps "veil social and economic inequalities".

Government land sales for executive condominiums and private housing developments that are located within predominantly HDB areas have also helped to integrate residents in the two distinct housing segments. The private developments that are located close to or within HDB towns have proven to be popular, as these locations also enable easy access to schools and public transport as well as to amenities and services within HDB estates (Liu and Tuminez 2015).

The ability of the HDB to integrate different groups across the income spectrum in its estates and new towns is, to a significant extent, due to its dominance in the Singapore housing landscape. With more than 80% of the resident population residing in HDB housing, there is no social stigma attached to public housing in Singapore. The majority of young Singaporean couples today start their homeownership journey at the corporate headquarters of the HDB. This is unlike the situation in most other countries, where public housing authorities provide shelter for mainly the marginalized and low-income groups.

HDB's Ethnic Integration Policy

After the 1969 Malay-Chinese race riots, the HDB allocated new flats in a manner that would mix the different races in the new housing estates. Then Prime Minister Lee Kuan Yew explained that this "prevented them from congregating, as they had been encouraged to do by the British" (Centre for Liveable Cities 2016, 26). However, by the mid-1980s, a trend of Malay ethnic regrouping through the resale market was identified as a social problem that could, over time, lead to the re-emergence of ethnic enclaves. In Bedok and Tampines HDB housing estates, Malay households made up more than 30% of the estate population.[5] Chua (2017) points to this spatial concentration as a valuable political material resource—a "home turf" as well as a vote bank to be mobilized to elect the group's own race candidates.

In 1989, the government moved pre-emptively to implement an Ethnic Integration Policy (EIP) under which racial limits were set for the HDB blocks and neighbourhoods. These quotas limit the proportion of flats in a block and in a neighbourhood that can be owned by a particular race. The quotas were set to approximate the composition of the population which was then 78% Chinese, 14% Malays, 7% Indians, and 1% Others. The neighbourhood limits were set at 84% Chinese, 22% Malays and 10% Indians/Others, respectively. In March 2010, in response to changing demographics, the neighbourhood limit for Indian/Others was raised to 12%. The block quotas are 3% above each neighbourhood limit (see Table 7.2).

Table 7.2 Ethnic limits under HDB's Ethnic Integration Policy

	Resident population 2016 (%)	HDB neighbourhood quota (%)	HDB block quota (%)
Chinese	74.3	84	87
Malay	13.4	22	25
Indian and others	12.3	12	15
Singapore Permanent Resident (SPR) HDB Homeowners		5	8
Non-citizen and SPR HDB tenants		8	11

Source: Singapore government and HDB websites

For new flats, a particular ethnic group will not be able to buy a flat from the HDB if the quota limit for that group has been reached for the particular block or neighbourhood (Ooi et al. 1993; Centre for Liveable Cities and HDB 2013, Chapter 5). For the resale market, when the set racial limits for a particular block or neighbourhood are reached, those wishing to sell their HDB flats in the particular block or neighbourhood are constrained to sell it to another household of the same ethnic group. At the time of implementation, 35 out of 125 neighbourhoods across 25 HDB new towns were affected by these quotas. To justify these restrictions, the government emphasized that "our multiracial policies must continue if we are to develop a more cohesive, better-integrated society. Singapore's racial harmony, long-term stability, and even viability as a nation depend on it".[6]

The government has attributed the idea behind the EIP to an unlikely source—a Harvard University economics professor, Thomas Schelling, who was awarded the Nobel Prize in 2005 (Dodge 2006). In a section of his 1978 classic book *Micromotives and Macrobehavior*, Schelling demonstrated how a slight-but-not-malicious individual preference to avoid being in even a slightly minority status (micromotive) would quickly lead to completely segregated neighbourhoods (macrobehaviour). This final outcome of segregation is in contrast to the moderate preferences of everyone who was happy to live in an integrated neighbourhood to start with. Schelling also studied how a neighbourhood's racial composition could change suddenly, "tipping" from one situation to another after a critical mass is reached. In his 2006 book *The Strategist: The Life and Times of Thomas Schelling*, Robert Dodge devotes an entire chapter to Singapore's EIP.

Changes in the composition of Singapore's population as well as HDB regulations over time have necessitated modifications to the EIP. In 2010, two decades after the EIP was first introduced, in response to the increase in the number of Singapore Permanent Residents (SPRs) purchasing flats in HDB estates, the government introduced a new SPR quota. The quota applies only to non-Malaysian SPR families buying flats, with the objective being to facilitate better integration and prevent new SPR enclaves from forming in public housing estates. The SPR quota is set at 5% and 8% at the neighbourhood and block levels, respectively. Malaysian SPR buyers are not subject to the SPR quota, as they are considered to have close cultural and historical similarities with Singaporeans. A non-Malaysian SPR household buyer must satisfy both the ethnic proportion and SPR quota to qualify to buy a resale HDB flat. The ethnic proportions and SPR quota for each block and neighbourhood are updated by the HDB on the first day of every month and buyers/sellers can check the status of a particular unit online.[7]

With liberalization of rules to allow HDB owners to sublet their flats since 2003, a pattern of voluntary segregation for SPRs and foreign tenants in certain HDB estates was observed. To prevent the formation of foreign enclaves in HDB estates, from 2014 onwards, non-Malaysian SPR or foreigners renting a whole HDB flat have had to first check if the Non-Citizen quotas for the block and neighbourhood have been reached. The Non-Citizen quota is 8% at the neighbourhood level and 11% at the block level. When the limits have been reached for the block and/or neighbourhood, flat owners are only allowed to sublet the flat to Singaporean or Malaysian tenants. This quota does not apply to the subletting of bedrooms. The eligibility of the non-citizen tenant to rent a flat from a homeowner in any block can be determined through an online check at the HDB website.

The HDB itself has faced difficulties in implementing the EIP quota for HDB public rental flats due to racial differences in demand for rental flats. Tenants of HDB's public rental flats need to meet stringent income eligibility caps to enjoy the highly subsidized rents. Malay households are disproportionately represented within the HDB rental households, which comprised 62% Chinese, 25% Malays, and 13% Indians/Others in 2012.[8] The Minister for National Development revealed that about 60% of HDB public rental blocks had reached their EIP block limit of 25% for Malay households.[9] The EIP quota has contributed to longer waiting times for rental flats for the Malays: the average waiting time for a public rental flat was approximately 4 months for Chinese, 6 months for Indians/Others and 7 months for Malays.

The restrictions on selling to the same ethnic group once the block or neighbourhood quotas are reached have resulted in some unhappiness and market-distortionary effects. Homeowners from the minority groups (e.g., Malay and Indian homeowners in a location popular with the Chinese, such as Bishan) have complained about difficulty in finding a buyer from the same ethnic group, as the potential market is much smaller. Similarly, Chinese homeowners in Tampines, a town that has reached the limit for Malay households, complained of difficulties finding a Chinese buyer. Difficulties that minority homeowners encountered when selling their flats were raised by MPs in Parliament on various occasions.[10] In his response, the Minister for National Development revealed that HDB received about 1200 appeals for a waiver of the EIP between 2013 and 2015, of which four in five appeals were unsuccessful.

In a careful study, Wong (2013) matched more than 500,000 names in the phonebook to ethnicities to calculate ethnic proportions at the apartment block level. She then investigated transaction price and time-on-market duration differences for constrained and unconstrained blocks using 35,744 transactions between April 2005 and August 2006. On average, Wong (2013) found the transaction prices in Chinese constrained units (the Chinese quota had been reached in the block or neighbourhood) to be 5% higher than transactions in comparable unconstrained blocks. Conversely, the prices for Malay and Indian constrained units were 3% lower. Using an average price of units sold (S$234,000), Wong (2013) estimated these price differences to represent 5 times the median monthly income of the Chinese (S$2335) and 3 times the median monthly income of the Malays (S$1790) and the Indians (S$2167). She also estimated longer time-on-market durations of between 1 to 1.4 months for constrained sellers.

As a result of the EIP that was introduced in 1989, residents of multiracial Singapore live in racially integrated housing estates. The desired policy outcome is that there should be no ethnic enclaves within HDB blocks and neighbourhoods where a minority group constitutes a majority. As the Chinese are a majority, the EIP ensures a Chinese majority in every block and neighbourhood. The government has consistently defended such social "engineering" through the HDB EIP as having contributed to the integration of the different races and social stability of Singapore. The requirement for an ethnic mix in every block and neighbourhood means everyday interaction of the different ethnic groups "in the corridors, and the markets. And critically, the majority of kids go to primary schools near their homes that consequently have an ethnic mix as well" (Shanmugaratnam 2014, 27). Deputy Prime Minister Tharman Shanmugaratnam has described this policy as "the most intrusive policy in Singapore" which "has turned out to the most important".[11]

Notes

1. In several Southeast Asian countries, the Chinese are the market-dominant minority. Chua (2003, 16) hypothesizes that the pursuit of free market democracy in a context of market-dominant minorities produces explosive instability. Democratization, "rather than reinforcing the market's efficiency and wealth-producing effects, leads to powerful ethno nationalist, anti-market pressures and routinely results in confiscation, instability, authoritarian backlash, and violence".
2. Dobby (1940), as cited in Huff (1994, 25).
3. Singapore's National Pledge is as follows: "We, the citizens of Singapore, pledge ourselves as one united people, regardless of race, language or religion, to build a democratic society, based on justice and equality, so as to achieve happiness, prosperity and progress for our nation."
4. Data on "Singapore Residents by Planning Area/Subzone and Type of Dwelling, June 2016" from Singapore Department of Statistics website. http://www.singstat.gov.sg/statistics/browse-by-theme/geographic-distribution. Accessed 1 Nov 2017.
5. "Racial enclaves forming – Dhana". *The Straits Times*, 7 Jan 1989.

6. See Singapore Parliamentary Debates, Official Reports. 16 Feb 1989.
7. See HDB website at: http://www.hdb.gov.sg/fi10/fi10296p.nsf/PressReleases/C515273FA068DD58482576DD00169155?OpenDocument. Accessed 1 Nov 2017.
8. See Singapore Parliamentary Debates, Official Reports. 10 Jul 2012.
9. See Singapore Parliamentary Debates, Official Reports. 14 Nov 2012.
10. The two most recent occasions being 6 Feb 2017 and 11 Jul 2016. See Singapore Parliamentary Debates, Official Reports.
11. The Deputy Prime Minister, Tharman Shanmugaratnam, in "An investigative interview: Singapore 50 years after independence", 45th St Gallen Symposium, 7 May 2015. https://www.youtube.com/watch?v=hpwPciW74b8. Accessed 1 Nov 2017.

References

Centre for Liveable Cities. 2016. *A Chance of a Lifetime: Lee Kuan Yew and the Physical Transformation of Singapore*. Singapore: Centre for Liveable Cities and Lee Kuan Yew Centre for Innovative Cities.

Centre for Liveable Cities and Housing and Development Board. 2013. *Housing: Turning Squatters into Stakeholders*. Singapore: Cengage Learning.

Cheong, Koon Hean. 2017. The Evolution of HDB Towns. In *50 Years of Urban Planning in Singapore*, ed. Chye Kiang Heng, 101–126. Singapore: World-Scientific.

Choe, Alan. 2017. The Early Years of Nation-Building: Reflections on Singapore's Urban History. In *50 Years of Urban Planning in Singapore*, ed. Chye Kiang Heng, 3–22. Singapore: World-Scientific.

Chua, Amy. 2003. *World on Fire: How Exporting Free-Market Democracy Breeds Ethnic Hatred and Global Instability*. London: Arrow Books.

Chua, Beng Huat. 2017. *Liberalism Disavowed: Communitarianism and State Capitalism in Singapore*. Singapore: National University of Singapore Press.

Dobby, E.H.G. 1940. Singapore: Town and Country. *Geographical Review* 30 (1): 84–109.

Dodge, R. 2006. *The Strategist: The Life and Times of Thomas Schelling*. Singapore: Marshall Cavendish.

Hodder, N.W. 1953. Racial Groupings in Singapore. *Malayan Journal of Tropical Geography* 1: 25–36.

Huff, W.G. 1994. *The Economic Growth of Singapore: Trade and Development in the Twentieth Century*. Cambridge: Cambridge University Press.

Lee, Kuan Yew. 1998. *The Singapore Story: Memoirs of Lee Kuan Yew*. Singapore: Singapore Press Holdings.

Liu, Thai Ker, and Astrid S. Tuminez. 2015. The Social Dimension of Urban Planning in Singapore. In *50 Years of Social Issues in Singapore*, ed. David Chan, 97–116. Singapore: World Scientific.

Matthews, Matthew, and Mohammed Khamsya Bin Khidzer. 2015. Preserving Racial and Religious Harmony in Singapore. In *50 Years of Social Issues in Singapore*, ed. David Chan, 75–96. Singapore: World Scientific.

Ooi, Giok Ling, Sharon Siddique, and Kay Cheng Soh. 1993. *The Management of Ethnic Relations in Public Housing Estates*. Singapore: Times Academic Press.

Phang, Sock-Yong. 1992. *Housing Markets and Urban Transportation: Economic Theory, Econometrics and Policy Analysis for Singapore*. Singapore: McGraw Hill.

Saw, Swee Hock. 1970. *Singapore Population in Transition*. Philadelphia: University of Pennsylvania Press.

Schelling, Thomas C. 1978. *Micromotives and Macrobehavior*. New York: Norton.

Shanmugaratnam, Tharman. 2014. Towards Equitable Cities. *Urban Solutions* (4 February): 20–30.

Singapore Department of Statistics. 2016. *Population Trends 2016*.

Singapore Parliamentary Debates. *Official Reports*. https://www.parliament.gov.sg/parliamentary-business/official-reports-(parl-debates). Accessed 1 Nov 2017.

Wong, Maisy. 2013. Estimating Ethnic Preferences Using Ethnic Housing Quotas in Singapore. *Review of Economic Studies* 80 (3): 1178–1214.

Wong, Aline, and Stephen H.K. Yeh, eds. 1985. *Housing a Nation: 25 Years of Public Housing in Singapore*. Singapore: Maruzen Asia for Housing & Development Board.

Yuen, Belinda. 2007. *Guiding Spatial Changes: Singapore Urban Planning*. Paper Presented at 4th Urban Research Symposium on Urban Land Use and Land Markets, 14 May. Washington, DC: The World Bank.

8

Redistribution and Housing Wealth Formation

Growing inequality and what to do about it has become of increasing social, political, and policy concern worldwide. Discussions about solutions to tackle the challenges of poverty and inequality have tended to revolve around higher taxes on wealth and labour market interventions such as minimum wages and universal basic incomes. As a city-state, with open capital markets and a high proportion of foreign workers in the labour force, Singaporeans are exposed to the vast inequalities of the global market place. To attract foreign investment, wealth and talent, the tax regime is one that is friendly towards globally mobile financial and human capital. The Singapore government has, instead, utilized housing welfare policies as an effective channel for wealth redistribution and income transfers.

Similar to other global cities such as New York, Paris, London, and Hong Kong, Singapore faces challenges of rising income and wealth inequality. The problems of inequality, housing affordability, and unequal housing wealth distribution are especially accentuated in large metropolises. There is a large body of literature linking city size to inequality (Baum-Snow and Pavan 2013; Hendricks 2011; Eeckhout et al. 2014; Behrens and Robert-Nicoud 2014). However, rather than using high

S.-Y. Phang, *Policy Innovations for Affordable Housing In Singapore*,
Palgrave Advances in Regional and Urban Economics,
https://doi.org/10.1007/978-3-319-75349-2_8

income tax rates to finance social welfare policies, Singapore has used a range of housing policies to mitigate inequality. Pro-homeownership policies have enabled low-income households to become homeowners. In addition, property tax rates and tax rebates differentiated by house values and stamp duties on property transactions have been used to mitigate inequality. In this chapter, we first compare inequality and housing affordability in Singapore with those of other top ranked global cities. We then discuss Singapore's range of redistributive housing policies and assess their impact on housing wealth distribution.[1]

Inequality and Housing Affordability in Global Cities

The topic of income and wealth inequality has been debated intensely in recent years, in particular, since the publication of Thomas Piketty's monumental book *Capital in the 21st Century* (Piketty 2014). From the perspective of cities, however, Piketty's treatment of inequality is, with respect, flawed in at least two aspects: first, the failure to take into account spatial variations in inequality and, second, the failure to treat households' housing wealth as distinct from production capital. National inequality measures mask considerable variations across cities within the *same* country. A country's biggest and most dynamic cities also tend to have the highest housing prices, highest concentration of housing wealth, and largest inequality gaps. Moreover, as noted in the recent study by Rognlie (2015), the rising share of capital in aggregate income in developed countries can be largely attributed to the rising share of owners of housing. The problems of inequality, housing affordability, and unequal housing wealth distribution are thus most accentuated in large metropolises.

In this chapter, the focus is on comparison of housing outcomes in Singapore with a particular subset of cities—the global superstar cities. The global city concept has been most associated with the work of Sassen (2001). Sassen defines a global city as a significant point where internationally oriented financial and producer services that make the global economy run are agglomerated. The term "Superstar Cities" has its origins in a study of housing price trends in US cities by Gyourko et al. (2013). In particular, their study notes the considerable differences in long-run house price appreciation rates across American cities after World War II. They define locations that experience persistently higher than average house price growth as superstar cities. In several global cities, housing price increases far exceed those of American superstar cities. The problems of housing affordability and housing inequality in the global superstar cities are the outcomes of a confluence of factors: inelastic housing supply together with higher rates of economic and population growth and concentrations of the global wealthy, top income earners, and unskilled workers.

This chapter is structured as follows: the next section provides a comparison of housing outcomes and income inequality for Singapore as compared to a selection of global cities. A brief overview of the distributional aspects of land and housing policies in Singapore follows. Using Singapore Household Balance Sheet data, we analyse the effects of Singapore's land and housing policies on households' housing wealth accumulation and housing wealth distribution. We find Singapore's gross housing wealth distribution to approximate capital ownership distribution in Piketty's "ideal society".

There are numerous ranking tables for global cities, each defining the meaning of "global" using a different list of characteristics. Leff and Petersen (2015) provide a review of the methodologies, definitions, data use, and conclusions of these rankings. New York, London, Singapore, Paris, and Hong Kong are five cities that consistently occupy the top spots in several of the rankings reviewed. In this section, we compare the inequality and housing statistics for these five global cities.

Global cities are invariably the largest city in the country that hosts them. Besides having higher than average house price growth, global cities also have higher levels of economic inequality. Various studies have shown that income inequality can be expected to increase with the size of the city. A recent study by Baum-Snow and Pavan (2013) for US cities shows the strong relationship between wage inequality and city size that developed from the 1980s. The study found that city size alone accounts for roughly 25–35% of the total increase in wage inequality from 1979 to 2007. Income inequality in New York Metropolitan Area is considerable higher than the US average.

A Euromonitor report (2013) provides evidence to support the hypothesis of city size as a key explanatory factor for income inequalities across the world's urban agglomeration. While Singapore's Gini coefficient for resident employed households (after taxes and transfers) is higher than the national Gini coefficients of the UK, US, and France, which are below 0.40, it is lower than the Gini coefficients of the global cities of New York and London and comparable to Hong Kong's, where income Gini coefficients are 0.4 and above (see Table 8.1). Amongst the five global cities, Paris has the lowest-income Gini coefficients at around 0.37. However, it should be noted that the income Gini coefficients for Singapore exclude foreigner households, while the data for Hong Kong excludes foreign domestic helpers.

Various explanations for the city-size income inequality nexus have been provided in the context of the US. Larger cities have different industry composition and a more skilled labour force (Hendricks 2011). Returns to skill increases with city size. Through spatial sorting, large cities attract a disproportionate share of households at both ends of the income distribution (Eeckhout et al. 2014). Also, large cities offer better public transportation access, and consequently attract poor households (Glaeser et al. 2009).

Behrens and Robert-Nicoud (2014) developed a framework that integrates natural advantage, agglomeration economies, and firm selection in

Table 8.1 Household income Gini Coefficients for 5 global cities

Global City Gini		Country Gini	
NY Metropolitan Area 2011	0.48	US 2015	0.39
Greater London Area 2011	0.44	UK 2015	0.36
Hong Kong 2016[a]	0.40	China 2016	0.47
Singapore 2016[a]	0.40	Singapore 2016[a]	0.40
Paris-Ile-de-France 2011	0.37	France 2014	0.30

Notes: [a]Gini coefficients are based on post-tax and transfer *per capita* household income. For Singapore, only resident employed households are included. For Hong Kong, only economically active households excluding foreign domestic helpers have been considered

Sources: Euromonitor (2013) for 2011 city data; OECD websites for OECD country data; government websites for Hong Kong, Singapore, and China data

order to explain why large cities are both more productive and more unequal than small towns. Historically, natural advantage first attracts firms and people to a location and induces agglomeration. The most productive firms cluster in the city and competition and *tougher selection* increases productivity, lowers consumer prices, increases choices, and attracts more people. Sorting occurs where the most highly skilled and talented people as well as the most productive, high tech, and creative firms cluster together in order to produce powerful economic advantages. The higher urban productivity thus generated provides incentives for rural-urban migration. Not everyone succeeds, and the less skilled or the unlucky fail and end up with incomes lower than in the countryside. However, other employment opportunities and the consumption diversity in the city provide incentives to stay on.

Just as large cities within a country provide larger markets to reward skills, the top global cities serve similar functions. Global cities have become much more valuable places in a globalized world. With globalization, an increasingly complex financial sector requires more sophisticated networks of lawyers, accountants, bankers, and traders. The global cities attract the top "one per cent" because they offer disproportionate rewards for the most skilled—a situation that is accentuated by the co-location of powerful and useful political, business, and social networks. A larger global city increases productivity as more skilled people are attracted to that location, and this further incentivizes migration not only from rural areas, but also from smaller cities and across borders.

Piketty's approach towards capital and wealth is an aggregative one and he does not treat real estate or land as a different or distinct form of capital. However, in the context of global superstar cities, land or location is scarce, capital not as scarce. Recent work by Atkinson (2015) and Rognlie (2015) point to the need to differentiate between the return on capital generated by the production side of the economy and the return to individual households in the form of investment income. The careful study by Rognlie (2015) disaggregates capital and finds that while the net capital share in developed economies has increased since 1948, this increase comes *entirely* from the *housing* sector. He therefore advocates that observers concerned about the distribution of income should keep an eye on housing costs.

Atkinson suggests that the most valuable asset for the majority of UK homeowners is likely to be their home, and increased housing wealth is a major reason for the rise in popular wealth in the UK (Atkinson 2015, 161). Bastagli and Hills (2013) also present evidence of the importance of housing in wealth accumulation and wealth distribution for Great Britain. Using British Household Panel Survey data from 1995 to 2005, they show that changes in wealth were heavily affected by changes in housing wealth, with the highest percentage increase in housing wealth taking place in the middle of the distribution.

Not surprisingly, the global cities are also superstar cities, with higher than national average house price increases and more serious housing affordability challenges. Inequality and higher housing costs in global cities have also been strongly linked to the presence of the global rich. Cvijanovic and Spanejers (2015) identify international demand for luxury consumption by non-resident foreigners as having a causal positive effect on housing price levels in Paris, as well as for other attractive locations worldwide.

Table 8.2 shows the annualized house price index increases for the five global cities for 2000–2017 in nominal and real terms, as well as in local currency and US dollars. In four of the global cities, the nominal house

Table 8.2 House price annualized growth rates for 5 global cities, 2000Q1–2017Q1

	In local currency		In US$	
	Nominal (%)	Real (%)	Nominal (%)	Real (%)
Hong Kong	7.19	5.57	7.19	5.57
Ile-de-France Paris – Flats	6.08	4.67	6.29	4.88
London	7.50	5.42	6.09	4.02
New York Condominiums[a]	5.72	3.61	5.72	3.61
Singapore – HDB Resale Flats	3.05	1.40	4.30	2.64
Singapore – Private Housing	1.92	0.26	3.17	1.51

Notes: [a]Refers to New York-Northern New Jersey-Long Island Metropolitan Statistical Area

Sources: Estimated using house price indices, CPI and exchange rate data from government websites (house price indices are from Hong Kong Government Rating and Valuation Department, France's National Institute for Statistics and Economic Studies, UK Office for National Statistics, Federal Reserve Bank of St Louis, Singapore Housing and Development Board, Singapore Urban Redevelopment Authority)

price indices (in local currency terms), have increased at average annual rates of above 5.50% for the period between 2000 and 2017: 7.50% for London, 7.19% for Hong Kong, 6.08% for Paris, and 5.72% for New York. For London, the annualized rates of increase are higher than Paris in local currency terms, but lower than Paris in US dollar terms, partly because of the decline in the value of the pound following the Brexit referendum. Hong Kong's annualized rates of increase are highest amongst the five global cities in real terms as well as in US dollar terms. Singapore's annualized growth rates in housing prices are lowest amongst the 5 global cities: at 3.05% for Housing and Development Board (HDB) resale flats and 1.92% for private housing in nominal local currency terms. The trends in nominal house price indices for the five cities from 2000 to 2017 are shown in Fig. 8.1.

To compare homeownership affordability, I obtained data from government websites and also from the Performance Urban Planning's *Demographia International Housing Affordability Survey* 2017. The chief

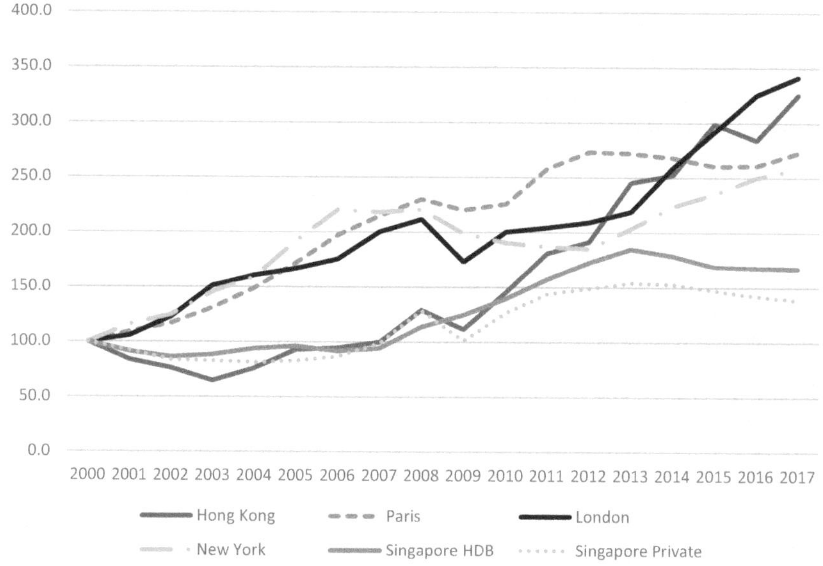

Fig. 8.1 Comparing nominal house price indices for global cities, 2000–2017 (Sources for data: As for Table 8.2)

measure of affordability is the affordability multiple, which is the median house price divided by the median annual household income (pre-income-tax). Singapore's housing affordability, based on HDB resale housing prices, was a multiple of 4.8 in 2016,[2] which was more affordable than London (8.5), New York (5.7), Paris (10.5, for 2015), and Hong Kong (18.1). Singapore's 90% homeownership rate for its resident population is an outlier, and is in contrast to the lower homeownership rates for the other cities: Hong Kong at 51%, Paris and London at 48%, and New York at 32% (see Table 8.3).

Redistribution Through Housing

For eligible buyers of HDB flats, new flats are priced at below market values in order to ensure that homeownership is affordable to 90% of households. In Chaps. 2, 3, and 4 of this book and in other publications (Phang 1996, 2001, 2007, 2015b), I have described the land, housing supply, and housing finance policies, as well as institutions that have made this possible.

In addition to price subsidies, the effective subsidy for each first-time homeowner household is carefully calibrated. Similar HDB flats sell for different amounts based on a host of criteria that determine the housing grants for which buyers are eligible (see Table 8.4). These grants are generally known

Table 8.3 Comparing housing outcomes in 5 global cities, 2016

	Price-to-income ratio	Home ownership rate (%)	Social rental housing (%)
Hong Kong	18.1	51	30
Paris-Ile-de-France[a]	10.5[a]	48	25
Greater London	8.5	48	24
New York, NY-NJ-PA	5.7	32	5
Singapore	4.8	90	4

Sources: *Demographia International Housing Affordability Survey 2017* for 2016Q3 data on median house prices and household incomes for Hong Kong, London, New York City, and Singapore; government websites

[a]Paris-Ile-de-France 2011, average transaction data from Cvijanovic and Spaenjers (2015) and average household income data from e-communication with C. Spaenjers

Table 8.4 Types of housing grants for homeownership

Housing grants	Objectives and income ceilings	Grant amount in 2018
CPF Proximity Housing Grant (PHG)	Introduced in 2015 to replace the Higher-Tier CPF Housing Grant first introduced in 1994 to help families who want to buy a resale flat, to live in with or near their parents/ married child The proximity conditions are "buying a resale flat within 4 km of their parents or children". The income ceiling is $12,000 ($18,000 for extended families)	The PHG is $20,000 for families and $30,000 for extended families who choose to live together Eligible singles also enjoy a PHG of $15,000 if they buy a resale flat with their parents. Singles who buy a resale flat near their parents recieve a PHG of $10,000.
CPF Housing Grant for Family	Introduced in 1995 Demand-side subsidy introduced to help families who want to buy a resale flat instead of purchasing a subsidized flat directly from the HDB. The income ceiling is $12,000 (and $18,000 for extended families)	The Family Grant is $50,000 for purchase of 2- to 4-room HDB flats and $40,000 for purchase of 5-room or larger HDB flats
CPF Housing Grants for Executive Condominiums	Introduced in 1996 Only for first time homeowners of new Executive Condominiums, a form of supply-side price discrimination based on income The income ceiling is $12,000	Graduated according to income brackets. The maximum grant amount is $30,000 for families
CPF Housing Grant for Singles	Introduced in 1998 Demand-side subsidy introduced to help singles (aged 35 or older) to buy a resale flat	The grant is $25,000 for purchase of 2- to 4-room HDB flats and $20,000 for purchase of 5-room or larger HDB flats

(*continued*)

Table 8.4 (continued)

Housing grants	Objectives and income ceilings	Grant amount in 2018
Additional CPF Housing Grant (AHG)	Introduced in 2006 Both a demand-side subsidy to purchase a resale HDB flat and a supply-side subsidy to allow price discrimination based on household income The income ceiling is $5000	The AHG amount is graduated according to income brackets to offer lower-income earners a higher grant amount. The maximum grant amount is $40,000 for families and $20,000 for singles
Special CPF Housing Grant (SHG)	Introduced in 2011; for new 2-room to 4-room HDB flat in non-mature estate Only for new smaller HDB flats, extends supply-side price discrimination based on income to families with gross monthly income not more than $8500	The SHG amount is graduated according to income brackets to offer lower-income earners a higher grant amount. The maximum grant amount is $40,000 for families and $20,000 for singles
Step-up CPF Housing Grant	Introduced in 2013 To help homeowner families in subsidized 2-room HDB flats in non-mature estates upgrade to purchase a new 3-room HDB flat in a non-mature estate	The maximum grant amount is $15,000 for families
Fresh Start Housing Scheme	Introduced in 2016 To help second-timers with young children who have previously enjoyed a homeownership subsidy but have since sold their flat and are residing in a HDB rental flat to own a 2-room Flexi flat	The maximum grant amount is $35,000 for a 60 or 65-year leasehold 2-room Flexi flat The amount is lower for flats with shorter leases

Source: HDB website

as Central Provident Fund (CPF) Housing Grants, as they are credited into the CPF account of the individual when the purchase of a HDB flat is made. The grant types and grant amounts have been increased, and eligibility coverage has been expanded since housing grants were first introduced (see

Table 8.4). Other than household income, the basis for determining housing grant amounts include flat type, whether the flat is a new or resale flat, whether the flat is located in a mature or non-mature estate, marital status, if spouse is citizen, or if one is living near parents or married children.

The first housing grant was introduced in 1994 for the purchase of a resale HDB flat near parents Phang (2001, 2007). This was the beginning of a shift from total reliance on subsidies tied to new flats to a more comprehensive system that also encompasses demand-side subsidies for resale flats. When first introduced, the government provided the first-time applicant household with a grant of $30,000 to purchase a HDB resale flat close to either their parents' or married child's residence. In 1995, the grant was increased to $50,000. (This scheme was enhanced and renamed the Proximity Housing Grant in 2015). The government also introduced a more general grant of $40,000 for eligible households that purchase a resale flat which does not need to satisfy the criterion of being close to parents/married child's residence. From August 1996, the CPF housing grant of $40,000 was also offered to first-time homeowners who purchased new Executive Condominiums. In 1998, in the midst of the Asian crisis, the government introduced a $15,000 CPF housing grant for singles to purchase resale flats. As the crisis deepened and prices of resale flats fell further, the CPF grant amounts were reduced in stages over 10 months to $30,000 for couples and $10,000 for singles.[3]

With up to 90% of households eligible for housing subsidies, housing grants had to be more finely calibrated in order to better target grant subsidies based on household incomes. The Additional CPF Housing Grant (AHG) was introduced in 2006 (and enhanced in 2007 and 2009) to allow families with lower incomes to receive a higher grant amount which could be used for either a new flat or a resale flat (Cheong 2014). The amount of the AHG depends on the average gross monthly household income and provides a larger subsidy for lower-income households. Households with monthly household incomes of less than $5000 are eligible for the AHG. The AHG ranges from $5000 (for households with incomes from $4501 to $5000) to $40,000 (for households with incomes below $1500).

For a low-income household with a monthly income below $1500, housing grants to purchase a resale HDB flat can be as high as $110,000 (see Table 8.5 and $120,000 with the enhanced PHG). This is more

Table 8.5 Grant amounts for housing purchase by household income, 2018

Average gross monthly household income	Grant amounts for eligible citizen households[a]	
Eligible first-time buyers who purchase flats	Direct from HDB (Additional and Special Housing Grants)	In HDB resale market (Enhanced CPF + Additional + Proximity Housing Grants)[b]
$1500 or less	$80,000	$110,000
$1501–$2000	$75,000	$105,000
$2001–$2500	$70,000	$100,000
$2501–$3000	$65,000	$95,000
$3001–$3500	$60,000	$90,000
$3501–$4000	$55,000	$85,000
$4001–$4500	$50,000	$80,000
$4501–$5000	$45,000	$75,000
$5001–$5500	$35,000	$70,000
$5501–$6000	$30,000	$70,000
$6001–$6500	$25,000	$70,000
$6501–$7000	$20,000	$70,000
$7001–$7500	$15,000	$70,000
$7501–$8000	$10,000	$70,000
$8001–$8500	$5000	$70,000
$8500–$12,000[c]	$0	$70,000
Above $12,000[c]	Not eligible	$0
Eligible first-time buyers of new Executive Condominium Flats		
up to $10,000	$30,000	$0
$10,001–$11,000	$20,000	$0
$11,001–$12,000	$10,000	$0
$12,001–$14,000	$0	$0
Above $14,000	Not eligible	$0

Notes:

[a]These grant amounts are for households where both husband and wife are citizens. Amounts will be less for singles and for citizen and PR/foreigner couples

[b]For 2 to 4-room HDB resale flats; minus $10,000 for 5-room and larger HDB resale flats; minus Proximity Housing Grant (PHG) of $20,000 if not residing within 4 km of parents/married child's HDB flat or owner-occupied private housing. In February 2018, the PHG was enhanced to S$30,000 for extended families who buy a resale flat to live together. Eligible singles also became eligible for the PHG when they buy a resale flat with or near their parents' residence. The proximity condition was extended from 2 km to 4 km

[c]The monthly household income cap is increased to $18,000 for households comprising working adults and their parents living together as an extended family in a flat. Extended families also enjoy a higher PHG of $30,000 when buying a resale flat to live together

Source: HDB websites

than six times the annual income of a household with a monthly income of S$1500, and about one-third of the market resale price of a 3-room HDB flat in a typical HDB town (about $300,000).

The Special Housing Grant (SHG) was introduced in 2011. Similar to the AHG, it is intended for low-income households. Unlike the AHG, it only applicable for the purchase of new smaller flats in non-mature estates. The SHG was enhanced in 2012, significantly expanded in 2013, and expanded again in 2015. The amount of the SHG depends on the average gross monthly household income. Households with household incomes of less than S$8500 per month are eligible for the grant. The amount of the grant ranges from S$5000 for households with income from S$8000 to S$8500, to S$40,000 for households with income below S$5000.

While the above grants are for first-time homeowners, the Step-Up and Fresh Start grants provide low-income households assistance with upgrading and a second chance at homeownership. The Step-Up Housing Grant (of S$15,000) was introduced in 2013 in order to help families in subsidized two-room HDB flats in non-mature estates upgrade to purchase new three-room HDB flats in non-mature estates. The Fresh Start Housing Grant, available from 2016, helps households with young children who have previously enjoyed a homeownership subsidy but have since sold their flat and are residing in a HDB rental flat to purchase a new 2-room Flexi flat.

The net effect of the Special and Additional Housing Grants is to allow the HDB to price its flats based on a household's ability-to-pay, thus ensuring that even low-income households can afford to own a home. While the eligibility criteria for household monthly income is currently $12,000 for HDB subsidies, the cap is $8500 to qualify for Special Housing Grants (for the purchase of new 2- to 4-room flat in non-mature estates) and $5000 to qualify for Additional Housing Grants. For flats purchased directly from the HDB for which the HDB determines the price before grants, the grants are not demand-side subsidies. Instead, they are a form of price discrimination based on household incomes.

The choice of housing type has become a useful proxy for household income and wealth. The Singapore's government budget uses house type as a means of facilitating redistribution via the budget. This practice began from 1994, when the regressiveness of the new 3% Goods and Services Tax (GST) was offset by annual rebates (announced as part of the fiscal budget and varying with flat type), to households residing in public housing, in the form of waivers on rents as well as service and conservancy charges (S&CC). The number of months or amounts of rent, utilities, and S&CC rebates for HDB households decrease with flat size, and these have since become a regular feature of the government's budget. Since 2000, other fiscal transfers in the form of CPF Top Ups, New Singapore Shares, Economic Restructuring Shares, and GST Cash Vouchers also use house type or house value to determine the amount of transfers.

There is generally no wealth, estates, or capital gains taxes in Singapore; however, residential properties come under different treatment. There are three types of stamp duties on property transactions in Singapore: the basic buyer's stamp duty, the additional buyer's stamp duty (ABSD), and the seller's stamp duty (SSD). The latter two stamp duties were introduced from 2010 as part of macro-prudential measures to discourage speculative purchases Phang (2015b). Transaction taxes such as stamp duties are targeted at buyers who pay cash and are not reliant on loans for housing purchase.

The stamp duty regime in Singapore is also based on the number of properties owned as well as by citizen/Permanent Resident/foreigner status (see Table 8.6). The ABSD regime is a highly progressive housing transaction tax with the highest rate of 15% paid by foreign buyers. At the point of purchase, taxing wealthy property owners and investors at a higher rate and subsiding entry into homeownership for lower-income and new households have created a Singapore housing tax and subsidy system that is more complex than its income tax code. High rates of stamp duties, however, reduce transaction volumes and reduce market efficiency.

The seller's stamp duty (SSD) is meant to penalize short-term speculative purchases and sales of residential property. The rates have varied with property market conditions, and it can therefore be viewed as an instrument to maintain housing market stability. As of March 2017, the SSD is 12% for residential properties purchased and sold within a year, 8% for a 1–2-year holding period, 4% for a 2–3-year holding period, and zero if sold after 3 years.

Table 8.6 Buyer's stamp duties (BSD) payable for purchase of residential properties

Profile of buyer	BSD rates[a]	ABSD rates[a] (8 Dec 2011–11 Jan 2013)	ABSD rates[a] from 12 Jan 2013
Singapore Citizens (SC) buying first residential property	1% on first \$180,000 2% on next \$180,000 3% on next \$640,000 4% for the remainder	Not applicable	Not applicable
SC buying second residential property		Not applicable	7%
SC buying third and subsequent residential properties		3%	10%
Singapore Permanent Residents (SPR) buying first residential property		Not applicable	5%
SPR buying second and subsequent residential properties		3%	10%
Foreigners (FR) and entities buying any residential property		10%	15%

Source: Inland Revenue Authority of Singapore at: https://www.iras.gov.sg/
[a]% of actual price paid or market value of property, whichever is the higher

The residential property tax regime is calculated based on the annual value of the property. It was made more progressive from 2015, with higher value property owners paying a progressively higher rate. Table 8.7 shows the range of rates from 0% to 16% for owner-occupied residential properties depending on annual value. For HDB owner-occupiers, the range of annual property tax payable in 2017 was 0–18 for 3-room flats, 52–100 for 4-room flats, 83–131 for 5-room flats and 95–143 for Executive flats. Non-owner occupier tax rates for residential properties range from 10% to 20%. Non-residential properties are taxed at 10% of annual value.

Impact of Housing Policies on Household Wealth Accumulation and Distribution

In this section, we evaluate the impact of housing policies on housing wealth accumulation and distribution. The HDB's massive building programme as well as increase in homeownership rates in the 1970s and

Table 8.7 Progressive property tax structure for residential properties

Owner occupied residential properties		
Annual value (S$)	Effective 1 Jan 2015	Property tax payable (S$)
First $8000	0%	$0
Next $47,000	4%	$1880
First $55,000	–	$1880
Next $15,000	6%	$900
First $70,000	–	$2780
Next $15,000	8%	$1200
First $85,000	–	$3980
Next $15,000	10%	$1500
First $100,000	–	$5480
Next $15,000	12%	$1800
First $115,000	–	$7280
Next $15,000	14%	$2100
First $130,000	–	$9380
Above $130,000	16%	
Non-owner occupied residential properties		
Annual value ($)	Effective 1 Jan 2015	Property tax payable
First 30,000	10%	$3000
Next $15,000	12%	$1800
First $45,000	–	$4800
Next $15,000	14%	$2100
First $60,000	–	$6900
Next $15,000	16%	$2400
First $75,000	–	$9300
Next $15,000	18%	$2700
First $90,000	–	$12,000
Above $90,000	20%	

Source: Inland Revenue Authority of Singapore at: https://www.iras.gov.sg/

1980s (see Chap. 3) resulted in rapid housing wealth accumulation in the household sector. Although housing wealth is only part of overall household wealth, it nevertheless forms the most substantial component of wealth for the majority of households. Phang (2001) estimated that in 1980, gross housing wealth was 52% of GDP and net housing wealth was 42%. The HDB resale market during the 1970s and 1980s was tightly regulated, and the increase in housing wealth was primarily in the form of a large increase in HDB flats for sale to households.

In 2016, the ratio of resident household sector total assets to GDP was 4.73 while household net worth to GDP was 3.97. The ratio of housing assets owned by the household sector was 2.10 times GDP, and outstanding housing mortgage loans were 57% of GDP. Figure 8.2 shows the trends in these ratio series over the past two decades.

The Distribution of Housing Wealth Across Housing Segments

In 2016, housing assets comprised 44% of total household sector assets. Housing wealth in HDB housing was 48% of total housing wealth (see Fig. 8.3). Table 8.8 shows average gross housing wealth per household for the HDB sector and the private housing sector at 5-year intervals from 1995 to 2015. Households living in private housing have higher housing wealth, averaging S$1,788,699 per household compared to an average of S$408,675 per household for public housing in 2015. Table 8.8 also shows the changes in housing wealth distribution over time. Average

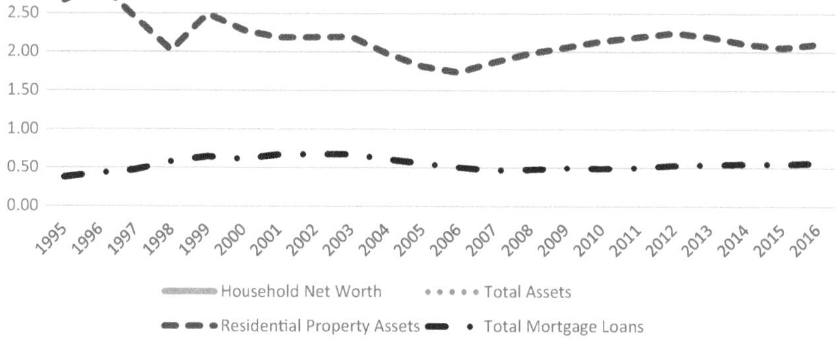

Fig. 8.2 Household sector assets and mortgage loans to GDP ratios, 1995–2016 (Source: Data from Singapore Department of Statistics)

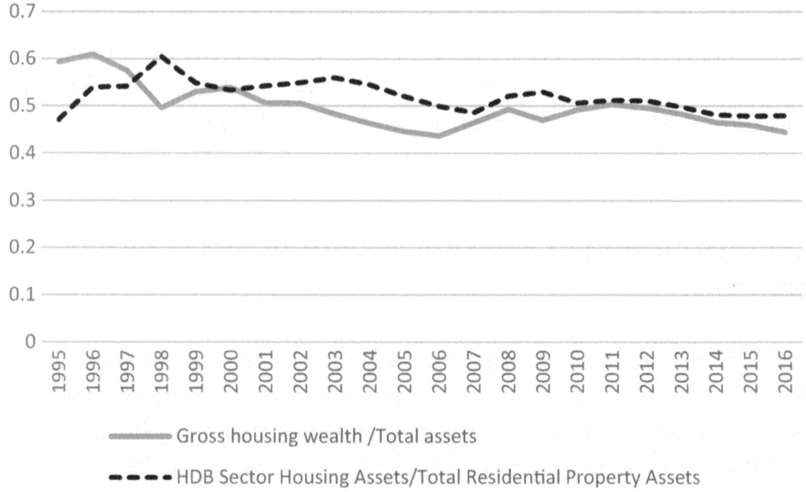

Fig. 8.3 Housing wealth ratios, 1995–2016 (Source: Data from Singapore Department of Statistics)

housing wealth per household in private housing has declined since 1995, whereas it increased by more than 100% (in nominal terms) for households living in public housing. Private housing became smaller in size as high-density condominiums replaced private landed and low-density landed housing. The proportion of 4-room and larger HDB flats in the housing stock, on the other hand, increased rapidly over the same period. The increase in housing wealth per HDB household over the 20-year period helped to reduce housing wealth inequality between HDB and private homeowners.

The major reason for the overall increase in housing wealth lies in the large price increases from 1990 to 1995—at over 190% in nominal terms—over the 5-year period, and over 160% in real terms (see Table 8.8). This was during the bubble period that preceded the Asian Financial Crisis of 1997. Between 1995 and 2000, during the worst period of the Asian Financial Crisis, HDB resale prices remained relatively stable (2.8% nominal change) while private housing prices declined by 19.5% in nominal terms and 23.4% in real terms. In general, over the 25-year period from 1990 to 2015, HDB resale price index

Table 8.8 Housing wealth and house price changes by HDB and private housing sectors

Nominal $						
Year	Aggregate gross housing wealth (S$m)	Resident Households ('000)	Gross housing wealth per household ($)	Change in gross housing wealth per household	Nominal housing price index change	Change in "quantity of housing services" per household
Public housing segment						
1995	156,472	680.1	230,072	n.a.	198.4%[a]	n.a.
2000	200,902	805.0	249,568	8.5%	2.8%	5.6%
2005	199,917	865.1	231,091	−7.4%	−3.0%	−4.4%
2010	349,156	943.7	369,987	60.1%	69.3%	−9.1%
2015	400,951	981.1	408,675	10.5%	8.4%	2.1%
Private housing segment						
1995	176,167	88.3	1,995,100	n.a.	192.6%[a]	n.a.
2000	175,581	110.1	1,594,744	−20.1%	−19.5%	−0.6%
2005	184,294	159.4	1,156,172	−27.5%	−11.0%	−16.5%
2010	340,195	202.2	1,682,466	45.5%	64.7%	−19.2%
2015	436,800	244.2	1,788,699	6.3%	1.7%	4.6%

Real $ (CPI=100, 2015 Q4)						
Year	Aggregate gross housing wealth (S$m)	Resident Households ('000)	Gross housing wealth per household ($)	Change in gross housing wealth per household	Real housing price index change	Change in "quantity of housing services" per household
Public housing segment						
1995	216,135	680.1	317,798	n.a.	165.9%[a]	n.a.
2000	264,189	805.0	328,186	3.3%	−2.1%	5.4%
2005	254,239	865.1	293,884	−10.5%	−6.2%	−4.2%
2010	387,922	943.7	411,065	39.9%	47.9%	−8.0%
2015	400,951	981.1	408,675	−0.6%	−2.5%	1.9%
Private housing segment						
1995	243,340	88.3	2,755,831	n.a.	160.7%[a]	n.a.
2000	230,892	110.1	2,097,111	−23.9%	−23.4%	−0.5%
2005	234,371	159.4	1,470,333	−29.9%	−13.9%	−16.0%
2010	377,966	202.2	1,869,266	27.1%	43.9%	−16.8%
2015	436,800	244.2	1,788,699	−4.3%	−8.4%	4.1%

Note: [a]Refers to change from 1990 to 1995

Source: Estimated using data from Singapore government websites

Table 8.9 Distribution of housing wealth by dwelling type, 2015

2015Q4	Households ('000)	Proportion by house type	Housing wealth (S$m)	Average house value (S$)	Housing wealth distribution
Resident Households	1,225.3	100%	837,752	683,711	100%
Total HDB Dwellings	981.1	80%	400,951	408,675	48%
1- and 2-room flats	68.8	6%	–	–	–
3-room flats	223.4	18%	73,722	330,000	9%
4-room flats	321.2	26%	136,508	425,000	16%
The HDB 4-room flat is the median house type by house value					
4-room flats	71.1	6%	30,218	425,000	4%
5-room & Exec flats	295.8	24%	160,501	542,600	19%
Total Private Dwellings	244.2	20%	436,800	1,788,699	52%

Source: Estimated using data from Singapore government websites

increases exceeded private housing price index increases during upturns; HDB resale prices were more resilient than private housing prices during downturns.

Table 8.9 shows the house type distribution for the resident population. The 80% of resident households that reside in HDB flats have a share of 48% of gross housing wealth. The median house type in Singapore is the 4-room HDB flat that is home to 32% of resident households. To estimate the proportion of gross housing wealth owned by the bottom 50% of households, we make the following assumptions:

(i) 1- and 2-room HDB flats are rental units and the 6% of households residing in these flat types have no housing wealth.
(ii) 3-room and larger HDB flat types are all owner-occupied. The average values of these HDB flat types are estimated from HDB resale flat prices.

Based on the above, and assuming that the bottom 50% of households reside in 4-room or smaller HDB flat types, their share of Singapore's gross housing wealth in 2015 was estimated at 25%.

The above analysis of housing wealth distribution in Singapore was motivated by Piketty's concern that "inequality of wealth is always and everywhere much greater than the inequality of income from labour". Piketty presents data for the US, which shows that in the early 2010s, the top decile owned 72% of America's wealth, while the bottom half's claim was just 2%. In France, the richest 10% owned around 62% of national wealth, the poorest 50% owned less than 4% (Piketty 2014, 257). In his view, this unequal ownership of capital is a prime driver of income disparities.

To quote Piketty, "To my knowledge, no society has ever existed in which ownership of capital can reasonably be described as 'mildly' inegalitarian, by which I mean a distribution in which the poorest half of society would own a significant share (say one-fifth to one-quarter) of total wealth... Of course, how one might go about establishing such an 'ideal society' – assuming that such low inequality of wealth is indeed a desirable goal – remains to be seen" (Piketty 2014, 258). Based on the above estimates, Singapore's housing policies have resulted in gross *housing* wealth distribution approximating capital ownership distribution in Piketty's ideal society.

Conclusion

US Supreme Court Justice Oliver Wendell Holmes, Jr. has opined that "taxes are what we pay for civilized society, including the chance to insure".[4] Singapore's policies demonstrate that taxes alone will be insufficient to bring about equitable housing outcomes in global superstar cities. A multipronged approach encompassing land and housing legislation, land use planning, land value capture, state housing developer and housing finance institutions, market regulations, taxes, and subsidies have been utilized in Singapore to bring about such outcomes.

The analysis in this chapter utilized data obtained from the Singapore government's Department of Statistics website, which refers only to the resident population—that is, citizens and permanent residents. As a global city, the number of foreigners in Singapore has been growing rapidly, and comprised 1.65 million or 29.3% of the total population in 2017. Official Gini coefficients, labour force, household and housing data released by government agencies do not include foreigners. The above findings on housing wealth distribution must therefore be interpreted as being valid only for 70% of Singapore's population. Despite this qualification, Singapore provides an interesting social and economic experiment of the wealth accumulation and distribution that has been achieved through interventionist land and housing policies in an open market economy.

Notes

1. This chapter is adapted from Phang (2016), which in turn grew out of the Celia Moh Professorial Chair Public Lecture delivered at the Singapore Management University on 23 Mar 2015 (Phang 2015a).
2. Singapore's affordability measure at 4.8 does not take into account housing grants for HDB resale flats. See Chap. 1 for discussion.
3. Ministry of National Development Press Release on "Revision of CPF Housing Grant Quantum", 11 Dec 1998. http://www.nas.gov.sg/archivesonline/speeches/view-html?filename=1998121101.htm.
4. The quote is from Justice Oliver Wendell Holmes, Jr.'s dissenting opinion in the 1927 court case of *Compañía General de Tabacos de Filipinas v. Collector of Internal Revenue.*

References

Atkinson, Anthony B. 2015. *Inequality: What Can Be Done?* Cambridge, MA: Harvard University Press.

Bastagli, Francesca, and John Hills. 2013. Wealth Accumulation, Ageing, and House Prices. In *Wealth in the UK: Distribution, Accumulation, and Policy*, ed. John Hills, Francesca Bastagli, Frank Cowell, Howard Glennerster, Eleni Karagiannaki, and Abigail McKnight, 63–91. Oxford: Oxford University Press.

Baum-Snow, Nathaniel, and Ronni Pavan. 2013. Inequality and City Size. *Review of Economics and Statistics* 95 (5): 1535–1548.

Behrens, Kristian, and Frederic Robert-Nicoud. 2014. Survival of the Fittest in Cities: Urbanization and Inequality. *Economic Journal* 124 (581): 1371–1400.

Cheong, Koon Hean. 2014. Promoting Social Equity Through Public Housing. *Urban Solutions,* Issue 4 (February): 66–70.

Cvijanovic, Dragana, and Christophe Spanejers. 2015. *Real Estate as a Luxury Good: Non-Resident Demand and Property Prices in Paris*. HEC Paris Research Paper No. FIN-2015-1073.

Eeckhout, Jan, Roberto Pinheiro, and Kurt Schmidhein. 2014. Spatial Sorting. *Journal of Political Economy* 122 (3): 554–620.

Glaeser, Edward L., Matt Resseger, and Kristina Tobio. 2009. Inequality in Cities. *Journal of Regional Science* 49 (4): 617–646.

Gyouko, Joseph, Christopher Mayer, and Todd Sinai. 2013. Superstar Cities. *American Economic Journal: Economic Policy* 5 (4): 167–199.

Hendricks, Lutz. 2011. The Skill Composition of US Cities. *International Economic Review* 52 (1): 1–32.

Leff, Scott, and Brittany Petersen. 2015. *Beyond the Scorecard: Understanding Global City Rankings*. Chicago: The Chicago Council on Global Affairs.

Performance Urban Planning. 2017. *13th Annual Demographia International Housing Affordability Survey 2017*. http://www.demographia.com/dhi.pdf. Accessed 1 Nov 2017.

Phang, Sock-Yong. 1996. Economic Development and the Distribution of Land Rents in Singapore: A Georgist Implementation. *American Journal of Economics and Sociology* 55: 489–501.

———. 2001. Housing Policy, Wealth Formation and the Singapore Economy. *Housing Studies* 16 (4): 443–459.

———. 2007. The Singapore Model of Housing and the Welfare State. In *Housing and the New Welfare State*, ed. Richard Groves, Alan Murie, and Christopher Watson. Aldershot: Ashgate.

———. 2015a. *Superstar Cities, Inequality and Housing Policies*. Celia Moh Professorial Chair Lecture, Delivered at the Singapore Management University, April 23, 2015. A summary of the lecture was published as "Home Prices and Inequality: Singapore Versus Other Global Superstar Cities" in *The Straits Times*, April 4, 2015.

———. 2015b. Singapore's Housing Policies: Responding to the Challenges of Economic Transitions. *Singapore Economic Review*, 50th Anniversary Special Issue on Singapore's Economy.

———. 2016. *Housing Wealth Accumulation and Distribution in Superstar Cities: The Case Study of Singapore*. Paper Presented at International Symposium on Land Policy and Housing Market. Co-organized by Hong Kong University, Lincoln Institute of Land Policy, and Peking University-Lincoln Institute Center for Urban Development and Land Policy, May 16–17, Hong Kong University, Hong Kong.

Piketty, Thomas. 2014. *Capital in the Twenty-first Century*. Cambridge, MA: The Belknap Press of Harvard University Press.

Rognlie, Matthew. 2015. *Deciphering the Fall and Rise in the Net Capital Share*. Brookings Papers on Economic Activity.

Sassen, Saskia. 2001. *The Global City: New York, London, Tokyo*. 2nd ed. Princeton: Princeton University Press.

Singapore Ministry of Finance. 2015. *Income Growth, Inequality and Mobility Trends in Singapore*. Occasional Paper.

The Euromonitor International. 2013. *The World's Largest Cities are the Most Unequal*. http://blog.euromonitor.com/2013/03/the-worlds-largest-cities-are-the-most-unequal.html#sthash.IUr4LPfD.dpuf. Accessed 1 Nov 2017.

9

Home Equity Extraction for Retirement Financing

Singapore's population is ageing rapidly. Fertility has declined to 1.2 children per female while life expectancy at birth has increased to 82.9 in 2016. There has understandably been increased policy focus on how to respond to the challenges for the economy as well as on how the growing numbers of older persons will manage in their retirement years. With a high homeownership rate of 91% for the resident population, a substantial portion of household wealth is tied up in housing. Home equity is however relatively *illiquid*. Moreover, leasehold housing, which declines in value as the lease approaches expiration, presents obstacles to introducing instruments such as the reverse mortgage in order to enable housing equity extraction. The leasehold feature of Housing and Development Board (HDB) flats led the Singapore government to introduce a policy innovation, the Lease Buyback Scheme (LBS), in 2009. This chapter

This chapter is adapted from Phang (2017), which was prepared for a Housing Roundtable organized by Singapore Management University, Centre for Research on the Economics of Ageing, on August 16, 2017. I thank Stephen Hoskins and Naqun Huang for their excellent research assistance. The research in this chapter (which draws on data from the Singapore Life Panel® survey) was supported by the Singapore Ministry of Education (MOE) Academic Research Fund Tier 3 grant MOE2013-T3-1-009.

S.-Y. Phang, *Policy Innovations for Affordable Housing In Singapore*,
Palgrave Advances in Regional and Urban Economics,
https://doi.org/10.1007/978-3-319-75349-2_9

discusses the challenges of financing retirement for senior homeowners, the instruments commonly utilized for home equity extraction, as well as Singapore's policies in the context of obstacles to utilizing conventional instruments.

The Singapore Life Panel® (SLP) survey is a high frequency longitudinal survey launched in July 2015 by the Singapore Management University's Centre for Research on the Economics of Ageing.[1] Its objective is to provide a better understanding of the myriad consumption, investment, employment, health, and other decisions of Singapore's resident population aged between 50 and 70. The SLP interviews approximately 8000 respondents from over 4000 households randomly selected from the population each month. The questions cover monthly household income and spending, labour force status, as well as health shocks. Over 30 categories of consumption spending are included. In addition to monthly online surveys, the SLP also conducts annual surveys to collect information on household assets and liabilities, pensions, and annual income from the respondents. The questions on assets include home ownership, mortgage loans outstanding, as well as property values. In this chapter, data from the SLP surveys are used to inform the discussion on housing wealth, consumption patterns, and attitudes towards home equity extraction amongst senior households in Singapore.

An Ageing Home-Owning Society

Population ageing is one of the most significant social transformations that Singapore is currently undergoing. This trend has been driven by reductions in birth rates and improved longevity, producing substantial shifts to the population age structure. Figure 9.1 shows the decline in total fertility rate from above 4 in the 1960s (the baby boomer generation) to around 1.2 in the past decade—one of the lowest rates internationally. Hong Kong (1.2), Macao (1.2), and Taiwan (1.1) have similar low fertility rates. The 2015 United Nations report on world population ageing shows slightly higher rates for South Korea (1.3), Japan (1.4), and Germany (1.4) (United Nations 2015). Rising singlehood, later marriages, married couples having fewer children, rising divorce rates, as well

Fig. 9.1 Singapore total fertility rate (children per woman), 1960–2016 (Source: Data from Singapore Department of Statistics)

as social norms against single parenthood contribute to the low fertility rates in East Asian societies.

At the other end of the life spectrum, along with rising incomes and wealth, improved access to education, health care, and medical technologies have extended life expectancy. Life expectancy at birth increased steadily from 72.1 years in 1980 to 82.9 years in 2016, an average of 0.3 years per year (see Fig. 9.2). The life expectancy in 2016 was 80.6 years for males and 85.1 years for females—comparable to figures for Japan and Hong Kong, which are amongst the longest life expectancy in the world. What was notable for 2016 was that for the first time in several decades, life expectancies at birth did not increase, remaining identical with 2015.

With declines in fertility and improvements in life expectancy, the ageing baby boomer generation (born between 1946 and 1965) has become proportionately the largest demographic group in the citizen population. Official statistics paint a sobering picture: the median age of the resident population increased from 18 years in the 1960s to 40 years in 2016; it is expected to increase to 47 years by 2030 and 53 years by 2050 (United Nations 2015). The old-age support ratio (citizens aged 20–64 years per resident aged 65 and over) has declined continuously from 13.5 in 1970 to 4.9 in 2015, and is expected to fall to 2.1 by 2030. The percentage of the population aged 60 or over was 17.9% in 2015; the 2015 United

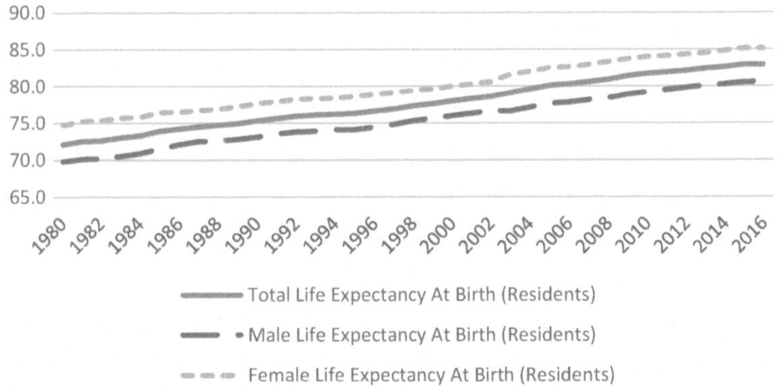

Fig. 9.2 Singapore life expectancy at birth (resident population), 1980–2016 (Source: Data from Singapore Department of Statistics)

Nations report on world population ageing projects the percentage to increase to 30.7% in 2030 and to 40.4% in 2050.

Population ageing is an issue of concern in many countries around the world, with today's over 60s being the world's fastest growing population group. In comparison to other countries, Singapore's rate of population ageing between 2015 and 2030 is especially rapid due to the sharp decline in fertility rates in the past two decades. Singapore has been identified by the UN as amongst ten countries with the fastest expected rise in the proportion of the population aged 60 years or over, between 2015 and 2030 (United Nations 2015, 32). Singapore does not have comprehensive social security or pension systems and a substantial proportion of households are financially unprepared for retirement. The SLP survey found the self-reported average chance of struggling in retirement to be 46%; 60% of households surveyed rated their financial preparedness for retirement to be "fair" or "poor". The implications of this surge in older persons and the policies needed to address the demographic challenges were the focus of a Population White Paper in 2013.[2]

Another dimension of population ageing that Singapore shares with other countries with high homeownership rates is the need for ways to facilitate home equity release for homeowners. This issue is of particular concern in Singapore due to its unusually high homeownership rate. SLP findings indicate that the homeownership rate remains high for older resident households aged between 50 and 70. In 2016, the homeownership rate was 86% for households residing in HDB flats, 93% for those residing in condominiums and apartments, and 90% for those residing in landed housing (see Table 9.1). There appears to be no significant decline of homeownership with age.

For homeowners, SLP data (see Table 9.1) show that more than 75% of HDB homeowners in the 50–70 aged group were mortgage debt free. For HDB households with mortgage debts, the median amounts were relatively low, at less than 20% of median home values. Analysis of household asset portfolios confirmed home equity to be a very significant proportion of total wealth for the group aged 65–69, the proportion being highest for households residing in 3-room HDB flats (see Table 9.2). A Singaporean resident, in the 65–69 age group, living in a 3-room HDB flat, has assets of approximately $367,000, of which 81% is in a fully paid up HDB flat worth $300,000, $52,000 is in illiquid Central Provident Fund (CPF) deposits, and only $15,000 is in other financial assets.

Figure 9.3a shows that for 4-room HDB households, while financial and CPF wealth declined with the age of homeowners, housing wealth remains little changed, showing no significant trend of home equity extraction insofar as senior homeowners are concerned. The proportion of housing equity in total net wealth increases with age, from around 70% for households aged 50–54, to above 80% for households aged 65–69—for both 3- and 4-room HDB flat owners. The increase in housing equity ratios with age for homeowners of 5-room and Executive HDB flats and those of private Condominiums and Apartments is broadly similar: from 57% for those aged 55–59 to 73% for those aged 65–69 for 5-room and Executive HDB homeowners, and from 56% for those aged 55–59 to 71% for those aged 65–69 in the latter category (see Fig. 9.3b). With housing wealth remaining intact, SLP data indicate that household spending declines with age as incomes fall (see Fig. 9.4), with possible negative impacts on wellbeing.

Singapore's high homeownership rate and high proportion of household equity in net wealth—for the vast majority of households—necessitates policies to help senior homeowners convert illiquid home equity into disposable income for old age wellbeing and to reduce the incidence of old-age poverty. For the vulnerable elderly, even a small increase in

Table 9.1 Housing wealth, mortgage debt, and housing equity by dwelling type, 2016

Dwelling type	Proportion of respondents in SLP sample (%)	Home ownership rate (%)	Median home values for homeowner households ($'000)	Proportion of homeowner households with mortgage (%)	Median mortgage debt for homeowner households with mortgage ($'000)	Median primary housing equity for homeowner households with mortgage ($'000)
1- & 2-rm HDB	3.7%	34%	150	3%	5	145
3-rm HDB	17.4%	87%	300	18%	60	240
4-rm HDB	33.2%	86%	400	20%	65	330
5-rm & Executive HDB	29.8%	89%	500	26%	80	410
Condominiums & Apartments	9.0%	90%	1000	29%	250	900
Landed housing	6.9%	86%	2200	23%	500	1920

Source: Data from Singapore Life Panel®

Table 9.2 Wealth components of households (aged 65–69) by dwelling type (homeowners, median values, $'000, 2016)

	Total wealth	Housing & other properties	CPF	Net financial wealth
1- & 2-rm HDB	201	108 (54%)	70 (35%)	23 (11%)
3-rm HDB	367	300 (82%)	52 (14%)	15 (4%)
4-rm HDB	493	400 (81%)	66 (13%)	27 (5%)
5-rm & Executive HDB	686	500 (73%)	108 (16%)	78 (11%)
Condominiums & Apartments	1770	1250 (71%)	175 (10%)	345 (19%)
Landed Housing	3328	2800 (84%)	168 (5%)	360 (11%)

Source: Data from Singapore Life Panel®

additional cash could help the them avoid unhealthy lifestyle choices such as limiting the intake of fresh fruits and vegetables and health supplements, turning off lights, delaying home repairs, or postponing much needed visits to the doctor or dentist.

Methods of Home Equity Extraction

The role of home equity as a funding source in retirement is well recognized in developed countries with homeownership rates above 60%. Home equity is often the largest proportion of retirement wealth for low- and middle-income homeowners. There is increasing policy interest worldwide to facilitate home equity extraction in order that society can better cope with the challenges of ageing, declining health, and old-age disability. Downsizing to a smaller home or selling and then renting are possible options. For seniors who eventually need some form of care, the home could be rented out or sold and the rental income or sales proceeds used to finance nursing home care.

However, there are those who prefer to stay in their own homes as they age. For this group of homeowners, there are various financial products that will allow them to borrow against their home equity, age in an environment they are familiar with, and at lower costs as compared to moving or nursing home care. The channels that can allow older people to borrow against their home equity include cash-out refinancing, a home equity

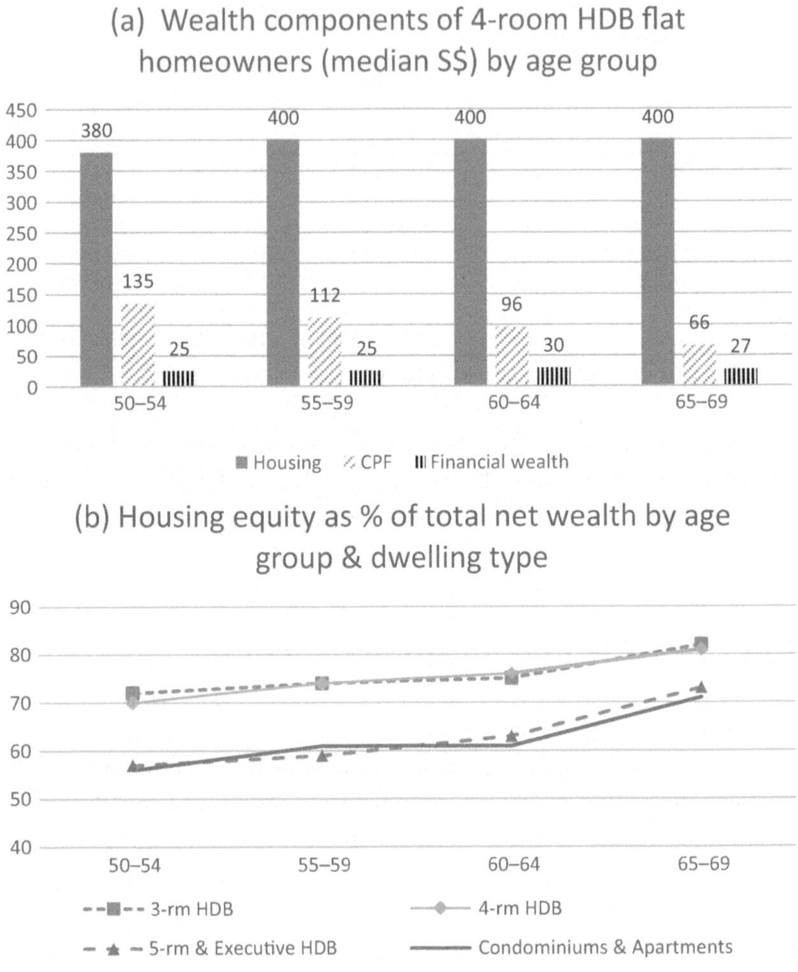

Fig. 9.3 Distribution of wealth components (median values) by age group, 2016. (**a**) Wealth components of 4-room HDB flat homeowners (median $) by age group, (**b**) Housing equity as % of total net wealth by age group & dwelling type (Note: Housing wealth includes the primary residence and other properties; Source: Data from Singapore Life Panel®)

line of credit loan, a second lien, or a reverse mortgage (RM). The first three channels are available to homeowners regardless of age, whilst an RM is designed specifically for elderly homeowners. The availability of these financial products differs in each country depending on the levels of

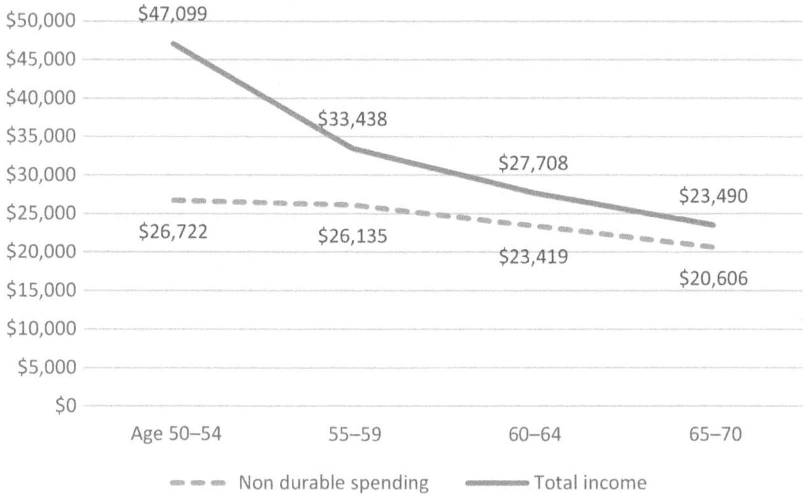

Fig. 9.4 Median annual income and nondurable consumption by age group ($), 2016 (Note: Annual income includes total income from investment, wage, CPF, annuities, pension, and government support in 2016; consumption only includes nondurable consumption from Jan to Dec 2016; Source: Data from Singapore Life Panel®)

financial education, the regulatory framework, and the willingness of governments to facilitate household debt in general and home equity extraction in particular. A brief description of each of these products is provided below:

(i) *Cash-out refinancing*

A homeowner with an existing mortgage may choose to prepay the mortgage by taking on a new mortgage that is of a greater amount. This enables the homeowner to cash-out the difference (minus the transaction costs) for the purpose of extracting equity from the borrower's home.

(ii) *Home equity line of credit*

A homeowner who does not have a mortgage on the home can extract housing wealth through a home equity loan or line of credit (often called HELOC in the US). The lender agrees to lend a maximum amount within an agreed period (draw period) with the borrower's home equity as collateral. The amount drawn can vary as long as it is no more than the credit limit. Repayment schedule and amounts depend on the terms of the loan, with repayment of principal plus interest due at the end of the draw period.

(iii) *Second lien*

A homeowner with an existing mortgage may take on an additional second lien mortgage. In the event of default, the second lien lender receives compensation from the sale of the property after the first lien mortgage is covered.

(iv) *Reverse mortgage*

An RM allows an elderly homeowner to withdraw home equity through a line of credit for as long as the owner or spouse lives in the home. The loan can be either in the form of an upfront lump sum payment, monthly payments (fixed or inflation-indexed) for life or for a fixed period of months (income stream products), a line of credit, or combinations of the above. What makes the RM different from the above three equity release products is that most RMs are designed such that *no repayment is required* until the last surviving borrower dies, sells the home, has not used the home as primary residence for a specific period of time, or fails to meet the obligations for the loan, such as paying property taxes and home insurance. When the home is sold, the contract is terminated, the loan amount, interest and other charges are repaid, and the balance of the proceeds goes to the owners, the spouse, or the beneficiary. Lucas (2015) describes it as a financial product where the borrowers are short a loan, and long a put option on their house, both with a variable maturity equal to their tenure in their current home.

The RM was introduced in the US from 1961, UK in the early 1980s, and Canada in the early 1990s (Warshawsky and Zohrabyan 2016).[3] In the US, the market did not grow much until 1987, when the Housing and Community Development Act introduced the Home Equity Conversion Mortgage (HECM) programme. The HECM programme is regulated by the US Department of Housing and Urban Development (HUD), with insurance provided by the Federal Housing Administration (FHA). Lenders can also sell the loans to the FHA as balances approach the insured limit.

The RM has gained much policy attention in the past decade internationally and has been introduced in Australia (2004), Spain (2006), South Korea (2007), Poland (2008), Hong Kong (2011), and Taiwan (2014). It is available in at least 10 EU countries and some cities in China.[4] Although several countries now offer the RM product, there is no "standard" RM and the design of the product varies, in particular, with regard to the risk-bearing party and the involvement of the government as risk-bearing provider.

A typical RM contract contains several risks, with the attractiveness of the instrument to the lender or borrower depending on how those risks are allocated or transferred to a third party. The multiple risks that need to be considered for allocation and pricing in the design of an RM include the following:

(i) *Non-recourse risk*: An important risk for lenders is that the loan balance on the termination of the contract may exceed the value of the property. If the RM is non-recourse, the borrower will not owe more than the value of the property and no assets other than the home must be used to repay the debt, that is, the borrower has a "no negative equity" guarantee. In the US, South Korea, Australia, and Spain, RMs are non-recourse. In the US, insurance is mandatory and is provided by the FHA. In South Korea, the government provides the guarantee through the state-run Korea Housing Finance Corporation. In the UK, mortgage loans are not automatically non-recourse and borrowers using an RM pay an extra fee to include a "no negative equity" guarantee (Warshawsky and Zohrabyan 2016). In the context of non-recourse HECM, Davidoff (2010) and Davidoff and Wetzel (2014) have shown that a borrower could adopt the following "ruthless" strategy: take out a line of credit and draw on it if the maximum loan limit exceeds the value of the house just before selling the house.

(ii) *Longevity risk*: The borrower may live longer and remain in the home for a longer period than the mortality assumptions used by the lender. If the rate of interest exceeds the rate of house price appreciation, the loan balance will exceed the collateral value when the loan becomes due. Cho et al. (2013) show lump sum RMs to be less exposed to longevity risk than life-annuity products, which helps explain why lump sum products are more popular internationally. As compared to a life-annuity RM, a fixed period annuity RM reduces the lender's exposure to longevity risk. The pension industry has developed solutions to manage longevity risk through risk transfer to insurance and reinsurance providers. However, the risk exposure to the RM lender is different from the annuity issuer, as the lender will continue to be compensated at the promised rate of interest as long as the mortgage is outstanding (Merton and Lai 2016). Despite the US having the most mature financial markets for risk transfer, it is notable that the US government saw the need to sponsor insurance for HECMs.

(iii) *Default risk*: In an RM, there are various channels for default to happen. The lender may default on making contractual payments to the borrower. Borrowers, who retain title to the property, are responsible for paying property taxes and homeowner insurance. A borrower who runs out of cash and fails to pay taxes or insurance is in technical default on the RM. Moulton et al. (2016) reports that in the wake of the financial crisis in the US, default rates for HECM loans rose and hit 10% in 2013.

(iv) *Interest rate risk*: The outstanding debt on an RM accrues at a contractual interest rate which can be variable (an interest rate index plus margin) or fixed. For lenders, interest rate risk for variable rate mortgages is less of a concern than fixed rate mortgages. Reflecting the higher risks, the interest rates for RMs are usually higher than those for conventional mortgages, higher for life versus lump sum RMs, and higher in countries where there is no government guarantee (Warshawsky and Zohrabyan 2016).[5] For US HECMs, the expected average interest rate is one of the factors that determines the maximum payment amount that the retiree can borrow. If the margins are too high or risk is overpriced, borrowers will find the product expensive. On the other hand, if the risk is under-priced or the risk premium capped by regulation, lenders will suffer losses or be unwilling to supply the product. If the risk is under-priced and transferred to a government insurer, as is the case of the US HECM programme,[6] the programme itself risks becoming insolvent. This was the case for the US HUD insurance fund, which suffered negative balances due to rising defaults and payouts (Moulton et al. 2016). Concerns over the programme's solvency led to major policy changes in 2013.

(v) *House price risk*: House prices fluctuate over time. When house prices increase, the lender has the assurance that the collateral value remains intact while the mortgagor or his/her beneficiary retains ownership and the upside to the price appreciation. When house prices fall, there is the possibility that the accumulated loan balances exceed the collateral value. The allocation of this negative equity risk to borrower, lender, or third-party insurer is crucial to the design of an RM.

(vi) *Maintenance moral hazard risk*: If reverse mortgagors do less home maintenance, the value of homes with an RM will be affected by the state of repair. This moral hazard risk is lower than the rental externality risk, as the mortgagor retains an equity stake and continues to live in the property.

(vii) *Selection risk*: In the context of RMs, Davidoff and Welke (2007) have suggested that adverse selection could be a concern in the sense that reverse mortgagors are more likely to be those who expect to remain alive and in their homes longer than the rest of the population.

Obstacles to Home Equity Extraction Through RM

Where various channels of borrowing are available, the decisions that ageing homeowners make on choice of product will have long-term consequences for financial wellbeing. The take-up rates for RMs have generally not been high, suggesting that there are numerous obstacles to home equity extraction. We first discuss the obstacles in the context of the US, where the HECM has been available for three decades, and then consider the obstacles in the context of Singapore.

The US Reverse Mortgage Puzzle

According to Moulton et al. (2016), only 2% of eligible seniors in the US have RMs, although demand has generally been rising over the past decade. The number of HECM loan originations totalled 1,040,323 between 1990 and 2017, and rose above 100,000 per year for 2007–2009.[7] This is despite the HECM's "no negative equity" and "no eviction" guarantees, which Davidoff (2010, 2015) describes as purchasing a put option on the house with an exercise price equal to the evolving maximum allowable balance. This allows borrowers to use the HECM line of credit to insure against both longevity risk as well as house price risk.

Given these attractive features, several researchers (Davidoff 2015; Lucas 2015; Merton and Lai 2016) have referred to the low adoption rates as the "RM puzzle": why is an insured financial product that offers a solution for older households so unpopular? Behavioural and other factors have been suggested: distrust and a lack of understanding exacerbated by the product's complexity; substantial upfront costs; limited need because of Medicaid coverage; as well as reluctance to spend bequests.

Lucas (2015) shows (using a stochastic model) that an explanation for the low demand could be due to the high financial cost of the product: she finds that the Net Present Value (NPV) of the typical HECM loan at origination averages *negative* US$27,000; the NPV of the government subsidy averages US$4000; while private lenders realize NPV of US$ 31,000 per loan—a profit rate of 21.4% of principal. In short, the largest winners are the private lenders who are offering an expensive product to the borrowers. For the HECMs, lenders collect origination fees and charge a spread over short-term interest rates of between 1% and 3%, despite bearing little risk. Lucas suggests that competition amongst lenders do not reduce these high profits as the industry is fairly concentrated, the market is opaque, and comparison shopping is difficult. However, Munnell and Sass (2014) suggest that the business is not particularly attractive to lenders after taking into account collection and foreclosure costs —as evidenced by the withdrawal of the three largest HECM from the market.

Davidoff (2015) points to the fact that the "high cost" explanation is incomplete as credit-line use is an elective for the borrower. He views the limited use of the HECM line of credit as put option insurance against house price depreciation (even near the house cycle peak) as puzzling and deserving of further research. Instead of buying an RM, older people prefer other alternatives that are easier to understand: downsizing to a smaller home or "sell-then-rent". Adult children may help with cash transfers to liquidity constrained parents, thereby preserving the value of the bequests. Moreover, seniors often do not keep their homes in good repair, extracting home equity by saving on maintenance (Davidoff 2004).

HUD is mandated to make the HECM programme self-funding and FHA insures lenders against negative equity by collecting a mortgage insurance premium for HECMs at loan closing as well as a percentage of the outstanding balances each month. However, the financial crisis of 2008–2009 led to a dramatic increase in originations to more than 110,000 in 2008 as well as in 2009, as more people turned to the HDCM as a source of funds. By 2012, nearly 10% of HECM borrowers were in default, with falling house prices also resulting in declines in the collateral values backing HECM loans (Munnell and Sass 2014). For HUD, the low take-up rate could therefore be considered a "blessing" as programme losses were correspondingly limited. Concerns over negative balances in the HUD insurance fund and programme solvency led to a major HECM reform in 2013. A number of changes were introduced: a moratorium on the fixed rate-full draw product; restrictions on amounts that could be withdrawn as lump sum in the first year; increase in insurance premium on outstanding balances from 0.5% to 1.25%; and introduction of underwriting standards to curb loans that pose excessive risk (Moulton et al. 2016).

The Reverse Mortgage Puzzle in Singapore

The first RM instrument was introduced in 1997 (albeit only for private housing) by a local insurance cooperative, NTUC Income. In 2006, following the government's announcement to allow HDB homeowners to obtain RMs, NTUC Income started to offer such mortgages for HDB flats. The second financial institution to offer the RM in 2006 was OCBC Bank, one of the "big three" commercial banks in Singapore. Both institutions have, however, discontinued their schemes since mid-2009, citing low demand. In the decade after first offering the product from 1997 to 2006, NTUC originated about 350 RM loans for private properties, a take-up rate of 35 a year. Between 2006 and 2009, when RMs were offered by NTUC Income to HDB homeowners, only 24 HDB homeowners took up an RM.[8]

The Singapore version of the RM puzzle centres on why the product failed to gain traction despite the housing asset-rich cash-poor problem for senior homeowners in Singapore. To help understand the reasons for the low demand, we compare the design of the Singapore RM with the US HECM. The differences in design features and particularly the treatment of risk for the HECM and NTUC RMs are stark (see Table 9.3).

First, the eligible age for the NTUC Income RM for HDB homeowners was higher—at 70 years or older. Second, only properties with a remaining lease period of 70 years or 50 years at the end of the loan period qualify. Third, the loan is recourse. Fourth, longevity risk falls on the borrower. At age 90, the loan is terminated: monthly payments cease and loan balances have to be repaid. Fifth, the maximum loan amount is reassessed every half year and a decline in house price will trigger the lender to seek repayment in order to avoid LTV in excess of a 70% cap. Sixth, unlike the HECM where there is a "no negative equity" guarantee provided by the FHA, the Singapore government is not involved. Yet, with borrowers bearing most of the risks for essentially a collateralized housing loan of a maximum 20-year tenure, NTUC offered the product to HDB homeowners at 5.0% interest rate in 2006. The then prevailing prime interest rate was 5.3%, and the HDB interest rate for a conventional mortgage was 2.6%.

The high risk to the borrower for the RM became apparent and received much negative media publicity in 2009, when an elderly couple sued NTUC Income, alleging wrongful seizure and sale of their property in 2006. The couple had applied for a reverse mortgage with NTUC Income in 1997 (close to the 1990s peak of the house price bubble) when their home was valued at $2.1 million. Based on an LTV ratio of 80%,

Table 9.3 Contrasting US's HECM and Singapore's NTUC reverse mortgage designs

	HECM	NTUC income RM
Eligibility and conditions	Homeowner at least aged 62; little or no outstanding loan on property, home is single family home or 2 to 4-unit home with one unit occupied by the borrower or HUD-approved condominium project; borrowers must be counselled by an independent third party	Homeowners aged 70–90, little or no outstanding loan on property; property must have at least 70 years of lease remaining; remaining lease at end of loan period should be at least 50 years; maximum loan tenure is 20 years; no requirement for third-party counselling
Repayment due	Upon death or sale of property	Upon age 90, death, or sale of property, whichever is earlier
Recourse?	Non-recourse	Recourse
Loan withdrawal options	Various options for variable rate loans: tenure (equal monthly payments for life); term (equal monthly payments for a fixed period of months selected); line of credit; combinations of line of credit and tenure or term	Term loan: equal monthly payments that cease upon age 90 or death, whichever is earlier or if LTV $\geq$ 70%
Loan amount	Maximum allowable loan amount depends on borrower age, current interest rate, and lesser of appraised value or $636,150. This amount is allowed to grow at the mortgage interest rate regardless of home price movements. At any date up to loan termination, borrowers may draw on the credit line up to the point at which the balance is equal to the outstanding balance if all available credit had been drawn at loan origination	The maximum loan amount is capped at 70% of the *prevailing* value of the property LTV of property is reviewed twice a year. If LTV $\geq$ 70%, monthly payout stops and the lender will take steps to recover the loan

(*continued*)

Table 9.3 (continued)

	HECM	NTUC income RM
Interest rates	Interest rate charged for outstanding balances = 1-year index rate + lender's margin (typically 1.5%) + FHA guarantee fee 1.25%	In 2006, the RM interest rate was 5% per annum, compounded monthly, and pegged to market interest rate (In 2006, the 1-year treasury bill yield varied between 2.8% and 3.2%, the HDB mortgage interest rate was 2.6%.)
Risk of negative equity at loan termination	Insured by FHA; borrowers may defer repayment of any credit used until death or extended absence from the home, and lenders cannot force early termination or reduce available credit in response to declining collateral value	No insurance; loan balances due at age 90; lender has recourse to recover negative equity from other assets of borrower even before loan termination and reduce or cease available credit when LTV exceeds 70%

Sources: US government Department of Housing and Urban Development website for HECM at https://portal.hud.gov/hudportal/HUD?src=/program_offices/housing/sfh/hecm/hecmhome; Davidoff (2015); Chia and Tsui (2009)

they were given $495,000 in cash to pay off their previous mortgage and payments of up to $2000 per month. Following the Asian financial crisis of 1997–98 and the SARS crisis in 2003, the borrowers were informed in 2004 that the house value had fallen to $1.1 million and that, with outstanding loan balances at $926,000, they were in breach of the 80% LTV cap. The borrowers were required to repay $46,400 to bring the LTV ratio back to 80% and had their monthly payments progressively reduced to $300 by 2005. In 2006, with outstanding balances at over $1 million, NTUC Income repossessed and sold the property, requiring the borrowers to continue making payments on a shortfall of approximately $55,000.[9]

The above "RM-gone-wrong" case highlighted the product offered in Singapore from 1997 to 2009 to be exceedingly risky and expensive for borrowers. It is hence no "puzzle" that the take-up rate was so low. Design features were retiree-unfriendly and, with the adverse publicity surrounding the product, it was doomed to failure. As mentioned above, both

NTUC Income and OCBC Bank stopped offering the RM in mid-2009. In September 2014, NTUC Income revealed that it was servicing only 38 private property and 10 HDB reverse mortgages.[10]

From the perspective of lenders, the reverse mortgage product is a risky product to offer for *leasehold* housing. The possibility that borrowers could outlive the remaining lease on their homes would constrain lenders to offer term RMs, with the need to stipulate terms that are shorter than the remaining leasehold. In addition, there is the reality of asset depreciation to zero value for leasehold properties upon expiry of the lease. For these reasons, offering an RM of similar design to the HECM would be unfeasible in a leasehold context (Koh 2015).

Housing Policy Innovations for Home Equity Extraction in Singapore

The private sector withdrew from offering RMs in 2009 when the government introduced the Lease Buyback Scheme (LBS). The HDB currently advises elderly households of three possible housing monetization options: (i) rental or sublet of room(s), (ii) downsizing to a smaller flat, or (iii) selling the tail end of the flat lease under the LBS.

During the earlier period of housing shortage, owners of HDB flats were not allowed to sublet their flats or even rooms within their flats without the HDB's permission. In 1990, they were allowed to sublet rooms in their flats—but not the entire flat—without having to obtain permission from the HDB. These rules have been relaxed to give flat owners greater flexibility to monetize their flat and to provide more rental housing options. From January 2003, HDB flat owners who owned a non-subsidized resale flat and who did not have any outstanding HDB loan, and who have occupied the flat for at least 10 years, were allowed to sublet their whole flat with the permission of the HDB. Later that same year (in October 2003), the rules were further relaxed to allow owners of all HDB flats who have occupied their flats for 15 years or more to sublet their whole flat. The objective was to allow flat owners in financial difficulty to generate some income to tide over their problems. In March

2005, the minimum occupation period for subletting of the whole flat was reduced from 15 to 10 years for all HDB flat owners, even if they have an outstanding HDB loan; and from 10 to 5 years for owners without an outstanding HDB loan.

The government facilitates downsizing through two HDB schemes: the Silver Housing Bonus (SHB) scheme from 2012 and the 2-room Flexi scheme. The SHB of $20,000 cash is provided to lower-income elderly households (aged 55 or above with gross monthly income of $3000 or less) who sell a larger home to buy a 3-room or smaller HDB flat, and use at least $60,000 of the net sale proceeds to top up their CPF retirement account in order to purchase a CPF life-annuity plan.[11] Another downsizing option is the 2-room Flexi scheme that was introduced by the HDB in 2015. It replaced the 2-room Flat and Studio Apartment Scheme for the elderly (introduced in 1998) and offers flexible shorter leases to applicants aged 55 years and above. Instead of a 99-year lease for a new flat, the lease period for the 2-room Flexi ranges from 15 to 45 years.[12]

The Lease Buyback Scheme

The Lease Buyback Scheme (LBS), announced in March 2009, represents a local housing policy innovation in the context of leasehold housing in Singapore. Similar to an RM, the LBS enables the elderly household to age in place while unlocking their home equity to finance retirement. The mechanics are, however, very different from an RM, as it involves the sale of the tail end of the lease. When first introduced, in order to be eligible for the LBS, homeowners had to be of retirement age (aged 63 or older) and live in 3-room HDB or smaller flats. Household income had to be lower than S$3000. HDB flat owners retain 30 years on their lease and sell the remaining years to the HDB. They receive a bonus of $10,000 for participating in the LBS. Proceeds from the lease sale are used to top up the CPF retirement account. Participating members are then required to purchase an annuity with their CPF retirement balance and receive lifelong payouts.[13] For the period between 2009 and February 2013, 471 households participated in the scheme, an annual take-up rate of about 117 households per year.

A February 2013 enhancement to the scheme raised the bonus to S$20,000 and also allowed homeowners the choice of withdrawing cash from the LBS proceeds if they have met the target retirement balance. Prior to the 2013 enhancement, all net proceeds, except for a maximum of $5000 lump sum cash, had to be used to purchase an immediate annuity with the CPF Board. The 2013 changes lowered the top-up requirement and allowed households to keep up to $100,000 of the net proceeds in cash.[14] Following this change that permitted lump sum cash withdrawal, demand for the LBS increased: 494 households signed on to the LBS between March 2013 and March 2015, averaging 247 households per year.[15]

On 17 August 2014, the Prime Minister announced further significant enhancements to the LBS, which came into effect in April 2015. The enhancements extended the eligibility for LBS to those who lived in 4-room HDB flats and raised the income ceiling from $3000 to $10,000 from April 2015 (and to $12,000 from August 2015).[16] 3-room HDB flat owners continue to receive a bonus of $20,000 for participating in the LBS, while 4-room HDB flat owners receive a bonus of $10,000.

In addition, the enhanced LBS allows households greater flexibility in choosing how much of their home lease they want to retain. Instead of a fixed 30-year term, the choice of lease to retain is from 15 to 35 years, provided that the retained lease covers the youngest owner until at least the age of 95 (see Table 9.4). Owners must have at least 20 years of lease remaining to sell. With the enhancements, the annual take-up rate for the LBS more than doubled to 541 households between April 2015 and March 2016, with 233 of these being owners of 4-room HDB flats.[17]

The following example, which is from the HDB website, illustrates the mechanics of the LBS scheme.[18] Consider a couple, both aged 65 years old, who had bought a 4-room HDB flat 34 years ago on a 99-year lease (see Table 9.5). There is no outstanding mortgage loan on the property. The remaining lease on the property is 65 years. The couple can retain 30 more years of the lease and sell the remaining 35 years of the lease to the HDB through the LBS. In this specific example, the HDB determines the current market value of the property to be $450,000 and estimates the current worth of the 35-year tail lease to be $190,000.

Table 9.4 Lease Buyback Scheme: options for lease period
A household that is eligible for the LBS will have the flexibility to choose the length of lease to be retained, based on the age of the youngest owner. The duration of the lease retained determines the amount of net proceeds unlocked

	Lease retained	
Age of youngest owner	Minimum	Other options
Eligibility age (currently 64) – 69	30	35
70–74	25	30, 35
75–79	20	25, 30, 35
80 and above	15	20, 25, 30, 35

Source: HDB website http://www.hdb.gov.sg/cs/infoweb/residential/living-in-an-hdb-flat/for-our-seniors/how-it-works. Accessed 1 Nov 2017

Table 9.5 Illustration of Lease Buyback Scheme
A couple, both 65-year-old Singapore citizens, are joint owners of a fully paid 4-room HDB flat worth $450,000, with a 65-year remaining lease. They chose to keep a 30-year lease, and sell the tail-end 35-year lease to HDB for $190,000

	Husband	Wife
Initial Retirement Account (RA) balance	$20,000	$5000
Current age-adjusted Basic Retirement Sum determined by CPF	$83,000	$83,000
LBS proceeds of $190,000 split equally	$95,000	$95,000
Top up CPF RA to $83,000 from LBS proceeds	$63,000[a]	$78,000[a]
Cash proceeds after RA top-up	$32,000	$17,000
Total cash proceeds for couple	$49,000	
Total RA[a] balance after top-up is placed into a CPF LIFE annuity to enjoy additional CPF LIFE monthly payout (based on Standard Plan)	$810	

Note: [a]As the household's top-up amount exceeds $60,000, the household is eligible for an LBS bonus of $10,000 that is paid into the RA
Source: HDB website http://www.hdb.gov.sg/cs/infoweb/residential/living-in-an-hdb-flat/for-our-seniors/how-it-works. Accessed 1 Nov 2017

The methodology used for the valuation of the tail lease when the HDB purchases the lease back from flat owners was not disclosed to the public, and questions were raised by Members of Parliament in a Parliamentary sitting on 8 September 2014. In his reply, the Minister for National Development clarified that the valuation of the tail lease is based on established industry-accepted standards and valuation practices and involves a number of steps[19]:

- The first step is to assess the market value of the flat with its full remaining lease. This valuation is done by a professional valuer from the HDB's panel of private valuers after a physical inspection of the flat, and then with reference to recent comparable market transactions.
- The second step is to estimate the value of the "X" years of lease retained by the household. Adjustments are also made to reflect the restrictions placed on the LBS flat, namely, no subletting of whole flat and no resale. (This adjustment for restrictions lowers the value of the retained lease, generating higher LBS proceeds.)
- The depreciation method used is not a straight line, as properties with very short outstanding leases tend to depreciate faster than properties with very long remaining leases.
- The current worth of the tail lease is the market value of the flat minus the value of the retained lease of the flat and is also dependent on the discount rate used for computation of the present value of the tail lease.
- The proceeds to the household from the LBS is the current worth of the tail lease minus any outstanding housing loan.

In the above clarification on the valuation methodology used, the Minister for National Development omitted to mention the values of key financial parameters used in the computation: the depreciation schedule used for properties with different length of remaining lease, the adjustment for restrictions on use of property, the discount rate used in computing the present value of an asset to be transferred in a few decades. Kwek and Hoh (2017) reference the publicly available Singapore Land Authority's Leasehold Table[20] for valuation of leasehold land (as percentage of freehold land values) and suggest that the HDB has adopted a similar principle that the value of the flat during the initial years (for the seniors' immediate use and occupation) is higher than the value in the remaining tail-end years, with an implicit discount rate of 3.5% (which provides a good approximation of the values reflected in the official Leasehold Table).

Returning to the illustration provided by the HDB (see Table 9.5), the proceeds from the LBS of $190,000 are split equally between the husband and wife, that is, $95,000 each. As the required basic retirement sum in 2017 as determined by the CPF Board is $83,000 per person, the lease payout is used to top up their individual retirement account to $83,000 with the remaining available as a cash payout. In the example provided by the HDB (see Table 9.5), the total cash payout is $49,000, and the CPF retirement balances of $83,000 each is used to purchase a standard CPF annuity plan (CPF LIFE), which pays a fixed monthly amount of $810 to the household for life.

The current design of CPF LIFE plans includes a bequest feature such that the unused annuity premium, if any (without interest), is paid to beneficiaries upon death or premature termination of the lease. If the retained lease is terminated prematurely, the flat has to be returned to the HDB, and the owner (or inheritors) will receive a refund for the remaining lease, pro-rated on a straight-line basis. Conversely, should the owner outlive the retained lease of the flat, the HDB has given the assurance that he or she will not be left homeless. The HDB will look into the circumstances of each case to determine the appropriate housing arrangement.[21]

The Lease Buyback Scheme Puzzle

Since the launch of the LBS in 2009 to March 2016, a total of 1504 households have signed up for the scheme. The General Household Survey 2015 reports that 50.2% of the 1.2 million resident households reside in 3-room or 4-room HDB flats and that 29.1% of resident households had at least one member aged 65 years or older. Assuming that 13% of households are Permanent Resident (and not citizen) households, back-of-the-envelope estimations point to a potential base of 156,000 households that could have qualified for the LBS scheme based on house type and citizenship status (in 2015). The take-up rate from 2009 to 2016 of about 1500 thus represents only approximately 1% of this base.

Of a sample of 8326 respondents in the SLP survey, analysis of household characteristics indicates that the number of respondents that were eligible for the LBS was 872, or 10.5% of the sample (see Table 9.6). A total of 8 respondents (or 1% of the 872 eligible) are participating in the LBS. The LBS take-up rate of 1% for the SLP sample is consistent with our earlier estimation based on the overall take-up rate. The puzzle is why

Table 9.6 Eligibility for Lease Buyback Scheme

Eligibility criteria	Number of respondents	% of total respondents
Total respondents	8326	
& own their home	7309	87.8%
& both owners are 64+	1332	16.0%
& at least one owner is citizen	1321	15.9%
& household income is <$12,000	1305	15.7%
& home is 4-room HDB flat or smaller	926	11.1%
& have lived there for more than 5 years	894	10.7%
& no ownership of secondary property	889	10.7%
& more than 55 years of lease remaining	872	10.5%

Source: Data from Singapore Life Panel®, 2017

the demand for the government sponsored LBS has been so low despite repeated enhancements and sign-on bonuses that help defray origination costs.

The SLP survey on senior households' views of the LBS and how they are monetizing housing equity can help to shed light on the LBS puzzle. Conditional to being eligible, 98% of respondents rate the probability of participating in the LBS to fund their retirement at below 40%, with 62% indicating below 20% probability. These findings are consistent with the low take-up rate of the LBS. The main obstacles to participation in the LBS was understanding how it works, followed by desire to leave a bequest, and family objections (see Fig. 9.5).

By selling a remaining lease to the flat to be delivered in the future, the LBS participant divests from the housing market in return for ageing in place with an annuity income. While financial literacy, product complexity, bequest motives, and objections from family members are obstacles to participation in the LBS, two strong underlying factors would be the mandatory life-annuity purchase requirement and the issue of house price expectations.

Unlike the HECM, which has various loan options including a lump sum withdrawal, cash constrained households are unable to withdraw the full amount of the proceeds from the LBS as they are required to top up their CPF account to purchase an annuity for life. Prior to 2013 programme reforms, 70% of HECM borrowers between 2010 and 2012 took out the maximum amount available as a lump sum loan at origination (Munnell and Sass 2014). (From 2014, the HECM programme limits

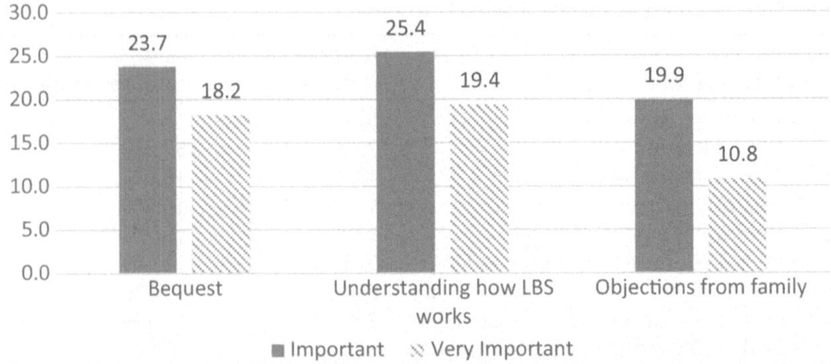

Fig. 9.5 Obstacles to participating in the Lease Buyback Scheme (% of respondents), 2017 (Source: Data from Singapore Life Panel®)

borrowing to not more than 60% of the maximum loan amount at closing or in the first year after closing.)

The requirement for part of LBS proceeds to be annuitized presents an obstacle for those who prefer to have a larger sum of cash upfront from monetizing their housing equity. The benefits, risks, and costs of annuitizing savings apply similarly in the context of the LBS. The direct connection between the LBS and annuities thus relates the LBS puzzle to the "annuity puzzle". Simply described, lifetime annuities offer retirees the benefits of insurance for longevity and investment risks, but the puzzle is why so few individuals voluntarily buy an annuity with their retirement savings (Yaari 1965; Friedman and Warshawsky 1990).

There is a large and growing literature on the reasons for the "annuity puzzle", most of which are also relevant to explaining the LBS puzzle. These include the following: lack of consumer awareness, lack of incentives, bequest motives, default risk, incomplete annuity menus, decreased flexibility in accessing one's money, health risk, expected large out of pocket medical and health care expenses, health shock leading to reduced life expectancy, unfair annuity pricing, as well as behavioural factors such as loss aversion and fear of unexpectedly dying early (Peijnenburg et al. 2016; Lockwood 2012). From the *psychological* perspective, Salisbury and Nenkov (2016) present evidence that the task of choosing an annuity is anxiety provoking, as it forces people to consider their own deaths. This makes people's mortality salient and motivates them to escape thinking about their mortality by avoiding the annuity decision so as to remove death-related thoughts from their consciousness.

The mechanics of the LBS also differ from the conventional RM in its treatment of housing price risk. The HECM provides a put option against a price fall with its no negative equity feature and provides the homeowner (or beneficiary) the benefits of house price appreciation. The LBS similarly provides an assurance against price decline (taking into account price depreciation as the lease runs down) but, in contrast to the HECM, also removes the benefit from the owner of future housing price appreciation. The HDB, by providing the LBS to owners, takes on the property value risk and interest rate risk, but not the longevity risk.

Owners who expect housing prices to appreciate substantially from current levels would be reluctant to forego the expected future appreciation while those who expect their house price to decline in the future would do well to lock in current values through the LBS. Expectations on house price trends tend to be backward looking and present expectations, if based on the very significant past appreciation in HDB resale prices, that would deter owners (and their families) from taking up the LBS. HDB 3- to 5-room flat homeowners rated the chances of their property appreciating in value over the next 5 years to be around 50%; private housing owners were more optimistic (54% for non-landed and 57% for landed), while owners of 1- and 2-room HDB flats were more pessimistic (39%) (Hoskins 2017).

Another factor working against LBS is the uncertainty concerning the value of leasehold properties when leases expire. This is despite policy pronouncements that the value of leasehold properties will fall to zero at lease termination.[22] LBS valuation is thus based on the value of the property being worth nothing when the lease expires. However, households may have expectations that leases will be extended. There is also the expectation of older estates being selected for renewal under the HDB's Selective En bloc Redevelopment Scheme (SERS). SERS flat owners enjoy the benefits of moving to a new home with a new 99-year lease, with a package of compensation and rehousing benefits. An LBS participant whose estate is selected for SERS would likely see reduced SERS "windfall" benefits.

Part of the explanation for the LBS puzzle could thus rest on house price appreciation and SERS expectations. The LBS may be unpopular with HDB flat owners because they expect housing prices to appreciate in the next three decades (despite the leasehold nature of their interest) as has been the case for the past three decades. They may also expect the HDB to redevelop housing estates through the SERS and present affected households with the choice of buying new flats at discounted prices.

Rather than participate in the LBS, older people (and their children) may opt for other ways of financing retirement that do not close off potential benefits and which do not require the purchase of a lifetime annuity. These include the following:

(i) *Rental income*: From 1989, HDB homeowners have been allowed to invest in private housing after fulfilling the 5-year minimum occupancy period. They have also been allowed to sublet rooms in their flat since 1990 (without the need for HDB approval), and to rent out their whole flat since 2003 (see Chap. 6). The data indicates that this is the favoured monetization option for senior households. 16.0% of households in the sample own more than one property, with 8.5% of households earning income from renting out a second property; 8.7% of households sublet rooms in their primary residence for rental income.

(ii) *Downsizing*: While respondents estimate a 1 in 3 chance of having to sell their house to fund their retirement, actual mobility for seniors is very low. Over 79% of respondents are living in a house they have owned for over 10 years. Only a total of 29 households or 0.6% of households in the sample had sold their previous house in 2016. Downsizing involves high search and monetary costs. Not surprisingly, rather than "attachment to current house" and "bequest motive", the more important barriers to selling their present home to fund retirement were "problems with finding a cheaper house" and "the cost and effort of searching" (see Fig. 9.6).

(iii) *Downsizing to shorter lease HDB studio and 2-room Flexi flats*: The HDB's studio apartment scheme for the elderly (1998–2015) and

Fig. 9.6 Self-reported barriers to selling housing to fund retirement (% respondents), 2017 (Source: Data from Singapore Life Panel®)

the 2-room Flexi scheme (from 2015) allow an elderly household to purchase a smaller flat (36 sq m–45 sq m) with a shorter lease, and that is fitted with elderly friendly features. There is no requirement to top up the CPF retirement account or purchase an annuity. However, these units cannot be sublet or sold on the open market. Despite the restrictions, these schemes have been more popular than the LBS: as of March 2017, HDB had built and sold 8530 elderly studio apartments (HDB Annual Report, 2016/2017), which is more than 5 times the total take-up for the LBS. Between November 2015 and March 2017, the HDB offered about 10,000 2-room Flexi flats for sale, and is committed to supply more of these flat types.[23]

(iv) *Cash transfers* from adult children and other family members may also serve to preserve the value of bequests. SLP findings indicate that 62% of HDB households aged 64–70 enjoy some amount of cash transfer income from family and friends. Median cash transfer income for households aged 64–70 in 4-room or smaller HDB flats was about 40% of total income.

New Proposals for Home Equity Extraction for Retirement

The ageing demographic structure of Singapore has necessitated changes to housing policies to help HDB homeowners unlock their housing wealth for retirement. The changes have included (i) removing regulatory barriers against subletting and rental of HDB flats, (ii) the supply of shorter lease studio and 2-room HDB flats for elderly homeowners, (iii) incentives for homeowners to downsize to smaller flats (SHB), and (iv) the LBS. In this concluding section, I review other suggestions for housing equity extraction in retirement, categorizing them into those that facilitate downsizing and those that enable "ageing in place".

Downsizing

The availability of affordable options for downsizing is rather limited in Singapore. It is a small city-state with housing supply largely determined by government policies. Homeowners who own 5-room or Executive HDB flats or private housing may find it feasible to extract housing wealth by downsizing to a lower value home. Downsizing for owners of HDB 4-room and smaller flats may not be an attractive option as the sizes of these units are not particularly large: HDB 4-room flat sizes are in the range of 85–105 square metres, 3-room HDB flat sizes are 60–65 sq m, while studios and 2-room Flexi flats sizes are 36–45 sq m. To further facilitate downsizing for HDB homeowners, introducing flexi-leases for 3-room HDB flats would provide a larger size option.

Rental flats provided by the HDB under the Public Rental Scheme are restricted to low-income households (household gross monthly income less than $1500) and are largely confined to 1- and 2-room flat types. In Phang et al. (2014), my co-authors and I highlighted the need to develop more affordable and feasible rental options for downsizing. We proposed the development of residential REITs consisting of HDB residential and commercial units that would meet both the need of households for affordable rental housing and their demand for real estate investment. A proportion of new units developed by the HDB can be sold to this REIT for rental. The REIT will be an active participant in rental and lease back market in the HDB sector. REIT shares can be sold to Singaporean CPF members in units of SGD1, with the HDB or approved banks as financier and an HDB subsidiary as the REIT manager (with some form of rental adjustment regulation to ensure that rental increases are managed and are not fully market driven).

The REIT can provide higher rental yields for shareholders due to the tax-free dividends that are aligned with market rental yields. This will help to reduce household housing investment demand as an instrument for hedging asset price inflation. Such an REIT arrangement would facilitate elderly households to invest as well as monetize their housing assets in more optimal ways. The REIT can facilitate retirement planning through homeowners selling their HDB unit to the REIT, with the option of renting the same unit, and owning REIT shares to neutralize the rental payment. The REIT can also act as a source of financing for the HDB Lease Buyback Scheme or for a shared-ownership housing scheme (see below).

Ageing in Place

To facilitate ageing in place, variations of the reverse mortgage have been introduced in several countries, with limited success. The common reasons that are cited as reasons for the disappointing growth include hefty upfront costs, high discounting of the home value, and high interest rates, together with unique layers of additional challenges specific to each country (Warshawsky and Zohrabyan 2016). In South Korea, the RM is fully guaranteed by a state-run financing firm, the Korea Housing Finance Corporation (KHFC). It is a "no negative equity" loan and the KHFC levies insurance premiums and also regulates the interest rate for the reverse mortgage. In Hong Kong, the wholly government-owned Hong Kong Mortgage Corporation Limited plays a similar role as the KHFC. In the UK, in addition to the RM, a home reversion plan is available that involves the sale of the entire or part of the home equity (with transfer of ownership) at the time the reversion plan originates. The elderly person continues to live in the house without paying rent until he or she dies. Australia has several home equity release schemes: reverse mortgages, home reversion schemes, as well as shared appreciation mortgages.

Merton and Lai (2016) highlight the challenges on the supply side—funding availability must be deep and reliable if RMs are to become a mainstream systematic source of retirement funding. They propose modifications to the current HECM design to facilitate standardization of contracts and securitization of the products into different risk tranches (housing equity, debt, and mezzanine) so as to attract private sector investors with different needs. They view the government as "rarely the best institutional provider" as it is inefficient, and are of the view that the private sector would do a better job in terms of efficiency because of higher profit incentives. In their view, the government's role would be best confined to regulation and coordination improvement, including consumer and usury law exemptions. Merton and Lai's proposals are made in the context of the US, where securitization and secondary markets are deep and mature, and consumer protection laws are highly developed. The immaturity (or lack) of secondary markets for mortgage securities in Asia, greater volatility of housing prices, as well as the heterogeneity of housing stock, present major obstacles to the adoption of their proposals in most Asian countries.

In the nascent stage of product development, governments have taken the lead to launch RM or RM-like products in Korea and Hong Kong, as well as in Singapore. In the Singapore context, there may be a need to allow more flexibility in methods of extracting funds by retirees. This could include higher lump sum withdrawals under the LBS and introducing an RM product with the government initially as the insurance provider. The earlier (1997–2009) failed RM episode discussed earlier in this chapter has generated much negative publicity for RMs, and any new RM product will require effective communication and marketing to overcome lingering public scepticism. Kwong and Tse (2017) have proposed a shared equity scheme where, instead of the HDB purchasing the tail end of the property's lease, the HDB buys a percentage share of the property. This proposal would work as well if the buyer is a residential REIT that is permitted to enter into such transactions.

In conclusion, the need to provide channels for housing equity extraction is integral to improving overall funding of retirement for lower-income homeowners in Singapore. Governments in countries with high homeownership and a growing population of retirees are similarly struggling with policy challenges for how to facilitate such extraction in ways that are beneficial for retirees as well as sustainable in the longer term. Singapore's LBS is the outcome of a housing context where leasehold homeownership is the dominant tenure form. There is no perfect solution, but there is certainly a need to approach the complex challenges with a multipronged policy framework that encompasses both general as well as targeted assistance.

Notes

1. Details of the SLP can be found at CREA's website at https://crea.smu.edu.sg/ Accessed November 1, 2017.
2. Singapore National Population and Talent Division (2013). The White Paper included proposals for immigration and foreign worker policies to support population projections of between 6.5 and 6.9 million by 2030. These projections generated much public debate and a series of public protests.
3. For a literature review and international comparisons, see Warshawsky and Zohrabyan (2016).
4. Ibid., the UK, Germany, Malta, Italy, Sweden, the Netherlands, Romania, Spain, France, and Hungary.
5. As UK RMs are not guaranteed by the government, they have much lower loan-to-value ratios and higher interest rates. See Warshawsky and Zohrabyan (2016), Table 39.
6. The FHA insurance charges comprise two components: a mortgage insurance premium (MIP) at closing and an annual MIP for the entire life of the loan. The MIP charge at closing is calculated on the lesser of the appraised value of the home or the HECM loan limit (US$625,500) and is 0.5% in most cases. The insurance premium throughout the life of the loan is 1.25% of the balance. See the HUD website at https://portal.hud.gov/hudportal/HUD?src=/program_offices/housing/sfh/hecm/hecmabou.
7. Data from https://www.nrmlaonline.org/2017/07/06/annual-hecm-endorsement-chart Accessed November 1, 2017.
8. "OCBC enters RM fray", *Business Times*, August 28, 2006; and "RM to be revisited", *The New Paper*, October 9, 2014.
9. "Couple sue NTUC Income over RM deal gone sour", *Business Times*, July 28, 2009. The case was eventually settled out of Court.
10. "Reverse mortgages in the spotlight", *Business Times*, September 17, 2014.

11. Refer to the HDB website for details of other eligibility criteria and requirements: http://www.hdb.gov.sg/cs/infoweb/residential/living-in-an-hdb-flat/for-our-seniors/right-size-with-silver-housing-bonus Accessed November 1, 2017.
12. Flat applicants aged 55 and above can choose units with shorter leases ranging from 15 to 45 years, in 5-year increments. The lease length chosen must last the applicant and his/her spouse until they are at least 95 years old. See HDB website for details of eligibility criteria and other conditions: http://www.hdb.gov.sg/cs/infoweb/residential/buying-a-flat/new/2room-flexi-flats Accessed November 1, 2017.
13. For details of annuity schemes, see CPF website at https://www.cpf.gov.sg/Members/Schemes/schemes/retirement/cpf-life Accessed November 1, 2017.
14. Joint Press Release by the Ministry of National Development, HDB and CPF Board, "Silver Housing Bonus and Lease Buyback Scheme made more attractive for elderly", December 27, 2012.
15. "Sharp rise in take-up of HDB Lease Buyback Scheme after enhancements", *Today*, May 15, 2016.
16. This is out of an estimated 42,000 owners of 3- and 2-room HDB flats who met the age and other criteria. "Lease Buyback Scheme: emotional barriers to retirement adequacy", *The Straits Times*, September 2, 2014.
17. "Sharp rise in take-up of HDB Lease Buyback Scheme after enhancements", *Today*, May 15, 2016.
18. HDB website at http://www.hdb.gov.sg/cs/infoweb/residential/living-in-an-hdb-flat/for-our-seniors/how-it-works Accessed November 1, 2017.
19. Minister for National Development (Mr Khaw Boon Wan), in response to questions by Members of Parliament on the valuation of leases under Enhanced Lease Buyback Scheme, Singapore Parliament, September 8, 2014 sitting.
20. The value of leasehold land falls to zero at the end of the leasehold period. See the Singapore Land Authority website for the table showing leasehold values as a percentage of freehold value at: http://www.sla.gov.sg/Portals/0/Services/Land%20Lease%20Conditions/DP%20policy%20wef%2031%20Jul%202000.pdf Accessed November 1, 2017.
21. See the HDB website on LBS at http://www.hdb.gov.sg/cs/infoweb/residential/living-in-an-hdb-flat/for-our-seniors/lease-buyback-scheme Accessed November 1, 2017.

22. "Don't assume flat will be picked for Sers, buyers told", *The Straits Times*, March 25, 2017.
23. The flats are priced according to the lease tenure and elderly buyers finance the purchase of the flats through cash or CPF savings, instead of a mortgage loan. Of 6,070 2-room Flexi flats offered in four sales exercises in November 2015 and early 2016, 87%, or 5,289 units, were booked. Of those who booked a flat, 47% were elderly buyers aged 55 and above. The rest were families and singles. "Response to 2-Room Flexi Scheme 'encouraging', 85% of elderly buyers went for short leases: HDB", Channel News Asia, March 5, 2017.

References

Chia, Ngee Choon, and Albert K.C. Tsui. 2009. *Monetizing Housing Equity to Generate Retirement Income*, Working Paper No. 2009/01. National University of Singapore, Singapore Centre for Applied and Policy Economics.

Cho, Daniel, Katja Hanewald, and Michael Sherris. 2013. *Risk Management and Payout Design of RMs*. Paper Presented at the Actuaries Summit, Sydney, 20–21 May.

Davidoff, Thomas. 2004. *Maintenance and the Home Equity of the Elderly*, Working Paper. University of California, Berkeley, Hass School of Business.

———. 2010. Home Equity Commitment and Long Term Care Insurance Demand. *Journal of Public Economics* 94: 44–49.

———. 2015. Can High Costs Justify Weak Demand for the Home Equity Conversion Mortgage? *Review of Financial Studies* 28: 2364–2398.

Davidoff, Thomas, and Gerd M. Welke. 2007. *Selection and Moral Hazard in the Reverse Mortgage Market*. Paper Presented at the 12th Annual Asian Real Estate Society Conference, Macau, July 2007.

Davidoff, Thomas, and Jake Wetzel. 2014. *Do Reverse Mortgage Borrowers Use Credit Ruthlessly?* Working Paper. University of British Columbia.

Friedman, Benjamin M., and Mark J. Warshawsky. 1990. The Cost of Annuities: Implications for Saving Behaviour and Bequests. *Quarterly Journal of Economics* 105 (1): 135–154.

Hoskins, Stephen. 2017. *Housing Data in the Singapore Life Panel®*. Presentation at Housing Roundtable, Singapore Management University, Centre for Research on the Economics of Ageing, 16 Aug.

Koh, Chee Wee. 2015. *Financial Sustainability of Monetising Housing Equity in a Leasehold Environment*, Senior Thesis. Singapore: Singapore Management University, School of Economics.

Kwek, Sian Choo, and Dionne Hoh. 2017. *Determining the Value of Leasehold Land: A Closer Look at 'Bala's Table'*. Centre for Liveable Cities, Singapore, Commentary. http://www.clc.gov.sg/documents/books/research-workshop/2017/balas-table.pdf. Accessed 1 Nov 2017.

Kwong, K.S., and Yiu-Kuen Tse. 2017. *Modelling Equity Release Products*. Presentation at Housing Roundtable, Singapore Management University, Centre for Research on the Economics of Ageing, 16 Aug.

Lockwood, Lee M. 2012. Bequest Motives and the Annuity Puzzle. *Review of Economic Dynamics* 15: 226–243.

Lucas, Deborah. 2015. *Hacking Reverse Mortgage*, Working Paper. Cambridge: Massachusetts Institute of Technology, Center on Finance and Policy.

Merton, Robert C., and Rose Neng Lai. 2016. *On an Efficient Design of the Reverse Mortgage: Structure, Marketing and Funding*. Paper Presented at the American Economic Association Conference, Chicago, IL, 6–8 Jan 2017.

Moulton, Stephanie, Donald R. Haurin, and Wei Shi. 2016. *Reducing Default Rates of Reverse Mortgages*. Center for Retirement Research at Boston College, Jul (16–11).

Munnell, Alicia H., and Steven A. Sass. 2014. *The Government's Redesigned Reverse Mortgage Program*. Center for Retirement Research at Boston College. January 2014, no. 14-1.

Peijnenburg, Kim, Theo Nijman, and Bas J.M. Werker. 2016. The Annuity Puzzle Remains a Puzzle. *Journal of Economic Dynamics and Control* 70: 18–35.

Phang, Sock Yong. 2017. *Monetization of Housing: 3 Puzzles*. Presentation at Housing Roundtable, Singapore Management University, Centre for Research on the Economics of Ageing, August 16, 2017.

Phang, Sock Yong, David Lee, Alan Cheong, Kok-Fai Phoon, and Karol Wee. 2014. Housing Policies in Singapore: Evaluation of Recent Proposals and Recommendations for Reform. *Singapore Economic Review* 59 (3): 1450025.

Salisbury, Linda C., and Gergana Nenkov. 2016. Solving the Annuity Puzzle: The Role of Mortality Salience in Retirement Savings Decumulation Decisions. *Journal of Consumer Psychology* 26 (3): 417–425.

Singapore Ministry of National Development. 2012. Silver Housing Bonus and Lease Buyback Scheme Made More Attractive for Elderly. *Press Release*, December 27.

Singapore National Population and Talent Division. 2013. *A Sustainable Population for a Dynamic Singapore: Population White Paper*. Singapore: National Population and Talent Division, Prime Minister's Office.

United Nations. 2015. *World Population Ageing 2015*. United Nations Department of Economic and Social Affairs, Population Division. http://www.un.org/en/development/desa/population/publications/pdf/ageing/WPA2015_Report.pdf. Accessed 1 Nov 2017.

Warshawsky, Mark J., and Tatevik Zohrabyan. 2016. *Retire on the House: The Use of Reverse Mortgages to Enhance Retirement Security*, Working Paper. Cambridge: Massachusetts Institute of Technology, Center on Finance and Policy.

Yaari, Menaham E. 1965. Uncertain Lifetime: Life Insurance, and the Theory of the Consumer. *The Review of Economic Studies* 32 (2): 137–150.

Singapore Newspaper Articles

OCBC Enters RM Fray. *Business Times*, 28 Aug 2006.

Couple Sue NTUC Income Over RM Deal Gone Sour. *Business Times*, 28 Jul 2009.

Reverse Mortgages in the Spotlight. *Business Times*, 17 Sep 2014.

RM to Be Revisited. *The New Paper*, 9 Oct 2014.

Lease Buyback Scheme: Emotional Barriers to Retirement Adequacy. *The Straits Times*, 2 Sep 2014.

Don't Assume Flat Will Be Picked for Sers, Buyers Told. *The Straits Times*, 25 Mar 2017.

Sharp Rise in Take-Up of HDB Lease Buyback Scheme After Enhancements. *Today*, 15 May 2016.

10

Transferability of Singapore's Housing Policy Innovations

Singapore's housing welfare model and urban planning practices have attracted much international attention and accolades from policymakers elsewhere. The Housing and Development Board (HDB) and Central Provident Fund (CPF) host numerous visitors from foreign governments and international organizations who visit Singapore to learn about its housing policies and practices. Singapore has "exported" its town planning and housing development expertise to rapidly urbanizing developing countries through government assistance programmes, and state-owned as well as private companies. Surbana-Jurong, Mapletree, CapitaLand, and Ascendas-Singbridge (all urban development companies owned by the Singapore government's Temasek Holdings) have developed HDB style townships, commercial, retail, and industrial parks in several countries and cities. The Surbana-Jurong group in 2016 had a global workforce of 13,000 employees in 113 offices across 44 countries in Asia, Australia, the Middle East, Africa, and the Americas.[1] The Singapore housing model itself remains a dynamic one, with constant policy changes and tinkering in response to changing economic conditions and demography. In this concluding chapter, I assess the transferability of Singapore's housing policy innovations.

S.-Y. Phang, *Policy Innovations for Affordable Housing In Singapore*,
Palgrave Advances in Regional and Urban Economics,
https://doi.org/10.1007/978-3-319-75349-2_10

Land Acquisition by the State

Compulsory acquisition of land by the Singapore government has been central to the efficient redevelopment of the central area, the success of the housing programme and the provision of necessary space and infrastructure for economic growth. Large-scale high-density urban redevelopment projects often require the assembly of contiguous land parcels into a larger buildable site. In many instances, fragmented ownership of land can become an insurmountable barrier in the land assembly process. When developers try to purchase the required minimum area of land through a private bargaining process, a few owners may decide to hold out by refusing to sell or insisting on a higher price without taking into account the costs imposed on the other owners or on society at large. This situation can be described as the tyranny of the minority. The result is gridlock and a tragedy of the anti-commons—the land is underutilized, its real value cannot be unlocked, and the redevelopment of the city is made more difficult (Heller 2013). Government intervention to exercise compulsory acquisition in such context can be justified as a means of overcoming the market failure of gridlock (Phang 2013, 33–35).

Singapore's land acquisition by the government at below market values for economic development is consistent with land value capture as proposed by Henry George's land tax (George 1879). At a critical juncture in its postcolonial history, it allowed the government to appropriate land values for public purposes, to redistribute through housing provision, and also to eliminate the potential profits of land speculators. In the process, affected landowners suffered wipe-outs, with actual financial losses in some unfortunate cases.

Whether such a policy is transferable is highly debatable from ideological, political, as well as legal standpoints. It is likely be a controversial and emotive issue as it will be considered by private landowners as an outright infringement of their property rights. Without the dire circumstances facing Singapore during the 1960s, such a radical reform of property rights would have been almost impossible to implement. The social context and legitimacy of the government in making such acquisitions would need to be considered carefully. The potential abuse of such powers for private benefit rather than public purpose is not a remote possibility in other contexts where corruption is rife. Moreover, where land use decisions are made by the public sector, this can easily result in inefficient allocation and outcomes as was the case for socialist cities (Bertaud and Renaud 1997).

In Singapore's context, the government paid careful attention to market signals, utilized tenders in government land sales, and eventually adjusted compensation for land acquired to market rates in line with norms in other countries. In countries or cities where government land ownership is high (such as in socialist and former socialist countries), the allocation of land for provision of affordable housing is more feasible without the need for acquisition and expropriation of private land use rights.

A Government-Owned Housing Developer

The HDB is Singapore's largest town planner, housing developer, estate manager, as well as mortgage lender (in terms of number of households served). Is it possible or even desirable for other cities to consider establishing such a dominant state-owned housing developer, mortgage lender and estate manager? Although the HDB has performed well despite being a state-owned enterprise (SOE), it bears repeating that SOEs operating in other contexts may not enjoy the same degree of success. As discussed in Chap. 3, the macro context under which the HDB operates is not easily replicated in other settings. The organizational practices adopted by public sector agencies and government-owned or government-linked companies in Singapore are much more aligned with private sector corporations, as compared to SOEs operating in other contexts where inefficiencies could be more common and better tolerated.

Excessive governmental control over SOEs may result in a more bureaucratic culture instead of a more corporate one. On the other hand, poor governance can lead to weak accounting systems, lax risk management practices, accountability deficiencies, and no incentives for innovation. More importantly, there may be corruption and rent-seeking activities. Also, being more susceptible to political interferences, SOEs may be hindered from achieving their initial social and economic objectives. SOEs may crowd out or prevent the emergence of more efficient private sector enterprises, particularly private developers and commercial banks in the case of housing institutions. SOEs may require subsidies for their continued operation—resources which could have been better allocated elsewhere.

Once established, there is a need to periodically review the performance, market impact, and continued relevance of SOEs. Where SOEs are dominant in the industry, they may need to be subjected to regulatory oversight. Exit strategies will need to be considered for poorly performing SOEs and even for successful ones that have fulfilled their initial purposes and objectives. A larger-scale reorganization or transformation of SOEs may entail partial or full privatization.

On the surface, partial privatization or a hybrid type arrangement such as a Public-Private Partnership (PPP) may furnish plausible alternatives: it involves private partners or shareholders who will require profitable results and risk-based management, whilst the government can guide the general strategy for the sector. In September 2017, India's central government announced a new PPP policy for affordable housing, providing eight PPP models for private investment in affordable housing.

These arrangements supposedly encourage market discipline and sound economic business strategies, while simultaneously enabling social objectives to be met. However, the risks of agency and moral hazard problems remain and could even be amplified. Private investors/management may be rent seekers who exploit privileges rather than pursue sound business or development strategies. The dual mission enterprise may lead to moral hazard risk taking behaviour as both management and investors implicitly believe that profits would be privatized and losses socialized.

In cities where HDB style townships have been established, these have been affordable housing for sale rather than for rental. Singapore's model of affordable homeownership has helped meet the needs of the growing middle-class rather than low-income households in rapidly urbanizing developing countries. As a city-state, Singapore is able to control its population growth while other cities are less able to control rural-urban, inter-city, or even foreign immigration. Cities in China however have been able to effect some degree of control of population growth through China's "hukou", or household registration system. For cities of a similar scale to Singapore (fewer than 6 million population), the Singapore experience has shown that it is organizationally feasible for a single housing authority to build, sell, and manage housing estates for a majority of the population.

Housing Provident Fund

Singapore's model of housing provident fund (HPF) for housing finance has been adopted in several countries including Malaysia, China, Nigeria, Philippines, Fiji, Mexico, and Brazil (Chiquier 2009). Similar to Singapore's Central Provident Fund, HPFs are specialized financial institutions that collect mandatory savings from employees, expressed as a percentage of their salary. Sometimes, employers are also required to make additional proportional contributions. The HPF then manages these accrued long-term savings, which are often remunerated at below market yield. This permits the contributing members of the HPF to withdraw the savings as a down payment for a housing investment and to receive a long-term housing mortgage loan usually at a preferential rate (either from the HPF or through another lending institution).

The World Bank has notably not been a strong advocate of HPF, highlighting the costs and problems in countries that have adopted HPFs. In particular, the list of concerns raised by the Bank include unrealistic and regressive cross-subsidies, interest rates below market levels for both savings and credit, HPF poor portfolio performance, exposure to political pressure and interference from changing governments, inefficient corporate governance structure, lack of transparency leading to abuses and corruption, as well as deterring the rise of private mortgage markets (Chiquier and Lea 2009). We consider how some of these concerns have arisen in China's HPF programme which has been described as the largest social housing finance program in the world (Chen and Deng 2014).

The HPF was introduced initially in Shanghai in 1991 as a pilot programme to kick-start a housing finance system that could help effect the housing reforms which began in 1988. It was subsequently implemented in most large Chinese cities, and there are over 400 HPF management centres under the control of the local authority. Most HPF management centres commission designated banks to administer collections, disbursement, and serving of mortgage loans (Chen and Deng 2014). Initially mandatory only for public sector employees, it required the participation of both the public and private sectors from 2005. Both the employer and employee are required to contribute at least 5% of the worker's wages into his/her individual provident fund savings account. The actual contribution rates are determined by local governments, with ceilings on contributions, and actual practices even within cities differing across sectors.[2]

HPF participants can withdraw their HPF savings for retirement purposes, or for purchase or major repairs of housing. The HPFs played an active role in popularizing basic knowledge of housing finance and promoting homeownership. However, there have been problems with HPF performance that include inefficiency, fraud, and the misuse of funds for other priorities (Deng et al. 2009). Despite its mandatory nature, actual HPF coverage is low at about 10%, according to Tang and Coulson (2017). As such, this precludes the HPF from making a significant difference in Chinese mortgage markets.

For the segment covered by HPF, regressive lending policies have also resulted in only a small proportion of contributors benefiting. The utilization rate of the HPF scheme by contributors varies across regions, but is generally low, owing to complicated and time-consuming loan application procedures and regulations on usage of the funds when compared to commercial banks. In 2011, Chen and Deng (2014) estimate that 20% of HPF contributors, at the most, received HPF mortgages. A large group of low-income renters, whose deposits are too low to make them eligible for loans, effectively cross-subsidize the low interest mortgage loans of a smaller group of middle-income homeowners (Burell 2006). Since higher-income earners receive larger contributions to their savings accounts, they would also be able to qualify for larger loans.

Regulations include caps on the amount of HPF loans, as well as a minimum down payment of 20% for units smaller than 90 sq m, and 30% for units larger than 90 sq m. Indeed, commercial banks appear to be a more important source of finance for housing purchase and have therefore not been crowded out by the HPF scheme. Tang and Coulson (2017) report findings that HPF participants are more likely to be owner-occupiers, but that they also purchase smaller properties than they otherwise might have due to the down payment restrictions on HPF mortgage loans.

Land Use Planning for Affordable Housing

The supply of new housing in cities can either be facilitated or obstructed by the land use planning regime at the local level. Singapore's long- and medium-term land use planning framework has been developed to ensure adequate supply of competitively priced commercial and industrial space for economic growth and affordable housing for all segments of its growing population. In the 1990s, land use planners made bold changes to the land use planning process in order to accommodate higher-density development for the future. Changes in zoning and permitted density together with public investments in Mass Rapid Transit infrastructure incentivized private landowners to sell their properties to developers for new higher-density developments. The density of HDB towns as well as plot ratios for sites sold by the government have increased over the years. The strategies adopted by land use planners to increase density and supply of affordable housing, with policies for integration of households of different income groups and ethnicity in HDB towns contributed to a more equitable and stable society.

The objectives of land use planners in other contexts often differ markedly from the objectives pursued by land use planners in Singapore. Land use planning agencies and powers could be overly fragmented and decentralized, resulting in resistance to mixed use and/or higher-density developments. The not-in-my-backyard (NIMBY) behaviour of homeowners and natural preferences for households to live amongst others with similar preferences and views can contribute to rising inequality, increasingly unaffordable housing, segregation, and social tensions in cities. Bishop (2009) and Florida (2017) have called attention to these urban challenges in their books on "The Big Sort" and "The New Urban Crisis", respectively. Singapore's experience has demonstrated that land use planning and policies can be part of the solution rather than the source of these urban problems.

Regulation of Housing Markets

Singapore has had a few decades of experience with careful regulation of, first, its HDB housing sector and, more recently, regulation of its private housing sector. While the objectives of housing market regulations have changed over time, the underlying motivations of restraining speculation, ensuring homeownership affordability for residents, and curbing housing bubbles have become more pronounced in the past decade.

In the wake of the 2008 global financial crisis, the US Federal Reserve Board's quantitative easing and zero interest rate commitment had led to massive capital flows into Asian countries and contributed to the Asian housing boom. Foreign investors have moved into real estate investments in cities favoured by immigrants and foreign students such as Hong Kong, Singapore, Sydney, Vancouver, Toronto, and selected US cities. A number of countries have implemented macro-prudential policies to counter capital inflows into their real estate sectors, in particular, foreign inflows (BIS 2017). The list of countries includes China, Hong Kong SAR, India, Korea, Malaysia, Thailand, Canada, and Australia. In some countries, measures are specific to cities, districts within a city, or specific market segments within the housing market.

As supply elasticity numbers can vary widely across a country and housing bubbles are often localized geographically, these targeted policies are justifiable to contain real estate booms that affect housing affordability for local residents. Two additional important objectives of policies to deal with real estate booms are: (i) prevention of real estate booms and associated build-up of leverage at households and banks, and (ii) increasing the resilience of the financial sector to a real estate bust. The toolkit available includes monetary, fiscal, and macro-prudential tools that can be used to dampen the housing cycle.[3]

However, monetary policy is too blunt an instrument to use in order to lean against a housing bubble (Phang 2013). Fiscal instruments such as transactions taxes and capital gains on real estate gains can be adjusted in a countercyclical manner in order to dampen the housing cycle and to discourage speculative activity during the boom phase. These measures have been used in South Korea since the late 1970s; they have been geared towards being location specific, for example, being applicable only to

Seoul, or even districts within Seoul (Chang 2010). Hong Kong SAR and China also introduced higher stamp duties to discourage speculation during the housing boom. In August 2016, British Columbia introduced a 15% property transfer tax on foreign real estate buyers in metro Vancouver, which was also adopted by Toronto in April 2017. The tax was one of 16 measures announced by the Ontario government, and was aimed at cooling the real estate market.

These fiscal measures can be considered as part of macro-prudential policy to contain housing bubbles that might affect the stability of the financial system as a whole.[4] Amongst the tools of macro-prudential regulation that affect households directly are caps on loan-to-value and debt service-to-income ratios to limit mortgage loans. The policy concern is not only with housing affordability, but also the financial sector's resilience—should there be a housing bust. A significant challenge, however, is that the risk of financial instability could build up even when bubbles are mild. If the financial sector expands credit and increases leveraged exposure to the housing sector, even a mild downturn could lead to financial distress. Conversely, a boom in housing prices does not always signal the build-up of risks in the financial system and the economy at large. The emerging international policy consensus is that countries need a wide range of early warning indicators and models to assess systemic risks. Quantitative indicators need to be combined with qualitative information and market intelligence for an effective macro-prudential framework (IMF/FSB/BIS 2016). For the housing sector, pre-emptive policy action to lean against a boom will need to take into account the underlying causes, as well as the specific and broader economic contexts, with policy responses tailored accordingly.

Inclusive Policies: Integration, Redistribution, and Housing Equity Extraction

With globalization, cities increasingly comprise diverse multiracial and multi-religious populations. The challenge of growing inequality is also more evident in large cities. Singapore's solution to these challenges has been to use its social housing system to spatially integrate households of different income groups and races. A housing welfare system heavily biased towards homeownership has enabled low- and middle-income households to own their homes despite high market prices for housing. This has been achieved sustainably through a land, housing, and property tax system that is highly progressive. With an ageing population, various housing policies have been implemented to facilitate housing equity extraction for retirement. These social housing policies have been possible as the HDB sector houses 80% of the resident population, with that sector being able to determine the social and spatial norms for the city.

Although its urban planning and housing finance system have been adopted elsewhere, Singapore's policy attention to these social issues, derived from its socio-political context, is not as easily transferable. Housing policies in many developed countries such as the US, UK, France, Germany, and Sweden do promote mixed income neighbourhood as a goal, although success is difficult to measure. Explicit racial integration, however, is much more challenging and it is correspondingly more difficult to articulate a policy objective.

Housing systems that are biased in favour of homeownership can have distribution effects that are regressive. Mortgage interest tax deduction in the US is a prime example of such a regressive policy that subsidizes bigger houses for the upper-middle income. However, Singapore's experience has demonstrated that it is possible to combine homeownership bias policies with a tax regime that is progressive in its impact through the careful calibration of housing grants, stamp duties, property taxes, and rebates.

In the area of schemes for home equity extraction, cities in China share with Singapore high homeownership rates, a concentration of housing wealth in the asset portfolio of households, as well as a leasehold system for housing ownership. Housing equity extraction for retirement in the context of leasehold housing is a challenging financial issue in search of a solution. The policies in this area are still being developed, and experiments in Singapore can help inform on future solutions to the problem.

Conclusion

Singapore's housing policy innovations have resulted from the need to optimize existing resources within extreme constraints. In the absence of workable models that could be adopted, policymakers experimented with feasible solutions—improving, removing, recalibrating, as well as innovating as conditions change. The housing institutions and policies have evolved from their colonial origins to become a distinct Singapore housing framework. The success of the framework demonstrates that affordable housing is an achievable goal. However, the chapters in this book also demonstrate the extensiveness and multipronged nature of the approach needed to deliver the affordable housing outcome. It has involved close attention to both the supply and the demand side: government acquisition of land, government as the dominant housing developer, mobilization of high levels of mandatory savings, extensive and intrusive regulation of housing markets, as well as large grants to lower-income households as market prices rose.

Numerous city governments in former socialist countries and in Asia are also major landowners. However, while similar approaches have been adopted by governments elsewhere, it is difficult to find strong advocates for government-centred housing welfare systems. The transferability of Singapore's experience need to be juxtaposed with the local political and social context, in particular, the city-state's high economic growth rates, low unemployment rates, and ability to control the entry of migrants who can impose a strain on the housing service sector. I conclude on this cautionary note—that the same set of policies adopted in another context can very easily lead to a very different set of outcomes.

Notes

1. See Surbana-Jurong's website at: https://surbanajurong.com/about-us/. Accessed 1 Nov 2017.
2. Employer's contribution ratios vary across provinces. In Beijing and Shanghai, employers matched 8–10% of the employee's salaries. In other provinces however, this figure may not reach 5% despite the minimum requirement imposed by governments. See Deng et al. (2009).

3. See Phang (2013), Chap. 10. For the pros and cons of alternative instruments and countries that have utilized these instruments to deal with real estate booms, see joint report by IMF/FSB/BIS (2016).
4. In contrast, micro-prudential regulation concerns itself with the risk of individual asset classes, the stability of individual entities and the protection of individuals. See Bank of England (2011), and IMF/FSB/BIS (2016).

References

Bank for International Settlements. 2017. Macroprudential Frameworks, Implementation and Relationship with Other Policies. BIS Papers No 94. Basel: Bank for International Settlements.

Bank of England. 2011. *Instruments of Macroprudential Policy: A Discussion Paper*, December.

Bertaud, Alain, and Bertrand Renaud. 1997. Socialist Cities Without Land Markets. *Journal of Urban Economics* 41 (1): 137–151.

Bishop, Bill, with Robert G. Cushing. 2009. *The Big Sort: Why the Clustering of Like-Minded America Is Tearing Us Apart.* New York: Houghton Mifflin Harcourt.

Burell, Mattias. 2006. China's Housing Provident Fund: Its Success and Limitations. *Housing Finance International* 20 (March): 38–49.

Chang, Soon-taek. 2010. *Mortgage Lending in Korea: An Example of a Countercyclical Macroprudential Approach.* Policy Research Working Paper 5505. Washington, DC: The World Bank.

Chen, Jie, and Lan Deng. 2014. Financing Affordable Housing Through Compulsory Saving: The Two-Decade Experience of Housing Provident Fund in China. *Housing Studies* 29 (7): 937–958.

Chiquier, Loic. 2009. Housing Provident Funds. In *Housing Finance Policy in Emerging Markets*, ed. Loic Chiquier and Michael Lea. Washington, DC: The World Bank.

Chiquier, Loic, and Michael Lea, eds. 2009. *Housing Finance Policy in Emerging Markets.* Washington, DC: The World Bank.

Deng, Lan, Qingyun Shen, and Lin Wang. 2009. *Housing Policy and Finance in China: A Literature Review.* Washington, DC: US Department of Housing and Urban Development.

Florida, Richard. 2017. *The New Urban Crisis: How Our Cities Are Increasing Inequality, Deepening Segregation, and Failing the Middle Class—and What We Can Do About It*. New York: Basic Books.

George, Henry. 1879. *Progress and Poverty: An Inquiry into the Cause of Industrial Depressions and of the Increase of Want with Increase of Wealth … The Remedy.* San Francisco: Author's Proof Edition. Edition referred to: 1971, New York: Robert Schalkenbach Foundation.

Heller, Michael. 2013. The Tragedy of the Anticommons. *The Modern Law Review* 76 (1): 6–25.

International Monetary Fund, Financial Stability Board, and Bank for International Settlements. 2016. *Elements of Effective Macroprudential Policies: Lessons from International Experience*. https://www.imf.org/external/np/g20/pdf/2016/083116.pdf. Accessed 1 Nov 2017.

Phang, Sock-Yong. 2013. *Housing Finance Systems: Market Failures and Government Failures*. Basingstoke: Palgrave Macmillan.

Tang, Mingzhe, and N. Edward Coulson. 2017. The Impact of China's Housing Provident Fund on Homeownership, Housing Consumption and Housing Investment. *Regional Science and Urban Economics* 63: 25–37.

Appendix: Singapore's Consumer Price Index, Exchange Rate (S$/US$), and Interest Rate for Housing Loans, 1988–2017

	Consumer price index (2014 = 100)	Exchange rate (S$ per US$, average for period)	Finance Companies' Interest Rate for 15 Year Housing Loans (% per annum)
1988	59.59	2.01	6.11
1989	60.96	1.95	6.15
1990	63.06	1.81	7.36
1991	65.23	1.73	7.36
1992	66.69	1.63	6.64
1993	68.22	1.62	6.48
1994	70.33	1.53	7.05
1995	71.54	1.42	6.95
1996	72.53	1.41	6.81
1997	74.00	1.48	7.17
1998	73.80	1.67	7.31
1999	73.81	1.69	6.15
2000	74.81	1.72	6.15
2001	75.57	1.79	6.40
2002	75.27	1.79	6.09
2003	75.64	1.74	5.98
2004	76.90	1.69	5.40
2005	77.26	1.66	5.56

(*continued*)

S.-Y. Phang, *Policy Innovations for Affordable Housing In Singapore*,
Palgrave Advances in Regional and Urban Economics,
https://doi.org/10.1007/978-3-319-75349-2

(continued)

	Consumer price index (2014 = 100)	Exchange rate (S$ per US$, average for period)	Finance Companies' Interest Rate for 15 Year Housing Loans (% per annum)
2006	78.01	1.59	5.73
2007	79.65	1.51	5.73
2008	84.93	1.41	5.56
2009	85.44	1.45	5.56
2010	87.85	1.36	4.41
2011	92.46	1.26	4.26
2012	96.69	1.25	2.87
2013	98.97	1.25	2.93
2014	99.98	1.27	2.93
2015	99.46	1.37	3.22
2016	98.93	1.38	3.41
2017	99.50	1.38	3.16

Sources: Official data from Singapore government agencies' websites

Index[1]

[1] Note: Page numbers followed by 'n' refer to notes.

S.-Y. Phang, *Policy Innovations for Affordable Housing In Singapore*,
Palgrave Advances in Regional and Urban Economics,
https://doi.org/10.1007/978-3-319-75349-2

The manufacturer's authorised representative in the EU is Springer
Nature Customer Service Centre GmbH, Europaplatz 3, 69115 Heidelberg,
Germany. If you have any concerns regarding our products, please
contact ProductSafety@springernature.com

Printed and bound by CPI Group (UK) Ltd, Croydon, CR0 4YY
05/10/2026
02228128-0004